ESSAYS
IN
ARGUMENT

ESSAYS
IN
ARGUMENT

RICHARD ANDREWS
AND
SALLY MITCHELL

Middlesex University Press

First published in 2001 by Middlesex University Press

Middlesex University Press is an imprint of
MU Ventures Limited
Bounds Green Road, London N11 2NQ

© Richard Andrews and Sally Mitchell

A CIP catalogue record for this book is available from
The British Library

ISBN 1 898253 35 8

Cover Photograph by Rachael Calder
Manufacture coordinated in UK from the Authors CRC
by Book-in-Hand Limited, London N6 5AH

ACKNOWLEDGEMENTS

All the chapters in this book have grown from our involvement with other people, most especially the teachers, lecturers, pupils and students who have worked with us and given us access to their classrooms and work. We'd like to take the opportunity that this volume provides to thank them for their generosity in allowing our research to go forward. The support of the Leverhulme Trust and the Esmée Fairbairn Charitable Trust has clearly been crucial to the research we've been able to do over the past ten years and we are immensely grateful for the opportunities they have provided.

In addition, we have to thank certain particular critical friends: Stephen Clarke, who acted as external evaluator on the 5-16 project and was a valued member of sixth form and higher education project's steering committee; Mike Riddle who has assumed an important incisive and creative role within the Middlesex Project; Peter Medway, acting with a keen eye from a distance; and Mark Reid, for Sally, a critical support closer to home.

Many other colleagues have been generous with their intellectual support for - and challenge to - the research. In these respects we would like to thank the members of our steering committees: Judith Atkinson, Jerry Booth, Martin Brooks, Stephen Clarke, Paul Drew, Alan McClelland, Patsy Stoneman; Trevor Corner, Carol Costley, Lynn Hale, Judith Harding, Roger Harris, Barry Jackson, Peter Newby, Chris Osborne; and others at the University of Hull and Middlesex University: Steve Burwood, Sandra Carter, Aram Eisenschitz, Amanda Jacobs, Tammy McLorg, Vicky Marks, Lesley Morris, Carlos Sapochnik, Arthur Williams, Cris Woolston; and Dodi Beardshaw, Russ Coleman, Catherine Grant and Simon Hollington, amongst many others.

We would like to thank Howard Gibson, Jeff Mason and Mike Riddle for permission to reprint their material in the book and for the ideas they have brought to exchanges with us.

On the administrative side, we are very grateful to Audrey Rusling, Maria Paschali, Jackie Lison, Caroline Johnson, Laura Rustill and Christine Thompson for their hard work and eye for detail, and without whom we would not have brought to fruition many of the papers and manuscripts that form the basis of this book.

Thanks must also go to Trevor Corner, John Annette and Marion Locke of Middlesex University Press for supporting the idea of this book.

Chapters in the present book have appeared in earlier versions in the following journals and books: *Learning and Teaching Genre* (edited by Aviva Freedman and Peter Medway) and published by Heinemann-Boynton/Cook; *The Journal of Art and Design Education* (UK), *Educational Review* (UK), *English in Education* (UK), *Curriculum* (UK), *English Journal* (USA), *English in Australia* (Australia), *English in Aeteroa* (New Zealand), *Typereader* (Australia), and *Seminariernes Engelskloererforening* (Denmark). We are grateful to the editors and publishers of these journals for permission to reprint.

Thanks to Faber and Faber Ltd for permission to reprint 'Poem' for *Kid* by Simon Armitage.

Other material was published by The University of Hull and Middlesex University; we thank them both for support and permission to reprint.

Richard Andrews and Sally Mitchell

York and London 2001

Trevor Corner

Essays in Argument, the third in the *Research in Education* Series from Middlesex University Press, carries forward the major intention of bringing educational research findings to a wider readership. The series aims to articulate links between research and practice thus adding impact to the work of educational researchers in schools, colleges and universities.

In *Essays in Argument*, Richard Andrews and Sally Mitchell describe the research into argument within educational settings at primary, secondary and tertiary levels. They discuss, in detail and with admirable clarity, a great deal of the research in the field that has been done over the past ten years. The authors present the theoretical background, show how argument helps learning in schools and higher education, and give many examples and illustrations which help to clarify and amplify understanding. Their work is a distillation of research enquiry into the nature and process of argument stretching over ten years and four major research projects at Middlesex University and elsewhere.

There is much in this book for researchers and teachers working across the educational spectrum to debate and discuss. The topics presented affect the way we think of learning and give insights on how we can improve teaching and communication to children and adults alike.

The titles included in the Research in Education Series are chosen with a view to inform policy-making in education, support practice in formal and informal education and to stimulate debate. Authors wishing to contribute to the series should contact the Series Editor.

Titles in the Research in Education Series:

Interpreting the New National Curriculum
Edited by Richard Andrews (1996)

Partnerships: Shaping the Future of Education
Edited by Kenneth Stott and Vernon Trafford (2000)

Living the Past
By Gavin Baldwin and Beth Goodacre

The collected extracts, articles and chapters that comprise this volume derive from over ten years of research into argument within educational settings at primary, secondary and tertiary levels. In putting together this volume our intention has been to draw out the distinctive features of this work by gathering a number of short publications – articles, chapters, papers — that have appeared disparately over the last few years in Britain and abroad. The work, focussed around four discrete research projects (see below), has included examination of the processes by which students learn to argue and the products by which their achievement is assessed. It has involved working with teachers to develop their awareness of argument and to improve teaching and learning. And to some degree also it has been a theoretical and philosophical enquiry into the nature of argument.

In undertaking the task of compiling this volume, we have found that certain influences and ways of looking have been dominant in our work and that there are central concerns to which we have repeatedly returned. These are concerns, amongst others, with the potential contribution of argument to education in its broadest social and moral senses; with the links between the ability and permission to argue and the development of individual, social and disciplinary identities; with the way subject curricula are framed; with the lived practices of education that may encourage or inhibit the expression of argument; and with practical ideas for improving the place and quality of argument in education.

We anticipate that these are concerns shared by educationalists of all kinds – teachers in schools and universities, postgraduate students and educational researchers. Argument is not a narrow specialism in education, relevant only, say, to linguists and philosophers, but is a central process – social and cognitive – in all learning. It should be of interest to teachers of all subjects and at all levels of the educational system.

In editing the collection we have grouped pieces into four – not entirely watertight – sections. The first section is designed to allow readers to familiarise themselves with the conceptual frameworks we have used and which influence the way argument is dealt with in later sections. The pieces it contains represent attempts to articulate understandings of argument that are suited to the multi-dimensional 'lived-in' contexts in which our investigations have taken place, and that are suited, too, to the practical aims of improving the teaching and learning of argument that we have often been pursuing. Thus these pieces do not represent final or categorical positions on the nature and uses of argument but rather are speculative and contingent, aiming mostly to move thinking on in the projects they represent rather than to close it down. They contain discussions of our central 'lens' – argument itself – as well as concepts, such as genre and dialogue, which we have found to occupy a similar theoretical area.

In the second section of this book are pieces that speak more or less directly to and from the tradition of English teaching, in Britain and more widely. In many ways English Studies (rather than, say, philosophy, psychology or linguistics) has been the 'spiritual home' of much of our research. In fact, the bias towards English Studies, both as a way of thinking about teaching and learning and as the subject to which we have applied our research with most relish, is evident not just in section 2 but throughout the book. We have found it to be a subject well suited to the expression and exploration of argument. At the same time, we have noted how, in other, less well acknowledged ways, English can put constraints on the expression of difference, for example, in privileging certain interpretations of texts and in treating the primary vehicle of academic argument — the essay text — as neutral and untouched by ideology.

The long chapter, 'Questions and Schooling: classroom discourses across the curriculum' which begins the third section was written after a period of immersion in classrooms at the start of the third project listed below. It records a sense of how dominant the question form was in classroom talk and focuses on this as a way of gaining insights into both the relations between teachers and students and the nature of the subjects being studied. As with the other chapters in this section, this piece reflects the observation that argument is shaped by wider discourse practices and that to learn to argue successfully involves learning the ways in which educational and disciplinary communities recognise and value argument and the ways in which their discourses shape what can be argued, how and by whom.

The title of this book, *Essays in Argument*, reflects the close affinity in Western education between argument and the essay form. At the same time it tries to hint at the provisionality contained in the origin of the term 'essay' — *essai*, a trying out. This provisionality is frequently in conflict with the summative assessment function accruing to the essay in many educational contexts. As a result, argument, in its fullest dialogic expression, can be stifled by the 'default' essay genre. The pieces in the final section of this book are attempts to look critically at the essay and to develop suggestions for the diversification of writing practices that involve argument.

The Projects

The pieces contained in this book derive from the work of the following four research projects:

An exploration of narrative and argumentative structures in writing, with particular reference to the work of year 8 students.

The work of this project (Richard Andrews' doctoral thesis) arose from an interest in the relations between argument and narrative as modes of discourse. Its focus was on the writing of 12-13 year olds in a town in northern England. It took place at a time when interest was being generated more widely about these two modes amongst those interested in the 'arts of discourse' in education; an interest which gave rise to Richard's (1992) edited collection *Narrative and Argument*. The research, which is recounted in part in Chapter 7, provided the inspiration to apply for the funded project grants which supported a further three projects.

Improving the Quality of Argument, 5-16

Funded by the Esmeé Fairbairn Charitable Trust, this project ran between 1991 — 93 under the direction of Richard Andrews and Patrick J.M. Costello at the University of Hull. Teachers from ten primary and ten secondary schools in the local area participated as practitioner researchers, identifying their own objectives, working out detailed plans and devising ways of assessing improvement amongst their pupils (Andrews & Costello, 1993). The project took place at a period when the National Curriculum was seeming to narrow the definitions for language use and to close down possibilities for expression, a situation explored in Chapter 8. Several of the projects developed by teachers and their pupils highlighted relations between argument and democracy, the school and the wider communities of which it is part. These strands of thinking are developed in Chapters 9 and 10.

The Teaching and Learning of Argument in Sixth Forms and Higher Education.

Running concurrently with the 5-16 project was another focussing on post-compulsory phases of education. It was funded from 1991-94 by the Leverhulme Trust, directed by Richard Andrews, with Sally Mitchell as the researcher. Rather than aiming to change and develop practice, this project took a more investigative approach, using a range of ethnographic methods to find out about the nature and functions of argument in a number of 'academic' disciplines up to degree level study. The work of the project was recorded in two reports (Mitchell, 1992 and 1994) and is represented in a number of chapters in this volume. The opening chapter 'Key concepts', for example, reflects the project's way of seeing argument as complexly embedded in the forms and practices that teaching and learning take. The chapter attempts to lay out some of the conceptual tools used to elucidate the situations that were the project's object of study.

Improving the Quality of Argument in Higher Education

The final project (1995-2000) from which the chapters in this volume derive was again funded by the Leverhulme Trust, with Richard Andrews and Sally Mitchell in their respective positions as director and researcher. This time, however, the location had moved from Hull to Middlesex University in London. Greater emphasis was placed in the project's objectives on practical outcomes, ways of *improving* the quality of argument and this brought its methods closer in spirit to the 'action research' of the 5-16 project. Chapters 2 and 4 reflect attempts in this project to pin down the concept of argument with the aim of creating a minimum shared understanding amongst research participants in the research and a basis, therefore, from which the effort to improve could be judged. At the same time chapter 3 gives expression to a continuing curiosity about the meanings of argument and a commitment to keeping open creative possibilities for conceiving of and practising with it[1].

[1] Further developments are to be found in an edited collection, *Learning to Argue in Higher Education* (Mitchell and Andrews, 2000) which resulted from an international conference held in 1997 during the course of the Middlesex project, and in the project's final report (Mitchell and Riddle, 2000).

CONTENTS

CHAPTER ONE

SOME KEY CONCEPTS IN ARGUMENT*

Sally Mitchell

This chapter introduces some theoretical tools for exploring the role and nature of argument in educational settings. It begins by setting out a situated contextual approach to the study of argumentative reasoning, starting 'big' with the pervasive notion of ideology. Drawing attention to the difficulty of distinguishing 'text' from 'con-text', the chapter points to the value and relevance of rhetorical and dialogic frameworks for understanding how argument works. It goes on to suggest that, even where argument is valued as a considerable cognitive achievement, in the academy it also performs the important cultural function of creating and justifying new knowledge. Overall, then, this chapter attempts to indicate the multi-dimensional factors involved in learning to argue successfully. Recognition of such social and cognitive complexity sets the frame for much of the research reported later in this book.

Context

In *The Uses of Argument* (1958), Stephen Toulmin made an important distinction between a notion of logic as somehow universal – both as a science, uncovering the laws of right reasoning and an art, offering tips on how to argue rightly – and a more situated approach to logic or argument, which looks at the ways in which cases are made in the furtherance of certain purposes. He suggested that:

> ... validity is an intra-field, not an inter-field notion. Arguments within any field can be judged by standards appropriate within that field, and some will fall short; but it must be expected that the standards will be field dependent, and that the merits to be demanded of an argument in one field will be found to be absent (in the nature of things) from entirely meritorious arguments in another (p. 255)

What sorts of things make up a context? There seem to me to be a number of ways in which context comes to bear. All of them can be seen as ways in which

---

* First published in Mitchell, S. 1994. *The Teaching and Learning of Argument in Sixth Forms and Higher Education*. Hull: The University of Hull, Centre for Studies in Rhetoric.

an action is framed: some, like ideology, are very extensive and indeed difficult to see beyond; others, like form, are more limited (or can be made to seem so) and so can be more closely addressed. They can also be the means by which to uncover ideology.

Ideology is very much an all embracing term (and idea), which describes the invisible structures and beliefs by which we operate and which appear as natural unchallengeable ways of doing things. Ideologies are associated with dominant forces and positions within our culture, which nonetheless keep the conditions and premises upon which domination rests invisible, precisely because they are seen to be natural. Ideologies are thus seen to be normative, conservative and also context-free. Challenges to ideology come often from marginal groups within it, which seek to overturn its assumptions by making them visible. So, for instance, feminists have critiqued the dominant ideology of patriarchy and this has included, incidentally, a critique of academic argument and discourse as patriarchal (see Lamb, 1991; Meyer, 1993). Meyer names the impersonal authoritative and objective stance associated with writing a formal academic essay as an 'illusion' and characterises the 'for and against' notion of argument as polarising and aggressive. Like Lamb, she wants to challenge the way we think of 'argument' and her critique is therefore not only of practices but also of definitions.

Ideological approaches are those which seek to name and undermine the forces of ideology, rather than to uphold it. Brian Street's (1984) approach to literacy, for example, is ideological because it seeks to supplant the 'autonomous' model which suggests that literacy is not affected by social context with an approach in which what counts as literacy varies between situations and according to the value and position accorded to it by ideology. His critique emerges from attention to what has been named as *other* within the dominant ideology, in this case, those who have been named as illiterate (the passive tense is no accident here) and considering the possibility of alternative interpretations and namings.

It is virtually impossible to be free of ideology in some form or other and I take it to frame in more or less evident ways all the examples of argument I have come across.

Discourse is the mouthpiece of ideology. It describes the way language is used, the way its components are organised to create knowledge and relationships. It allows things to be said, but also contains what can be said: it enables and constrains the kinds of meanings we can make about the world. Foucault (1972) said of its determining role: 'one cannot speak of anything at any time; it is not easy to say something new ...' (p. 64). Michael Billig (1991) has also made this point by commenting that when we hold an attitude or opinion about something we are indicating both something personal about ourselves and at the same time locating ourselves within a wider controversy. Our opinion is a 'dual expression' (p. 43) which owes as much to current debate as our own thinking.

Discourse can also be more widely defined than as a particular form of language use and this is useful to bear in mind:

At any moment we are using language we must say or write the right thing in the right way while playing the right social role and (appearing) to hold the right values, beliefs and attitudes. Thus what is important is not language, and surely not grammar, but *saying (writing) – doing – being – valuing – believing combinations*. These combinations I call 'Discourses', with a capital 'D' ('discourse' with a little 'd', to me, means connected stretches of language that make sense, so 'discourse' is part of 'Discourse'). Discourses are ways of being in the world; they are forms of life which integrate words, acts, values, beliefs, attitudes, and social identities as well as gestures, glances, body positions and clothes. (Gee, 1989, pp. 6–7)

There is not just one discourse; there are discourses; different ways of using language and creating meanings which vary according to context. Academic discourse, for example, construes the world differently from everyday discourse and, within academia, different **disciplines** (Toulmin's term is 'fields') operate with different discourses. Disciplines therefore also constitute contexts. Concepts which enable meaning to be formulated in, say, sociology, are different (though there will be overlaps) from those in, say, psychology. A discourse may allow communication between fields (as is witnessed when people from a variety of disciplines come together to share a sense of what it is like to be within an academic community). In this sense, then, becoming part of one discipline (learning the operation and validity of its arguments) is also acquiring what has been called 'trained incapacity' to think outside the parameters of the field. Again the way in which knowledge and learning are compartmentalised by institutional structures and discourses can be seen as a manifestation of ideology and has in fact been critiqued by such movements as feminism which, in drawing from a number of disciplines, seeks as one of its aims to disrupt specialised disciplinary claims to knowledge (and, therefore, power). So what individuals do within and between fields may also change the nature of and shift the boundaries of that field.

Learning a discipline involves *learning* to speak and be heard in a particular discourse. Individuals are not simply located but become located. Neither do individuals come to learning discourse-free, but must manage transitions between discourses, learning what Sheeran and Barnes (1991) have called the **'ground rules'** – appropriate ways of speaking, writing, reading, thinking.

There are often tensions experienced in such transitions. A mature student on a philosophical methods course I observed hinted that the new ways in which she had been encouraged to consider the question of 'What is love?' had begun to alienate her from her family and friends; her identity, she felt, was somehow changing. Most people can be assumed to have something to say about love and find some relevancy for it in their own experience, but this 'common sense' discourse was not much help in the philosophy course or at least only in a limited way. The lecturer explained that in this course the topic of love was not a straightforward appeal to experience, though students should draw upon what they knew. This knowledge would not be personal or particular, but somehow general. From such general knowledge it would be possible to generate hypothetical or imagined examples, as distinct from actual lived experiences. At one step removed from experience, then, the approach becomes disinterested and cool. Philosophy demands that the question be looked at systematically and in a certain rigorous way. Succeeding attempts to define love are overturned and rejected, shown through a process of systematic reasoning to be merely synonymous with sexual desire or the 'will to live'. For all its rigour, though, the philosophical approach does not reach conclusions as to what love is: it removes certainty and replaces it with a relentless process of questioning. To adapt to this way of behaving, students either achieve a separation between the disinterested disciplinary approach and their own interested beliefs and experiences, or take over the philosophical approach altogether. Most academic disciplines have this type of enculturation – or at least the display of it – as an important aim[1].

Physical setting, persons present, time allotted all have an impact on the kinds of argument that are possible. The size and layout of a room for instance affects the kinds of grouping and social interaction that are possible as does the contact time available. If time is short, the teacher may feel that she must pursue her own agenda more rigidly to ensure it is covered. Teachers tend to have different views about the kinds of space and group size they like. Some, for instance, sense that their presence amongst a group of students may inhibit students' contributions to discussion, and for this reason, dislike the enforced intimacy of tutorial groups – both because the group is thought to be too small to have a dynamic of its own and because the setting – the tutor's own office – is wrong. The role of the teacher in this setting is felt to be ambiguous and uncomfortable. Other teachers prefer the intimate arrangement as it allows the kind of discussion in which the teacher models for the students the kind of disciplinary discourse they need to learn. In this case the different dynamic and feel of a small group discussion from which the teacher is absent may not be thought to suit the purposes of disciplinary learning. The role and presence or absence or the teacher, both as 'expert' and 'authority' is a considerable factor in determining the type of argument which might take place. But the impact of the setting is open, to some degree, to the interpretation of those present, not only the teacher but the students as well. A teacher who asks a question in a lecture, for instance, in order to stimulate debate, may well be greeted with passive resistance by students who have understood the social rules of the situation differently. Similarly the impact of time on learning to argue will vary according to the value placed on the activity by the discipline, by the prevailing pedagogy and by the individual teacher.

---

[1] A significant argument against modularised degrees is that they do not allow sufficient experience within a particular discipline for a Discourse to be adequately learnt. Students, as a result, learn something *about* the discipline (an outsider's point of view) without learning what it is to be *within* the discipline.

Form and conventions might also be seen as part of the context for argument, though, like discourse and ideology, they are also intrinsic to what is produced. A form is an accepted way of doing something. In schooling, for example, written argument is generally seen as taking the form of an **essay** and again this form frames what can be argued and how. There is a nice example of this in a paper by Roz Ivanic and Denise Roach (1990), which tells the story of how, when Denise first began her academic course as a mature student, she answered an essay question directly with 'no', though she realised she would have to write more than this:

> With reference to the above question I could answer with namely one word NO – However for the purpose of this essay a deeper analysis is called for. (p. 14)

Noting the incredulous responses of her friends and after several redraftings the 'no' disappeared from the first paragraph to be replaced by the phrase 'is incorrect' in the final paragraph:

> So despite Firestone offering what she believes is a comprehensive analysis, her assumption that women's oppression is brought about through women's reproductive capacity is, as I argue, incorrect. (p. 15)

Denise's disagreement ends up, then, in the conventional place for the expression of opinion within the essay form – the conclusion – and is expressed in a cooler academic discourse. Ivanic and Roach pose this question: 'Is this superior argumentation, or is it a different set of discourse conventions for the same intellectual process?' (p. 15) The answer to this is complex, I think. When Denise answered the question with 'no', she was engaged in argument only in so far as she was expressing an opinion or making a statement. She was not however demonstrating the reasons why she arrived at that conclusion, nor giving any sense of alternative positions which might need to be taken into account and/or refuted in order to locate her opinion and the place she gave to that expression in the essay. Education is only rarely about intellectual, as divorced from social processes, and in a sense, what Denise was intellectually capable of was not at issue here. Her first introduction was wrong because she did not understand the 'way of saying', the discourse which properly constituted the social practice she was engaged in; she did not understand what Bazerman (1988, p. 320) has called its 'decorum'.

There is, it seems, a distinction to be made between the mode of thinking that Denise needed to engage in (argumentative) and the form and discourse she needed to adopt the 'valid' expression of this thinking (see Andrews and Mitchell, 1994). This introduces a new key idea: **argument as a mode** – a 'way of doing', which can at some level be distinguished from its form of expression. Mode and form often *need to be* distinguished when learning to argue, in order for attention to be given to ways of generating argument as well as presenting it. It seems to me that an emphasis on argumentative *product* tends to fuse mode and form unhelpfully and can result in writing which though formally and rhetorically appropriate falls short in terms of argumentative content.

The point about the example above is that Denise was not simply being called upon to argue, but to argue in a certain way for a certain audience/readership. Her writing had, that is, a particular **rhetorical purpose**.

Rhetoric

The notion of rhetoric is closely tied to argument and argumentative contexts since it is concerned with the effectiveness of arguments and the way they persuade. Taking a rhetorical perspective on writing is to ask questions about *purpose* (see Andrews, 1992b and 1994) such as whom am I writing *for*? Who am I writing *as*? For what *purpose*? What options are open to me to be effective? Asking such questions as these may denaturalise the processes of writing and bring them to a level of consciousness where they can be reflected upon. The rhetorical task may involve, or be perceived to involve, for instance, the construction of an impersonal objective stance, for the purpose of persuading a particular disembodied academic audience. Denise came to understand her writing task this way though she experienced it uneasily as 'fabricating a sort of detective story for the reader' (p. 15). Or, on another occasion in a different sort of context, it may involve speaking (as if) from the heart – as in the following example from a first year biology undergraduate's speech to her tutor group. Below is the entire speech as Helen prepared it to speak. I'm including it here, as it illustrates several of the points that have been made about argument so far, as well as others that will take the exploration further:

TO LIVE AND LET DIE

One of the basic human rights enjoyed by everyone of us is the right to live. Surely as death is part of life – we all die eventually (look at Fred – point at the skeleton) – the right to live also means the right to die.

But what does life mean to you?
(brief pause and audience response – probably nil)

To us (indicate group) life means:
i   eating chocolate cake
ii   missing lectures
iii the morning after the night before
iv freedom of expression in all its forms
v   feelings and personality

What does death mean to you?

(brief pause and audience response – probably nil)

To us (indicate group) life (sic) means:
i.   a total lack of awareness
ii.   becoming an object, a non-person
iii.   having no purpose – you are useless
iv.   no interaction with the community
v.   being a temporary collection of organic ingredients, soon to be broken down and reassembled in another form

The medical definition of brain death includes the following criteria:
1.   Apnoea – no spontaneous breathing i.e. if respirator turned off
2.   Unresponsitivity – no movement to any stimulus
3.   Absence of cephalic reflexes (no pupil response, no eye movement when head is turned, no coughing when throat is stimulated)
4.   Flat EGG recording – electrocerebral silence
5.   Confirmation test of absence of cerebral brain flow for 30 minutes

The main subject on whom our case is based is Tony Bland.

Nearly four years ago he was crushed in the Hillsborough disaster. The result of this tragedy was that Tony suffered brain damage so severe that it left him in a permanent vegetative state – known as PVS. To all intents and purposes he became a living corpse. The person who was Tony Bland died that day at the Hillsborough stadium. The happy, vibrant, football loving young man has gone forever. All his family and friends have to remind them of Tony is a body which bears no resemblance to the former essence of his personality. This living corpse cannot comprehend its surroundings, cannot move, and is maintained by machines. Its vital signs are prolonged but it is in no way a prolongation of life. Tony can never be released from within this mound of flesh because Tony and all that he was has gone.

The only thing being preserved by his dependence on machines is his family's suffering. The essence of Tony has gone. Why preserve its mortal prison? It is time to allow Tony to die with his last dignity intact. If he had not had the operations and machines in order to maintain him he would have ceased to function that fateful day at Hillsborough.

His family could have laid his memory to rest and begun the grieving process along with the families of the other tragic victims that died.

A doctor has a duty to sustain life where it is sustainable but has no duty – legal, moral or ethical – to prolong the distress of an incurable patient or their family.

Gastric tubes, intravenous infusions, antibiotics and respirators are all supportive measures for use in acute or subacute illness to assist towards recovery of health. To use such measures in the treatment of incurable patients is inappropriate as there is no expectancy of a return to health and therefore such practices can be considered bad medicine.

When deciding whether to prolong a life, a doctor must take into account:
i.   the patient's medical condition
ii.   their spiritual and emotional capacity
iii. their religious convictions
iv.   the degree of interaction with friends and family
v.   personal and social commitments of the patient
vi.   and finally and perhaps most controversial, the cost involved – what degree of care can be afforded on the patient's behalf – by the family and the state

Doctor Howe – Tony's doctor – took all these points into consideration in his case and concluded that:

'Medicine is not just a case of keeping people alive. We are not producing immortality.'

This was endorsed by one of the Law Lords involved in the historic ruling allowing Tony to die. He said:

'It is lawful to cease to give treatment and care to a PVS (persistent vegetative state) patient considering that to do so involves invasive manipulation of the patient's body and which confers no benefit upon him.'

To end our presentation we decided to use a poem about death, which we feel is appropriate to our case.

'Through vaults of pain,
Enribbed and wrought with groins of ghastliness,
I passed, and garish spectres moved my brain
To dire distress.
Where lies the end
To this foul way? I asked with weakening breath.
Whereon I saw a door extend –
The door to death
It loomed more clear:
At Last! I cried. The all-delivering door!'

There are a number of ways in which this speech shows awareness of rhetorical purpose. At the beginning the instructions in brackets anticipate the context in which the words will be spoken (a skeleton she knows will be in the room, a group – her team for whom she is spokesperson, an audience). Rhetoric is in this instance literally pointing, but one might use this as a metaphor for the way it designates audiences through language. The nature of the audience (other members of the tutor group) is also constructed or anticipated in the choice of examples of what life means. They are a humorous appeal to shared experience and bridge the gap between the point of view of the speaker and that which she assumes her listeners to have. They range over several levels from the concrete and frivolous (chocolate cake) to the abstractly meaningful (feelings and personality). These examples are a form of cliché: they appeal to what is common. The second set of examples which refer to death balances the first (there are the same number) and forms a contrast in tone. This contrast is an important part of the argument, which is based from the outset and throughout on the oppositional categories of life and death; 'feelings and personality' versus 'a temporary collection of organic ingredients'; 'the happy, vibrant, football loving young man', 'Tony Bland', the 'person' versus the 'living corpse' and the 'mound of flesh', 'he' versus 'it'. The opposition is built upon an appeal to (highly emotive) everyday definitions of what constitutes life and death.

Yet Helen is also a biologist speaking to biologists and indicates her awareness of this by bringing in the medical definition of brain death, which includes specialised terms and criteria. She also uses the opinions of experts to defend her view. This mix of discourses has to do, I think with the context for which the speech was prepared. The tutor was concerned that in order to study biology successfully at university his students did not need to grapple with its ethical and 'real world' implications and were not required to have experience of how to communicate their knowledge in other ways. He decided therefore to devote some tutorial time to 'for and against' debates on certain topical issues, which related to biology: 'Drugs and sport' and (this one) 'When to turn off life support'. Since the debates were taking place within the context of a tutorial rather than a seminar, lecture or laboratory session they were at the margins of disciplinary activity and this, it seems to me, contributes to making possible and legitimate the mix of the moral, ethical and commonsensical as well as clinical.

In addition the framing of the initiative as 'debate' with 'for and against' groups suggests that the topics may be treated in a general rather than specialised way and probably accounts for Helen's adoption of a 'public-speaking' type of form and tone. This carries with it certain interpretations of the audience. The students are invited to confront real world issues and they do so in real world terms (in which the spoken medium is certainly a factor). The framing sets up the topics as containing oppositions, two opposing points of view. What Helen produces conforms to this adversarial model of argument and may also account for the forcefulness of her rhetoric.

What can be made of the speech in terms of argument? The paragraph beginning 'Gastric tubes ...' conforms closely to the definition from the OED: 'a reason urged in support of a proposition'. There are two reasons (or premises) here: the first is that gastric tubes etc. are measures to *assist recovery* of health; the second is that incurables have no expectation of recovery. The proposition (or conclusion) which derives from these is that using such measures is inappropriate (and therefore not good medicine). So here is a neatly formulated argument which fits our definition.

Yet how much else is going on here in terms of argument with the purposes of influencing the mind (and heart)! The speech does all the following things in the service of argument: it lists, it conveys knowledge and asks questions, it establishes links with an audience, it tells a story (a very *current* one at the time), it uses authorities (quotes them), it employs a range of discourses, it appeals to emotion as well as reason, and it concludes not with a statement but a poem. An understanding of argument within context and as effective (i.e. as having effects), has to take into account these extra dimensions.

Helen's argument for the turning off of life-support in cases such as Tony Bland's took place on an occasion where an argument was also made for the opposite view. Both her team and the opposing one also faced questions from the audience. As I have noted, several of the features of Helen's speech gesture towards this larger event of which it was a part. I think it's easy here to conceive of Helen's speech as an *action* contributing to an *event*, because of its obviously performative nature. But this is perhaps less easy to grasp when it is proposed for all acts of communication, written as well as spoken: an essay as performing an action as part of an event. Yet this idea is clearly a part of the rhetorical perspective and also behind other ways of characterising language use: 'literacy practices' and 'literacy events' as ways of understanding literacy (Barton 1994), Gee's definition of Discourse, and, for text, a notion of *genre*, understood as 'social action'.

Genre as social action

This idea was coined by Carolyn Miller (1984) in a highly influential article of the same name. Charles Bazerman 1988), using Miller's work, gives this summary:

> A genre consists of something beyond simple similarity of formal characteristics among a number of texts. A genre is a socially recognised, repeated strategy for achieving similar goals in situations socially perceived as being similar (Miller). A genre provides a writer with a way of recognising the kind of message being transmitted. A genre is a social construct that regularises communication, interaction and relations. Thus the formal features that are shared by the corpus of texts in a genre and by which we usually recognise a text's inclusion in a genre, are the linguistic/symbolic solution to a problem in social interaction. (p. 62)

Amy Devitt (1993) gives some concrete examples of how a sense of genre might help to solve such problems in social interaction:

> ... consider what we know when, as readers, we recognise the genre of a text. Based on our identification of genre, we make assumptions not

only about the form but also about the text's purposes, its subject matter, its writer and its expected reader. If I open an envelope and recognise a sales letter in my hand, I understand that a company will make a pitch for its product and want me to buy it. Once I recognise that genre, I will throw the letter away or scan it for the product it is selling. If in a different scenario, I open an envelope and find a letter from a friend, I understand immediately a different set of purposes and a different relationship between writer and reader, and I respond/read accordingly. (p. 575)

Devitt goes on to argue that genre can play a mediating role with regard to traditional dichotomies which have dominated the way language use is understood:

Genre is an abstraction or generality once removed from the concrete or particular. Not as abstract as Saussurian notions of *language* or language system, genre mediates between *language* and *parole*, between language and the utterance. Not as removed as situation, genre mediates between text and context. Not as general as meaning, genre mediates between form and content. Genre is patterns and relationships, essentially semiotic ones that are constructed when writers and groups of writers identify different writing tasks as being similar. Genre constructs and responds to recurring situations, becoming visible through perceived patterns in the syntactic, semantic and pragmatic features of particular texts. (p. 580)

An important implication of this way of construing genre (as also of the rhetoric perspective which replaces the question 'what text is this?' with 'what persuasive action is this text performing ?') is that it helps to collapse fixed boundaries which close off certain textual forms from others (the fact/fiction and literature/non-fiction divides would be examples). As Miller says of this understanding:

It does not lend itself to taxonomy, for genres change, evolve, and decay; the number of genres current in any society is indeterminate and depends upon the complexity and diversity of the society. (p. 163)

But despite the flexibility, genres are recognisable and perform important communicative and identity-building functions. Thus as Swales (1990) has suggested the possession of one or more genres is one of the defining characteristics of a *discourse community*; a community, that is, which shares certain '*saying (writing)-doing-being-valuing-believing combinations*'. (Gee, 1989, p. 6)

What can be said about Helen's speech in terms of genre? The genre was not specified nor uniformly interpreted. Helen's speech conformed most to a recognisable public model (and was in fact highly thought of), but others were less carefully structured, less passionate or made more appeal to scientific discourses. These were closer perhaps to presentations than speeches. (My use of the term 'speech' itself indicates that I am distinguishing this text-type from something more general such as 'talk', or more distinct, such as 'paper'.)

What type of generic situation was this, in fact? Was it about the communication of lay or scientific arguments to a lay or specialised audience? Who did the speakers see themselves as? Questions of this kind might have been used as part of this activity to bring the type of situation to a level of reflection and collaborative definition. A matrix such as the one below could be used as a focus for discussion:

AUDIENCE → SPEAKERS ↓	LAY	SCIENTIFIC
LAY	Public speaking model? Ethical, common sense arguments?	Ethical, common sense arguments? Appeals to humanity?
SCIENTIFIC	Presentation, representation? Simplification of scientific arguments, plus ethics?	Paper, presentation? Scientific arguments and language? Objectivity?

The table is certainly both an over-simplification and over-generalisation, but it prompts an awareness of differences as well as overlaps in types of forms and arguments employed in various situations. The matrix might be extended or adapted to include other kinds of speaker and audience. It is a way of introducing to students possibilities for constructing and presenting arguments, which might otherwise not be available to them. The boxes do not contain answers, 'correct' ways of categorising speakers and audiences and the forms of communication that exist between them, but rather create the possibility of choice. The idea here is that language should empower as much as construct the individual.

However, as suggested, individuals are differently empowered to bring about change within their environment, and some environments (those at the margins perhaps) are also more open to negotiation than others. The difference may depend on the ways in which knowledge and learning are conceived (differently by different groups), as well as the kinds of institutional structures which support and embody these conceptions.

Dialogue

A rhetorical view of argument implies in a sense that all argument is dialogic, in that it orientates towards a position beyond itself, and seeks to persuade. It operates therefore on a principle of *otherness*: the otherness of the person spoken to, other points of view, other positions. This otherness has in a sense been present in much of the discussion so far: the notion, for instance, that giving an opinion is a 'dual expression' (Billig, 1991, p. 43). There are traces of otherness also in the dictionary definitions: 'a connected series of statements of reasons intended to establish a position (and hence refute the opposite)', 'a statement of reason for and against a proposition; discussion of a question, debate'. In the first of these definitions, the building of an established position carries with it an inbuilt defence mechanism, simultaneously a recognition and a warding off of alternative positions. The dialogism in this case is rather more implicit than in the second definition where more than one actual speaker is suggested. The definition from mathematics might also be understood as operating on a dialogic principle, since it describes how what is given or known ('the angle, arc or other mathematical quantity') is used to deduce or discover what is not given or known. This is rather like a dialogic understanding of the enthymeme (a syllogism with one premise unexpressed) which suggests that the omitted premise, rather than indicating an incomplete argument or an attempt to hoodwink the audience, represents rather a point of contact or dialogue with the audience: in order to understand the argument it must – and is trusted to – supply what is inexplicit.

The sense here is that the utterance is not meaningful in isolation but becomes meaningful in the context of its reception. This is what Bakhtin (1981) has called the 'activating principle':

> To some extent primacy belongs to the response, as an activating principle: it creates the ground for understanding, it prepares the ground for an active and engaged understanding. Understanding only comes to fruition in the response. Understanding and response are dialectically merged and mutually condition one another. (p. 282)

This description can be applied to actual situations in which words pass between individuals and is useful therefore in understanding what goes on in a spoken interchange and in reading texts. But for Bakhtin, language itself is dialogic, since it both carries with it a history of usage in different contexts and is again received and responded to in yet another context:

> ... actual meaning is understood against the background of other concrete utterances on the same theme, a background made up of contradictory opinions, points of view and value judgements – that is, precisely that background that, as we see, complicates the path of any word towards its object. Only now this contradictory environment is present to the speaker not in the object, but rather in the consciousness

of the listener, as his apperceptive background, pregnant with response and objections. (p. 281)

The understanding of language suggests that words do not simply have meaning, but rather that they *make sense*, or fail to do so, within contexts. As the example of Denise's 'no' suggested, there is not really such a thing as plain talking. For Bakhtin a communicative act is not *about a 'subject'*, as if the subject were somehow passive and inert, transferred intact from speaker to listener, but rather the subject, which he re-terms the 'hero', is a third active participant in the communication (see Schuster, 1985).

It seems to me that argument can be dialogic in each of the senses that are raised here – implicity, actually and/or as an internal feature of a single word or text. What, then, of Helen's speech? It appears to represent only one point of view and has a single speaker and thus to be a monologic utterance, yet it both anticipates and influences how others will respond by the kind of strategies it employs, and it is *actually* responded to by an opposing speech, by questions and by the assessment of peers. In these senses it is dialogic.

It also, as I noted before, includes a number of different voices within its internal structure, both those directly and indirectly quoted[2]. What Wertsch and Smolka (1993) contend is 'a basic question arising out of Bakhtin's work' can be applied quite straighforwardly to Helen's speech: 'This is the question, "Who is doing the speaking?" The Bakhtinian answer is "At least two voices"' (p. 74). Every word that Helen speaks is simultaneously spoken by another voice or combination of voices.

In learning to speak in the discourse of a discipline, students are engaging in specific dialogism of this kind; learning to make their voice heard through another voice:

> The word in language is half someone else's. It becomes 'one's own' when the speaker populates it with his own intention, his own accent, when he appropriates the word, adapting it to his own semantic and expressive intention. Prior to this moment of appropriation, the word does not exist in a neutral and impersonal language (it is not, after all, out of a dictionary that the speaker gets his words!), but rather it exists in other people's mouths, in other people's concrete contexts, serving other people's intentions: it is from there that one must take the word, and make it one's own. (pp. 293–4)

---

[2] But the form is also oppositional; it seeks to close rather than open up debate, to persuade and co-opt rather than to invite questions. Whilst in Bakhtin's definition, speaker and listener mutually influence each other, the form of the biology debate means that the possibilities for this are limited: Helen cannot easily revise her understandings, even in the light of questions. This argument might be said then to be, at some level, anti-dialogic. I think it needs to be remembered, that as well as operating upon otherness, argument can seek to subsume otherness, to coerce it into a position of sameness. It can be aggressive as well as playful. Amongst the dictionary definitions, this sense is certainly present. It returns us to the question of power with which this exploration started.

Students frequently encounter difficulty in both adopting the Discourse (what Bakhtin calls the 'social language') and adapting it, making it their own. Denise's sense that she was fabricating by not simply saying 'no' is a good example. She felt very acutely that the language she was expected to use was not her own, that it was *more than* 'half someone else's'. Issues of power and access to power are implicated here; the population of language with one's own meanings is not straightforward and unrestricted. Gee's (1989) distinction between primary and secondary Discourses helps to clarify these issues. Primary Discourses are those which 'we first use to make sense of the world and interact with others' (p. 7), whilst secondary Discourses are those which we acquire when we have access to social institutions and gain apprenticeships within them. However access to dominant social Discourses may be restricted, 'the word' protected. This, Gee argues, is more likely to be the case for individuals whose primary Discourse is not close to a dominant secondary one, than for those for whom primary and secondary Discourses share affinities. Even where institutional access to 'the word' is gained, such individuals may have further to go in making it their own. What emerges from Gee's analysis, for those involved in teaching, is the need to be aware of the constraints which can prevent the 'word' being appropriated and the dialogue being entered into. Dialogue between primary and secondary Discourses is an important way for transitions to take place.

I should like here to note that Bakhtin's notion of dialogic understanding can also inform the conception of genre I introduced earlier. Anne Freadman (1988) develops the metaphor of a tennis game:

> Imagine a game of tennis, preferably of course, (if you have any ball sense) singles. The players are not exchanging balls, they're exchanging shots [...] Player A plays a shot; player B plays it back. What is this 'it'? It is not useful to say '"it" is the ball'; and manifestly inaccurate to call it the same shot. Player B, let's say, the 'receiver', but to receive a shot s/he must return it, play, that is to say another. The same shot, then – Player A's serve – has a different value for each of the two players: a 'good shot' may win a point for its player, but, well-received, it may turn against s/him [sic], its speed, its turn, or its angle enabling an unexpected return. (pp. 91–3)

Freadman argues that, in her conception of genre as a game in which meaning is 'subject to play' and 'perpetual modification' (p. 93), it is important to move away from assumptions which concentrate on singularity and see a text 'in a genre' and a genre 'in a text'. Rather genre should be understood 'as consisting, minimally, of two texts, in some sort of dialogical relation' (p. 97). Dialogue is conceived of here as an agent of change rather than replication.

The link between genre and dialogue provides a useful way of understanding the function and value accorded to students' texts in educational contexts. A piece of writing, for example, prepared by a student *prior* to a class and perhaps intended to be read or paraphrased there as a stimulus for discussion will be in a different dialogic relation (and therefore a different genre) than a piece which is written as the *outcome* of a class discussion and perhaps awarded a grade or a short comment by the teacher. In the first case the students' text can quite literally be thought of as part as a dialogue; it is also more likely that the more provisional, exploratory role of the writing will produce more dialogic aspects within the text itself, speculations and questions for example. In the second case, the writing is less likely to be used in an open dialogue, since a new topic of discussion will by that time have been introduced. In consequence of this the text itself may have a more monologic character, seeking to convey the authority and resolution of its utterance.

The differences I have suggested between these two pieces of writing are not always recognised and as a result the pedagogical potential of each is not exploited. The difficulty is compounded where different pieces of writing (in terms of dialogic relation and function) bear the same generic (in the more traditional sense of the word) name. The *essay* is the obvious example; in the British system, it embraces writing undertaken before and after discussion, over varying periods of time – a week, a term, a pressurised examination hour – and in hugely varying conditions. The term is used in a large number of disciplines in the Arts, Humanities and Social Sciences, and also, as I discovered, in A level biology. Yet the criteria for 'essay' writing in these subjects is very different, in terms of structure, formal conventions and the argumentative (or other) content.

The ubiquitous use of the 'essay' means that the work students do in their writing appears to conform to some universal model, and, in a way, it not only appears to, it *does* conform, despite disciplinary variations. Writing, like speech, can, however, be freely adapted to context for a range of functions, processes and products. The potential of understanding genre, not as text-type, but as dialogue, is a diversification of contexts and forms employed as part of the learning process. Lev Vygotsky (1978) commenting that 'If one changes the tools available to a child, his mind will have radically different structure' (p. 126) implies that contexts (relationships, environment, forms) have a determining influence on thought and thinking processes. If the context (say, the essay as outcome) is reproduced over and over without variation, the thought patterns are likely to remain the same, but where they are varied (different forms of writing, different rhetorical tasks at different stages in the learning process) there is likely to be greater diversity of thought.

Mention of Vygotsky here brings my discussion to a consideration of argument as cognitive process.

Argument as cognitive process

There are close links between Bakhtin's theory of dialogue and Vygotsky's model of cognitive development, since both thinkers locate meaning in language and social interaction. For Vygotsky the development of the individual begins with the social: language structures are acquired in interaction and only later become internalised as 'inner speech' or thought. Thought therefore, has a dialogic quality. Inter-mental processes provide a model for intramental ones (see Wertsch and Smolka, 1993). Development, Vygotsky says, is dependent upon learning, by which he means guidance from or collaboration with others; it is not something which occurs independently. From this idea he derives the important notion of 'the zone of proximal development' (1978, p. 90), which indicates the difference between a child's mental ability in independently performed tasks and their ability when in interaction with an adult or more capable peers. Ability in interaction (learning) is in advance of development (which measures the internalisation of the socially learnt processes). If the zone of proximal development indicates the potential of interaction to extend the cognitive capacity of an individual, then the importance of dialogue in learning is clear. Beyond this, if argument is understood as dialogic process, it too takes a leading role in cognition and learning. As Billig (1991) puts it, 'the sound of argument is the sound of thinking' (p. 52).

Thinking can be broken down into a number of operations, which Bloom (1956), in seeking to formulate a taxonomy of educational objectives in the cognitive domain, listed as:

1 – knowledge
2 – comprehension
3 – application
4 – analysis
5 – synthesis
6 – evaluation

The objectives are hierarchically arranged, developing from simple to more complex operations. Operations like synthesis and evaluation are likely to make use of those found lower in the list. Something like this hierarchy appears to underlie most assessment at A level and undergraduate level. Put crudely, knowledge will receive a certain level of reward, which will be increased if it can be shown in relation to other knowledge or applied to some other situation, whilst the highest reward is reserved for the ability to take multiple sources of knowledge, show how they are related and critically evaluate them. If this is done in order to produce a new position or an 'original' argument (within the constraints of the discipline) then this will generally attract the highest grade. One way of thinking about the levels is in terms of the degree to which the material is dialogised, the degree to which otherness is assimilated and transformed into the 'own' voice of the student. One-sided (monologic) argument, tends, perhaps for these reasons, not to be highly credited in the academic system: it does not show awareness of multi-voicedness.

The A level Cambridge History Project (CHP) provides a particularly useful example of the way cognitive skills are differentiated in assessment terms and of the high value placed upon argument which can be seen to result from a combination of the skills. Teaching and assessment are arranged according to domains of historical concepts and skills of analysis rather than content. The following extract from the syllabus of the 1992 pilot scheme suggests the increasing cognitive complexity required to move between levels 1 and 3.

Domain 5: Change and development
[Concept domain]

Levels   *Descriptors*

1.   Demonstrates understanding of the way in which significance may be attributed to events as trends and turning points, 'dead-ends' and 'false dawns' within a line of development through time.

2.   Demonstrates understanding that lines of development are theories about as well as representations of the past, and that differing and competing lines of development may be advanced in order to describe and make sense of any part of it.

3.   Demonstrates understanding of the reasons why and the ways in which different and competing lines of development may co-exist and be integrated within a single historical account.

Domain 6: Constructing accounts
[Skills domain]

Levels   *Descriptors*

1.   Can select and organise material so as to construct developmental narratives.

2.   Can select, organise and interpret material so as to construct alternative developmental narratives.

3.   Can select, organise and interpret material so as to construct coherent narratives that make reference to concurrent sequences of events and different lines of development.

The project director commented about the importance of the ability to argue within this syllabus:

Candidates who do not put forward an argument and merely provide a narrative account are awarded level 1 on all domains.

Yet these criteria state that the highest achievement is the construction of 'coherent' *narrative*. The point is, though, that this narrative is developed out of an understanding of a 'different and competing line of development', it is the outcome of a process of argumentation and it is *new*.

Novelty and difference

The sense in which argument can be said to be about the creation of newness or novelty is an important one. Consider the following description of argument as contrasted with narrative and based around the idea of difference:

> All cultures need the categories of narrative and argument for dealing with two opposing, contradictory demands. On the one hand, a culture needs to provide institutionalised means of handling difference. Without difference there can be neither change nor new systems of values. Argument provides [...] the means for bringing difference into existence. At the same time, it provides conventionalised textual forms not just for maintaining and tolerating difference, but for culturally productive use of difference. Yet where there is only difference, the cultural group cannot attain stability, cannot reproduce itself or its values. Narrative [...] provides means of resolution of difference, of reproducing, in an uncontentious mode, the forms and meanings of a culture. Narrative serves as a major means of the reproduction of social and cultural forms and values.

> Narrative, in other words, is a form whose fundamental characteristic is to produce closure; argument is the form whose fundamental characteristic is to produce difference and hence openness. (Kress, 1989b, p. 12)

Narrative in the Cambridge History Project's scheme operates to close the process of argumentation, but the argument itself is still open to counter-argument (maybe in the form of competing narratives) and to change. The closure can be seen as a contingent moment in an on-going process. It is frequently tied up with written forms such as the essay (the primary vehicle through which the A level students express their argument) which require resolution in the form and position of the 'conclusion'.

'Bringing difference into existence' can be a difficult task: there is sometimes more than enough to do in trying to understand and reproduce – particularly when it comes to learning a new discourse. Academic essays and papers can often require students to take on the discourse of the discipline and additionally to manage the actual voices and meanings of others in the form of citations and references to existing writers within the field. Going beyond this to construct an argument out of and in response to these voices is not easy: how to appropriate the language and make one's own voice heard? How to produce a new and convincing account? Often the result of these demands is the suppression of the student's voice and the sense that it is 'other people' only who are speaking. The writing may contain the arguments of others, but is not itself fully argumentative. This, as I've suggested, will gain some credit in assessment terms, as the display of knowledge. In subjects such as philosophy, however, where citation and referencing is often not even a formal requirement, there is little escape from the need to argue – argument is here very much the thing itself. The problem is often compounded by the narrative form in which students are expected to write (beginning, middle and end of the essay, for instance). The task for students trying to construct arguments (dialogic thinking) in writing (generally monologic forms) is to manage the structure and the form in such a way as to manage multiple points of view and generate dialogue (answer and response) rather than to suppress it, and, in addition, to make the meanings 'their own'. This is not a simple task.

David Kaufer and Cheryl Geisler (1989) have examined the idea of novelty in relation to academic writing and describe it as less 'a process of winning adherence for one's new ideas' than 'designing to be new' (p. 287). They outline four 'definitional propositions about authorial newness':

1. Newness is less a property of ideas than a relationship between ideas and communities, and less an individual trait than a regularity of communal life and structure.

2. Authors in disciplinary communities rely on novelty claims to reference the complex processes by which they and their fellows learn and change through a shared epistemology. Authorial contributions are carefully tied to and shown to grow out of existing knowledge.

3. Members of a disciplinary community refer to newness as a shorthand for the standards they must follow to contribute to this growth [...] Synthesising the literature they want a place in, authors lay the ground on which they hope to make their imprint. They manage to be new when the imprint they make fits the community standard and when they can make it before their competitors have a chance to make it theirs.

4. The literature suggests that newness turns on a delicate balance between the inertia of the past and the drive to change it. (pp. 288–9)

These descriptions of how authors establish novelty add an intra-textual dimension to the sense in which argument is contextually embedded and exploitative of difference. The kinds of difference which can be successfully exploited are, in addition, dependent upon the aspects of existing accounts, knowledge and texts which are attended to within particular contexts. This presupposes that writers must have skills in identifying what counts as knowledge and discriminating how accounts differ.

In accordance with Bloom's hierarchy, Kaufer and Geisler suggest that novelty is developed out of a series of other operations upon texts. The first of these is the ability to 'inventory the stack of consensual knowledge in their target community' (pp. 289–90). But it is not the case that there is just one inventory possible within any community: there are variations in what writers know. As a result when writers synthesise what they know, they also have to *persuade* their readers that this represents the consensual/communal knowledge. As Kaufer and Geisler point out, there is a combination of both the cognitive and social here.

How are these gaps or inconsistencies in the consensual knowledge represented? Kaufer and Geisler note that gaps can be characterised as either '"inherent" to the knowledge itself or an interpretative scheme (a "heuristic") that writers opportunistically impose upon knowledge to find something new to say'. (p. 290) The way in which knowledge is explored to uncover gaps must generally also be transparent, signalled as particular 'tools of analysis' or 'method', which are legitimate within the community. And novelty claims are also of different magnitudes, from claims against an isolated fact to the subversion of a dominant theory.

The understanding of and ability to produce novelty claims constitutes, according to Kaufer and Geisler, a significant difference between expert writers and student or novice writers. They see the difference as in part due to the different status of these two groups within academic communities. The students do not have 'insider' status. They are generally taught 'to write an "original" essay, but by "original" is typically meant "free of plagiarism" or "in one's own voice" rather than new'. (p. 305) Students are not shown how to be 'poised in and against some intellectual community with the goal to talk back to it' (p. 306); how, that is, *to be in dialogue*.

CHAPTER TWO

WHAT IS THIS THING CALLED ARGUMENT?[*]

Sally Mitchell

One of the first problems of definition is that the term 'argument' is used variously to refer to an interpersonal activity in which each participant has a share (as in 'They were *having* an argument' or '*Their* argument was over x'); to denote a particular point of view from another ('My argument with what you've just said is ...'). We can think of these uses as a spectrum, at one end of which argument is the structure supporting the claim and at the other it is an active exchange between positions. The range is between a notion of argument as having an internally coherent logical shape, and a more dynamic social view in which argument is constituted in interaction and in which the validity of positions is less a quality of their internal logic than of the conditions of their reception.

To demarcate one end more clearly from the other, it may be useful to make a distinction between 'argument' and 'argumentation', in which 'argument' is the structure supporting a point of view or claim or can denote the claim itself. As the activity which gives rise to arguments, I would want to foreground 'argumentation' – the more active, social definition – as a starting place. Argumentation is an interaction between non-identical positions in and claims about the world. This interaction entails the revelation of reasoning (i.e. the steps by which a position can be reached or supported) that is shaped by a number of factors, including epistemology, situation and purpose. The revealed reasoning we can call the 'argument'. Having made the distinction, some definitions of 'argument' are close to 'argumentation': argument is *all about* encounters with other arguments.

In this essay, I want to chart some differences of conception, emphasis and use. I will start with a model of argument that can be located close to, but not right up against, the logic end of the spectrum.

Toulmin's model of argument

The work of Toulmin et al. (1984) is a good place to look for a comprehensive model of argument. Their model contains a number of related elements:

---

[*] First published in Mitchell, S. 1996. *Improving the Quality of Argument in Higher Education interim report*. London: Middlesex University, School of Education.

Claim: 'assertion put forward publicly for general acceptance'.

Grounds: 'the *specific* facts relied on to support a given claim'. 'Facts' is used here to suggest common ground between the person making the argument and the person receiving it, which enables the claim to go ahead. Less contentious terms might be 'data' or 'evidence'. If the information relied on is not agreed upon, but in dispute, then the grounds offered become in their turn a claim to be convincingly supported.

Warrants: 'statements indicating how the facts on which we agree are connected to the claim or conclusion now being offered' 'previously agreed general ways of arguing'. In science and engineering for example, warrants are generally exact and reliable, as in the case of deriving the value of an unknown variable (claim, or 'answer') from the values of known variables (grounds) via the application of a relevant formula (warrant). In other areas the basis on which we make claims from evidence is less easy to pin down precisely.

Backing: 'generalisations making explicit the body of experience relied on to establish the trustworthiness of the ways of arguing applied in any particular case'. This further level of authorisation or explicitness may be important where there are competing ways of warranting a claim. In other words, the backing validates the warrant.

These four elements, say Toulmin et al., need to be present or at least potentially present through close questioning. For an argument to be *strong*, two further elements are required:

Qualifier: 'phrases that show what kind and degree of reliance is to be placed on the conclusions, given the arguments available to support them'. We may use these phrases – e.g. probably, possibly, presumably – for a variety of reasons: 'to present our claims tentatively', 'to put them into debate in an uncommitted way, merely for purposes of discussion', 'to treat them as serious but conditional conclusions' and/or 'to offer them simply as a good bet'.

Rebuttals and exceptions: '*the extraordinary or exceptional circumstances that might undermine the force* of the supporting arguments'. These spell out the loopholes in the argument, the reasons why it does not apply in all cases or is in some other way partial.

The interconnectedness of the elements is represented in diagrammatic form. Figure 1 is my adaptation.

Figure 1

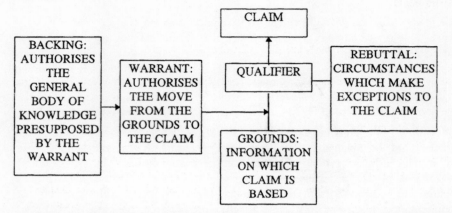

Adapted from *An Introduction to Reasoning*, by Stephen Toulmin, Richard Rieke and Allan Janik, Second Edition 1984, New York: Macmillan.

Figure 2

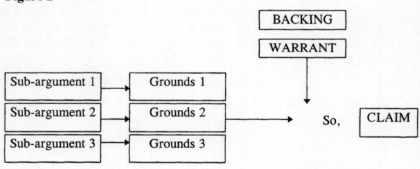

Toulmin et al. also look at the way arguments are chained so that statements which are grounds for one claim, when investigated become claims in others (Figure 2). Equally the claim in Figure 1 could be a ground in Figure 2. These diagrams depict a kind of verificational archaeology of argument, the actual or implied network of specific knowledge and more general ways of knowing on which claims are built.

As well as offering a 'vertical' underpinning, however, the various elements in Toulmin et al.'s model can also have a sequencing function in making linear texts; warrants, for example, can be seen 'not simply as a move to justify for a reader the logic of claims and data already at hand, but [...] a move to discover and create those links by developing inferences and elaborations in the process of planning and composing an argument' (Higgins, 1994). Higgins' work adds to what is a rather static model a generative dimension which applies more fully to the way people actually go about making arguments.

Voyage of discovery or travellers' tales?

It is important to note that argumentation for Toulmin is not about 'the getting of conclusions' but 'their subsequent establishment by the production of a supporting argument' (Toulmin, 1958, p. 17). 'Typically, reasoning is less a way of *hitting on new ideas* – for what we have to use our imaginations – than it is a way of testing and sifting ideas critically' (1984, p. 10). This emphasis on argumentation as a means of verifying knowledge is quite specific, but it tends to over-simplify what happens in the actual practice of argumentation. It does not account for the ways in which positions may change in the process of 'testing and sifting' and for the fact that this process may very well lead to arrival at new ideas.

A more formative, 'constructive' account of argument (see Higgins, 1994) sees it as critical exploration (which might involve the testing of alternatives) building towards or gradually uncovering a position. The following extract from an engineering student's lab book may not constitute an argument, but it does enact a process of argumentation. The student is embarking on a project to design a new mechanism for a cotton ginning machine and these are part of his 'Initial Design Considerations'. Most of the words are on the right-hand page of the book, with the 'Original drive for beater shaft' and 'Crankshaft and drive assembly' drawn and labelled on the left-hand page:

Why does the input drive have to be located where it is? When the motor is only driving the beater shaft? Assuming that the electric motor driving the machine is in a fixed position, i.e. simulating shafting or other driving means, in 'as field' conditions, different length drive belts could be used for different input drive positions.

Could a support [illegible word] be added to the end of the existing drive?
[Drawing to show this possibility].
REJECTED – 4 bearings 'in line' – alignment problems – support would have to be v. accurately made for stress free running. Is there physical room available to do this? – NO!

The student challenges the status quo; he envisages things being different and generates and tests new possibilities, using both verbal and visual modes to articulate his thinking. This is a hit and miss process, but it is the beginnings of the eventual solution that will be his 'claim'. Grounds (specific facts) and warrants (general rules) are certainly being employed.

Not to see what this student is engaged in as argumentation seems to limit the scope of the term too narrowly. Nonetheless it is useful to be aware of a distinction between research (working with hypotheses and thinking speculatively) and the demonstration or *representation* of a thesis or argument. The latter is the retrospective, rational process generally invoked by the academic essay, whilst the former is, as in the example, often recorded in a log book or field notes. Such forms of writing are generally closer to speech in their informality and open-endedness. In contrast, it is no coincidence that the argument 'proper' as Toulmin et al. would have it, is associated with high status written forms such as the academic essay, article or thesis, in which clarity of expression, structure and coherence are highly valued. I think it is true to say that the distinction is not often made clear to students and it is perhaps also true to say that teaching staff are not always good at deciding what kinds of argumentative thinking they want from their students and what kinds of writing and speaking might help them achieve it.

Regular and critical arguments

One further aspect of Toulmin et al.'s analysis which seems useful for much of the argumentation that occurs in university contexts, is the distinction between regular (rule applying) and critical (rule justifying) arguments. Rule applying arguments are those which are put forward as applications of theories that are not in themselves being challenged; backing is not called into question and warrants not evaluated. Rule justifying arguments seek to challenge the credentials of current theories and ideas and (perhaps) put forward refinements or alternatives in their place. Arguments can thus be both conforming and subversive.

This distinction seems useful because it allows us, firstly, to begin to characterise specific disciplinary uses of argument and, secondly, to notice whether there is a progression in the kinds of argument expected of students over a course of study.

Let me take literary criticism as an example. Scholes (1985) describes three activities expected of students in relation to texts: Reading, the construction of a text within a text; Interpretation, text upon text; and Criticism, text against text. Interpretation, I take here to be a rule applying activity, where the rules are the cultural codes that the reader and the text are assumed to have in common; for example, that characters can be read as morally accountable, that texts are internally coherent. Criticism is rule justifying in the sense that 'it involves a critique of the themes given in a certain fictional text, or a critique of the codes themselves out of which a text has been constructed' (p. 22). According to Scholes, criticism of a text can only be performed from a similar position of generality, i.e. another theory or paradigm: 'any group that has identified its interests as a class can mount a critical attack on a story's codes and themes from a position of its own system of values' (p. 23). As Toulmin et al. note, the regular arguments of one field may be the critical arguments of another. Thus, a coherent feminist position, say, may be used to critique the codes (warrants) of a realist textual interpretation: that is, the theoretical orientation of social science works to 'expose' the naturalised untheorised practice of interpretation. In a book by Con Davis and Schleifer (1991), a distinction is made between criticism and critique, where criticism is close to Scholes' interpretation and critique, his criticism. What the authors say of critique is instructive: it is self-reflexive in that it subjects its own methods to scrutiny – its warrants are therefore less secure and so pedagogy based on critique is not so much about what is already known, as about what can come to be known through the application of a certain system or perspective. In Toulmin et al.'s terms, in critique warrants and backing are taken as explicit starting points for generating knowledge.

If the regular/critical distinction differentiates, say, English as interpretative from English as theoretical and critical, it also enables us to trace the progress of students through the discipline. As part of the Hull project (Mitchell, 1994e), I was able to witness the change when students took a first year undergraduate course in Literary Theory, the starting point of which was to locate their own views of what it is to be a student of English within an historical context; that is, to name the warrants and backing by which they had been operating to that point.

Studies have suggested that 'expert' writers, in certain disciplines at least, tend to do more than apply rules; on the contrary, their motivation is to establish a position of difference from current ideas and thus to make a novel contribution (Kaufer and Geisler, 1989; Geisler, 1994). Citations and references to authority tend to be used negatively, so that an author's position is not constructed through equivalence to existing points of view, but through careful differentiation from them. Kaufer and Geisler capture this tendency with the notion of 'authorial newness': novelty is less 'a process of winning adherence for one's new ideas' than of 'designing to be new'. On the other hand, learning to become part of a discipline is a process of coming to share warrants. In the Hull project, I noted how Sociology undergraduates took on the principles or vantage points of the discipline (its discourse) that enabled them to talk as sociologists: argumentation was initiated from a consensual basis (Mitchell, 1995).

Where warrants can be assumed to be held in common, they are often not made explicit. An example from the Middlesex project, perhaps an extreme one, is of an occasion in interior design, where tutors were assessing students' work. They took one look at one student's drawings and started to utter phrases such as 'Love it!' 'He's got it just right'. As an outsider to the world of interior design and architecture I could not see behind these claims to what the arguments might be but at this stage, at least, the staff did not need to make them explicit. Interestingly, as the moment of communal enthusiasm passed and perhaps as they scanned the drawings more closely to see exactly what it was they liked so much, the initial claims were modified to some degree; there were after all things that the student could have done better. This was instructive: the search for evidence does not only support, it qualifies.

Change and difference

Toulmin et al. do not do so, but I want to suggest that rule-justifying, critical arguments are somehow more argumentative than rule-applying, regular arguments. Again, this move comes from attending to the social dialogic end of the definitional spectrum. 'Critical' argument chimes more closely with strong characteristics associated with the term in its everyday social and cultural uses: its association with challenging and being challenged, with the engagement with other, different points of view, with the impulse to change and the acceptance of being changed. According to this perspective on argument, the scientific example (specific data, general formula, specific result) cited earlier from Toulmin et al. to illustrate the concept of 'warrant', actually seems very little like an argument. As it contains no challenge and is unlikely to set an exchange in motion, it feels far more like an explanation (see Antaki 1994). In contrast, when warrants – 'the rules of the game' – are exposed to scrutiny, a distance opens up between one position and another, revealing their non-equivalence and giving rise to argumentation – the interactive process that fuels the search for arguments and brings about change in positions.

Locating argument

I said at the beginning of this chapter that Toulmin et al.'s view of arguments is not quite at the 'logic' end of the definitional spectrum. In fact Toulmin's early work (1958) could be said to represent a shift in argumentation theory from the rational to the reasonable. He achieved this, by insisting that no one abstract logical structure determines an argument's 'truth' or 'falsity', rather the validity of an argument is dependent on the field in which it is employed and from which it takes its backing. This means that, in order to argue successfully within a particular field, the arguer needs awareness of what counts as new knowledge, what as old, what valency claims have, when to hedge and so on. In the 1984 book, five fields are specified: law, science, the arts, management, ethics, each of these having typical goals and modes of resolution. These categorisations and typifications are useful in, for example, identifying where a student in a multi-disciplinary subject like geography may be adopting a management style of argument rather than a (social) scientific one.

In other ways though, the idea of a large-scale field of argument is rather rigid, unitary and generalised. I have found Goggin's work (1995) helpful in enriching (and complicating) the way context may be said to inform and validate a particular argument. She describes 'three intersecting historical perspectives': the macro-plane is 'the history of a context', which is constituted by the interactions of discourses, disciplines, institutions; the meso-plane is 'concerned with the individual personal histories of participants in a particular context (e.g. teachers, students and researchers in a discipline)'; the micro-plane is 'concerned with the immediate history of a given context (e.g. the duration of a particular class)'. Goggin's planes make it possible to consider how the argument I make is influenced by authoritative, 'given' ways of constructing arguments appropriate to the 'field' I am in; by individual influences and experiences, my own journey to and positionality within that field (as expert or novice, for example); and by the particular context of the interaction, including what the person before has just said that might influence what I then say.

The contingency of the micro level is particularly a part of argumentation because of the importance of otherness or difference in its operation: the way positions are formed in response to other positions. In Toulmin et al.'s model, by contrast, it is as though the argument is shaped 'from the outside in', the macro shaping the micro, which is neatly embedded within it. The Chinese Box type model, though neat, overlooks the hybridity of many situations in which arguments are made and the ways in which people actively make arguments to suit their purposes in particular situations. In her critique of Toulmin, Higgins (1994) comments that some fields are less formal (or formalised) than others and that in these 'participants [...] have not, in repeated interaction with each other, established the ground rules for arguing [and so] argument strategies may be developed and continually modified in the very act of arguing'. In these instances, fields are less 'stable entities that guide performance' than 'provisional agreements created in social interaction'. This recognition of 'new or ill defined argument situations' is of use when it comes to looking at a newly emerging discipline such as nursing, one which moreover is practically and professionally, as well as academically based. A model of argument in this area of practice and study, for example, needs to be able to take into account local pressures and influences that create the particular circumstances in which argumentation might occur. It needs to consider how individuals respond as much to social and power relations as to logic. 'Not all arguments are equal', not because of some impartial weighing of worth, but because of conditions in which they are uttered, by whom, to whom and for what purpose. For a model of argument to be useful in a discipline such as nursing it needs to include recognition of these factors.

To address the provisionality of situations and the micro level at which contexts change, I have found Bakhtin's (1981) account of the way utterances work illuminating. It provides another way of considering what Goggin is saying about context by starting with what happens when language is exchanged and extrapolating out to where that language has come from, its 'background'. For Bakhtin, an utterance is not meaningful in isolation but becomes so in the context of its reception; what he calls the 'activating principle'. Language is 'populated' by its history of usage, the situations it has been part of; at the same time the new unique meaning that a speaker gives to it is not realised until it is responded to – a kind of 'dialectical merging'.

> ... actual meaning is understood against the background of other concrete utterances on the same theme, a background made up of contradictory opinions, points of view and value judgements – that is, precisely that background that, as we see, complicates the path of any word towards its object. Only now this contradictory environment is

present to the speaker not in the object, but rather in the consciousness of the listener, as his apperceptive background, pregnant with response and objections. (p. 281)

In Bakhtin's work, a communicative act is not about a 'subject', as if the subject were somehow passive and inert, transferred intact from speaker to listener, but rather the subject, which he re-terms the 'hero' is a third active participant in the communication. In this view, argument becomes more like an event that occurs between speakers, listeners and the words they utter, rather than a stand-alone set of relations in language.

A rhetorical view of argument

With Bakhtin, we move decisively towards a rhetorical view of argument. Lanham (1993, p. 63) gives an idea of what this means when he writes of:

A broad-based willingness, if not proclivity, to look AT what we are doing, at its stylistic surface and rhetorical strategy, as well as THROUGH it, to the Eternal Truth which we all, at the end of the day, hope somehow we have served.

A rhetorical perspective embraces the external factors – the conditions of utterance, who is speaking, to whom and why – which impinge upon the internal logic or 'Eternal Truth' of a more philosophical approach. It takes argument firmly towards 'persuasion' and away from strictly intrinsic rational criteria for judging success or failure and it places meaning-making within an interactive context, so that an utterance is not so much shaped by what stands behind it in terms of abstract logical structure, as by the way (or ways) it is received and responded to.

Take, for example, an argument which appears to be presenting a single point of view, referring to no other positions. When audience and purpose are taken into account, this 'monologic' text can be reconstrued as dialogic, responding to a context of potentially conflicting positions. The very fact that the writer or speaker needs to argue, to attempt to construct a watertight position pre-supposes a context in which that position may be challenged. Having an opinion is at once an individual act and an acknowledgement of wider controversy (Billig, 1991).

This account of an argument responding to a context can be extended to a text which does not have the full internal structure of an argument. The example of the enthymeme is sometimes thought of as an incomplete argument structure, but a more rhetorical view suggests that far from being defective it may be extremely sophisticated. The second premise is not explicit, but is supplied by the listeners, thus enabling them to participate in the thinking being put forward and so be more readily persuaded by it. A second example takes this one step further and perhaps looks more outlandish. It comes from a book introducing students to *Academic Vocabulary and Argument* (Pearson and Phelps, n.d.) which gives the following two examples:

> The Vauxhall Astra has fuel injection, electric windows and power steering and is now available, at competitive prices, at your local dealer.

Writing clearly and grammatically is important. First of all it forces you to think clearly and secondly it allows the reader easily to follow what you are saying.

The first example, it is claimed, is not an argument because 'there is no reasoning involved'; the second is an argument because 'two statements are offered as a justification for the third':

1.   [writing grammatically and clearly] forces you to think clearly
2.   it allows the reader easily to follow what you are saying
                        THEREFORE
3.   writing clearly and grammatically is important

Viewed *grammatically* and as text alone, the first example 'simply asserts or reports facts or opinions', but there is something about it that tempts me to try it out as an argument, using the same syllogistic type analysis:

1.   the Vauxhall Astra has fuel injection, electric windows and power steering
2.   it is competitively priced and available now at your local dealer
                        THEREFORE
3.   you'd be wise to go along and buy one

It works as long as I supply a conclusion. It is my reasoning that construes it as an argument or more precisely an attempt to persuade, so the argument is dialogically constructed. True, other readers might not see the argument or might interpret it differently, but given the collective knowledge we share in the Western world about advertising, I don't imagine I would be alone. The words construct me as a potential buyer (the 'you' in 'your local dealer' is crucial), at the same time as I construct the words as an encouragement to buy. And although I can resist participation by not buying, I have already participated by reading the message that way.

If this account of the text seems plausible this far, then it becomes possible to see that it is not words alone that argue. If the description of the Vauxhall Astra were accompanied by a photograph of the car against an exotic backdrop and displayed above a busy roundabout I would even less doubt its message to me; or again, if I heard the words spoken on my television at the end of a film sequence showing the car driven by a bold young woman through a dramatic landscape to the sound of a famous aria, I would recognise and perhaps be persuaded that the Vauxhall Astra is not only good value for money but that, if I bought one, it would do great things for my lifestyle and image as well. You can see I am moving between conclusions: not one, but a string of them that I am generating from my encounter with the text.

The point is, I suppose, that rhetoric might play as fundamental a part in argument as reason. Each of us, in order to function in society, is a rhetorician. In different contexts we present ourselves in different ways according to the purposes we hold and the expectations we recognise others hold of us. If we want to argue successfully we draw consciously and unconsciously on all these factors. They affect not only the language we use, but the way we dress and use our bodies, or in writing, the kind of paper, format, script and so on, that we choose. The way discourse is constructed – whether, for example, writing is personalised or 'depopulated' – strengthens or diminishes the authority of argument in particular contexts.

Opening up the definition of argument through 'persuasion' to include implication and a constructive role for the recipient potentially makes a political point. The explicit propositional model of argument has been critiqued for the way it seeks to close down positions, to subsume the voices of others and to impose closure. This has been called 'the illusion of mastery' referring to the watertightness of traditional criteria for argument (see syllogistic scheme above) as patriarchal (Meyer, 1993). In forms which, for instance, work by juxtaposition or the free play of voices, the argument becomes the choice and activity of whoever chooses to engage.

At the beginning of this section, I used the phrase 'the revelation of reasoning' when talking about what argumentation is or does. But if what reasoning implies here is only the rational – what is amenable to logic – then it is not entirely useful for our purposes. Logic and reason are not the only ways in which a position may be supported. Support or 'legitimation' (van Leeuwen, n.d.) may be drawn from a range of dimensions including the affective and experiential, and evidence can be of many kinds. Put another way, there are many means by which we can be convinced. Relativising the role of logic in arguments starts to dismantle much of the framework by which they are traditionally judged good or bad. It threatens for example, the whole notion of fallacies since these exist only by a logical definition of argument. Instead, the emphasis shifts to whether the argument works or does not within certain contexts, problematising the criteria by which effectiveness is judged.

Further, the idea that argument is the 'revelation of reasoning' identifies it as a presentational tool rather than one to use in constructing: what is already made can be revealed, laid bare. Again this idea has its limits since it places argument always somehow after the event, rather than as an ongoing contingent process; archaeological rather than generative and interested in surface only as an index of depth.

If we take on board these challenges and extensions to the narrow view of argument, then we raise a number of questions: what works as argument? How do we tell and what criteria do we use for judging? What purposes can argument fulfil both in the university and beyond? Where do its parameters lie?

What are we looking for in argument?

It seems important that we are wary of the parameters of what can be counted as argument and at the same time that we are prepared to push at those boundaries. To this end, it is useful to shift to thinking of the kinds of purpose and practice that are part of argument. A list generated in part by the above discussion would contain some of the following:

- challenging evidence and claims; considering different kinds of evidence;
- making and supporting a case; generating evidence and claims;
- developing and testing ideas and alternatives;
- selecting and categorising from a range; evaluating alternatives;
- moving from wider to narrower perspectives and vice versa;
- being aware that what is being argued is part of a larger system; knowing where claims come from (how they are warranted and backed); seeing self and others as positioned in various ways; being able to imagine and explore alternative positions and look from a different vantage point;
- entertaining degrees of certainty; employing tentativeness, speculation; using questions to extend, as well as verify thinking; going beyond 'solutions' to imagine instances where the solution might no longer be valid;
- engaging in and sustaining dialogue; exploring differences, establishing connections;
- aiming to convince or engage an audience, or several audiences by various means; providing opportunities for the audience (reader, listener) to participate and respond;
- adapting the arguments of one context so that they operate effectively in another;
- judging the suitability of arguments for various purposes and contexts and being able to say why.

This is a 'brainstorm' rather than a definitive list; it includes several of the 'usual suspects' in thinking about argument and should be refined and extended to embrace the full range and complexity of what the term can offer in education. Nonetheless such a list provides a basis for generating questions and ideas for teaching and learning. What occasions are there for these practices to happen? How do students understand them? What else do they need to know (e.g. about how to structure a piece of writing) in order to carry them out? How can teaching and/or learning materials make clear what the requirements and possibilities are?

CHAPTER THREE

RECONCEIVING ARGUMENT[*]

Richard Andrews

Background

Research projects in the field of argument undertaken in the early 1990s, reported in Andrews (1992a), Andrews, Costello and Clarke (1993) and Mitchell (1994e), though very different in nature and methodology, worked broadly with a definition of argument that more closely approximated the term 'argumentation', defined in the OED as 'i) the action or operation of inferring a conclusion from propositions premised; logical or formal reasoning, ii) interchange of argument, discussion, debate and iii) a sequence or chain of arguments; a process of reasoning'. If these definitions seem circular, the circularity is not quite complete: *argumentation* is distinct from *argument* in that it describes the action and process of the phenomenon we call '*argument*'.

There are key terms in each of the definitions of argumentation that were distilled from these projects to form an overarching definition for the purposes of the research: terms like *action, reasoning, interchange, process* and *sequence.* In other words, the projects were concerned not so much with the product 'argument' (essays, transcribed debate or discussion etc.) as the action or process of arguing in school or academic contexts, though inevitably an exploration of the process of argument hammered out for that period of research (1990–94) was *a connected series of statements intended to establish a position and implying response to another (or more than one) position(s)*, sometimes taking the form of an actual exchange in discussion and debate, and usually presenting itself in speech and/or writing as a sequence or chain of reasoning (either 'at the time' or *post hoc*).

This isn't to say that the use of the term 'argument' treated it merely as an 'alias' for 'argumentation'; rather, the principal focus was on process rather than on product because the context was educational, not scientific. Indeed, many aspects of the existing definitions of 'argument' helped to direct and explore working practices and to refine the analytical tools developed to account for argument. The definition of argument as 'proof, evidence' was only partially helpful in that it failed to account for the generation and development of propositions; and the aspects of argument concerned with abstraction, as in the

---

[*] First published as Andrews, R. 1997. 'Reconceiving argument' in *Educational Review* 49 (3): 259-69.

summary or abstract of a book, suggested that distillation of concrete instances into a concept or proposition was an important element to consider. But the two aspects of 'argument' that proved to be most revealing were, first, from astronomy and mathematics: 'the angle, arc or other mathematical quantity from which another required quantity may be deduced, or on which its calculation depends'. The second develops the notion of argument being closely associated with narrative, as in the argument of a chapter that appears in, say, *Gulliver's Travels*: in that case, the argument *is* the narrative.

What kind of definition was one based on argumentation, and what were its underpinning ideologies? First, it was broad enough to cover the range from a tightly structured and formulaic essay (the formal 'default genre' in academic assessment) to a free-ranging discussion (at the informal end of the spectrum of discourses in academia) – text and discourse types that are generally considered to be argumentative forms. Second, it was specific enough to identify argument when it was encountered and to make comparisons between different kinds of argument as found in different contexts. Third, it enabled exploration below the surface of language (words, utterances) to look at the underpinning propositions that were operating in writing and/or speech. The research was informed by thinkers such as Bakhtin (for the dialogic element in speech and writing), Habermas (for the drive towards 'achieving, sustaining and renewing consensus' and for connections to rationality – see Andrews, 1995, p. vii) and Harré (for the view of argument as a process 'which enables the individual to engage with the collective, to appropriate and transform it' – see Mitchell, 1995, p. 133).

But what was missing from the working definition, both in terms of range and clarity? One aspect, which often caused difficulty, was argument that was not manifested in speech or writing, in two very different respects. First, in the philosophical dimension in which argument might be *informing* the actualities of speech, encounter or print; and second, in a not unrelated way, in argument that took other forms than the purely linguistic. In the latter case, I mean argument as expressed in movement, physical positioning, mathematical or musical form. And third, in the vernacular sense of argument associated with passion, feeling, tension and identity.

It seems now that each of these perspectives can shed further light on our definition of argument. I'll run through each of them in turn before coming back to a more representative definition of argument at the end of the chapter.

Philosophical perspective

According to the *Oxford Companion to Philosophy* (Honderich, 1995, p. 47) the term 'argument' has three main senses: as in a quarrel, when the neighbours across a courtyard argue from opposite premises; in mathematical parlance, and slightly differently from the astronomic/mathematical definition quoted above, an argument of a function is an input to it, or what it is applied to; and in the most important sense for philosophy, an argument is 'a complex consisting of a set of propositions (called its premises) and a proposition (called its conclusion)

... The conclusion must be marked, for example, by putting "because" or like before the premises').

This last sense – the central one to the practice of philosophy, according to the *Companion* – is, however, a relatively narrow one. An argument is seen to be valid when its conclusion follows from (is deducible from, is entailed by) its premises, as in 'Souls are incorporeal; therefore they have no location'.

There were two problems with such a definition as far as the Middlesex project (see Preface) was concerned. If such a syllogistic approach – the so-called 'method of argument' – is adopted, we fall into the trap of thinking that a syntactic formulation such as the example quoted above can actually apply in the real world of argument: the world in which propositions are asserted, negotiated and transformed or confirmed. Formulations at phrase, clause or sentence level (i.e. syntactic structures) do *not* translate neatly to the discourse level. If they did, linguistics would have stopped with Chomsky. That is to say, syntax-based linguistics cannot account for the complexities or even the basic nature of discourse, just as sentence-based premises and conclusions cannot readily translate into full-scale propositions and arguments as they occur socially or within people's minds. What syllogisms are revealed to be are micro-propositions cast in language, itself a highly contingent medium.

Rather than via the conventional 'sets of propositions' approach, philosophy contributes to a firmer sense of what argument is and does via a geometrical analogy and dialectic. Dialectic – the form of reasoning proceeding via question and answer – assumes the unity of opposites (the nature of everything involves internal opposition); a balance between quantitative and qualitative approaches (quantitative change always eventually leading to qualitative change or development); and the valuing of negotiation, in that secondary negotiations lead to further development and not a return to a first proposition. Dialectic's basic principles have much in common with the practice of argument – especially if argument is seen as driven by a negative mode of interpretation, characterised by Ricoeur (1970, p. 27) by 'a willingness to suspect' and a 'vow of rigour' – and are 'in harmony with the fundamental spirit of progressive, rational scientific thought' (Honderich, 1995, p. 199). While not subscribing to the rationalist, progressive tradition, Bakhtin's (1981) approach to the understanding of apparently monologic literary texts is underpinned by a principle of dialogism in even the most authoritarian utterances, and by reviewing print in the light of speech structures. His work provides a bridge between dialectic and rhetoric.

The geometrical, algebraic definition of argument, revived from its obsolete position as applied to astronomy or mathematics, allows a wider definition of argument within philosophy, as in this definition supplied by Walton (in Honderich, 1995, p. 49):

An argument is a set of propositions, one of which, the conclusion, is subject to dispute or questioning, and the others, the premises, provide a basis, actually or potentially, for resolving the dispute or removing the questioning. This definition is a little narrow, because it is possible for an argument to have several conclusions, i.e. in the case of a sequence of argumentation, where the conclusion of one subargument functions also as premises of another.

Walton's 'wider' definition sheds more light on the arguments we have encountered whose functions in academic contexts are variously to clarify, to demonstrate, to establish and/or question a position, to engage in critical enquiry and debate, to prove and to bring about consensus or resolution:

> Basically, in an argument, some key proposition is held to be in doubt, in contrast to an explanation, for example, where the proposition to be explained is generally taken for granted, or at least not subject to doubt or questioning as far as the purpose of the explanation is concerned. (ibid.)

What, then, can be gleaned from a consideration of philosophical approaches to argument that might inform a fuller definition of the term? The useful practice from philosophical enquiry is not so much the application of conventional syllogistic method (Toulmin's approach, discussed below, provides a more satisfactory approach to validity) as the affirmation of the negative, suggested by a dialectical approach: the notion that argument, like critical enquiry, will not let anything stand still, but is continually questioning its premises and conclusions via series of propositions and counter-propositions.

The projects between 1990 and 1994 (again, see Preface) focused largely on argument as manifested in print and in speech, although there was some consideration in the doctoral research (Andrews, 1992a) of arrangements of photographic images as arguments and some analysis of mathematical equations in the first Leverhulme project (Mitchell, 1994e).

The Middlesex project, 'Improving the Quality of Argument in Higher Education', deliberately set out to collaborate with two disciplines whose 'languages' were non-verbal: Visual Communication Design and Dance. The work in Dance has already identified four kinds of argument at play in the discipline: the argument embodied in *writing* about the practice and theory of dance; argument embodied in discussion and reflection about dance, before, during or after the dance itself; *choreography*, the semiotic system that depicts what is to be danced; and dance *per se*. It is clear that dance – suggested as a metaphor for argument to counterbalance prevalent metaphors based on battle and war on the one hand, and construction on the other – has much common ground with argument (even some of the language is shared, like 'taking a position', 'moves' etc.) and that much will come of a joint exploration in these fields. It may be that actual dances might be explored as *analogies* for arguments in the verbal/visual domain, or if we want to explore the application of thinking about argument to dance, that we can conceive of dance as a semiotic system *alongside* the verbal and visual (and thus subject to the same kind of analyses as arguments).

It is the visual dimension of argument on which I wish to concentrate here, however, in order to extend and refine the definition of argument itself. Central to the earlier definitions of argument was a notion of a 'sequence' of some sort, a 'chain of arguments', a 'connected series of propositions' and at the logic end of the spectrum, insistence on a particular sequence or series of propositions defining the nature of the argument itself. It is as if argument was seen as apparently time-based, like narrative, in that one proposition has to be entertained before another; but essentially the 'chain' is relational rather than temporal.

One of the findings of the doctoral research was that narrative sequences had an emotional logic about them that could not be altered without changing the narrative, whereas the elements of an argument could be arranged and rearranged with interesting rhetorical nuance, but without fundamentally affecting the direction of the argument itself. Such an observation was partly suggested by rearrangements of photographs offered to the students who were subjects in the fieldwork. The relationship between images and argument is even more removed from linearity and narrative. Images exist in time, yet by themselves their most obvious relationship to the viewer is 'vertical' rather than 'horizontal'; that is to say, although viewers may bring narrative preconceptions to a painting or sculpture, the work exists itself in a relatively time-free state. More important are its relationships within and without the frame, so that its argumentative power rests in its *difference* from what is around it, or what has come before it, but in a propositional way – a dialectical, physical, pleasurable way – rather than in series of abstract propositions or in a concrete narrative time-based sequence (unless we are talking about film).

Ostensibly, images and artworks (and dance) do not seem to argue. They operate like music, as part of first order symbolic systems – like speech, but unlike writing which has been characterised by Vygotsky (1962) as a 'second order symbolic system' prone to abstraction and therefore to reflection and argument. But artworks, at another level, *do* argue.

The relevance for argument of the visual, and the significance of the way the visual operates, is highlighted when words and images come together – as they do now in most printed communication. Consider multimedia screens and what they suggest about definitions of argument. Positions may be established and developed via a combination of image and word, sometimes following each other in a sequence, but more often than not, standing alongside each other. The *propositions* of argument (for that is still a good term to hold on to as we try to redefine 'argument') are there, as in the use of phrases like 'a visual proposition'. We will *infer* and *deduce*, often simultaneously, and always having to make connections between the images and words presented to us. We will also have to read behind the 'information' that is presented to us on the seductively sensuous screen in order to gauge the arguments that are being put forward.

Thus argument takes on a new dimension – one of positioning in space in relation to a frame and to other phenomena – when we consider it in the light of dance or the visual world. In this case, the original working definition of argument and argumentation is deepened and refined rather than radically altered, taking on i) multimodality, ii) the point of view of the 'reader' or 'viewer' and iii) openness to interpretation, where it is less constrained by a series or 'chain' of propositions. Each of these additional perspectives opens argument to rhetorical rather than logical analysis.

A paradigmatic perspective

One of the most helpful approaches to strengthening our definition of argument has been the work of Toulmin et al. in *An Introduction to Reasoning* (Toulmin, Rieke and Janik, 1984). The latter book sets out with a basic aim: to test the soundness or well-reasoned nature of arguments. It is important to point out, however, that the principal focus of the book is *reasoning* – as indicated in the title – rather than argument or argumentation. Toulmin et al. make an interesting distinction between reasoning and argumentation (1984, p. 14) in which argumentation is seen as the whole activity of 'making claims, challenging them, backing them up ...' etc. and reasoning is used 'more *narrowly*, for the central activity of presenting the reasons in support of a claim' [my italics]. The book takes an approach that although it sets *reasoning* as the overarching activity with which it is concerned, changes its focus in suggesting that reasoning is a sub-area of argumentation. To muddy the water even further, argument and argumentation are often synonymous.

The strength of the approach is that it provides a systematic way of gauging the soundness of arguments, and in order to do this it sifts out from the contexts and contingencies of argumentation what it takes to be the key elements: claims, grounds, warrants and backing, qualifiers and rebuttals. These elements are said to be analysable in any argument, whether in an informal everyday situation or in highly specific disciplinary contexts, like law. They also provide a formal characterisation of the context (more specifically, the 'field') in which the claims are made. To characterise the four essential elements briefly: claims are the assertions made or positions taken (confusingly called the 'destinations' of arguments); grounds are the foundation for the claim, often in the form of evidence or 'proof' of some sort; warrants indicate how you justify the link between the claim and the grounds for the claim; and the backing might be seen as degrees of justification for a claim (what underpins the backing?). As far as the Middlesex project is concerned, the system does provide an analytical tool for making comparisons between different manifestations of argument in order to answer the following questions: what are the common elements of argumentation in the disciplines that are being explored? What are the key differences between the way argumentation takes place in these disciplines? Does the Toulmin et al. model provide a satisfactory basis for analysis in these disciplines?

Its problems as far as the current project is concerned, however, are considerable. First, for a book that sets out to establish criteria to test the soundness of an argument, it admits later that 'context determines criteria' (p.

256). In other words, the attempt to establish a model that applies to a certain extent in a number of situations has to admit that, in the end, the situations are the determinants of the model. Second, it operates via a number of simple polarities – instrumental versus argumentative language, argumentation as advocacy or inquiry. The interesting thing about setting up an argument on such a polarised basis is that even if you represent the polarity as 'two ends of a continuum', you are still operating with a formulation that is unable to cope with the dynamics of argumentation in space; and essentially, you are also operating from a model whose backing is adversial (either/or). Britton's (1975) formulation of 'poetic' and 'transactional' language (cf. Toulmin et al.'s equally unsatisfying 'instrumental/argumentative' formulation) is not powerful enough as a theory or model to account for the actualities of argument as found in everyday and academic discourse.

Second, all the examples in the book are taken from propositions in the form of sentences or small clusters of sentences. Although that is how arguments may take shape in some contexts, as a method of explication it falls into the trap of the syllogistic approach, assuming that demonstration of argumentative development at an exemplary, simple-propositional level will somehow translate to arguments that are of a different size or nature.

Third, there are too many variables informing the nature and direction of arguments *as they happen* to be able to account for in a system that breaks down argument into four main elements. Toulmin's system is useful in that it provides a *post hoc* method of analysis to determine the underpinning of arguments. What it doesn't do is provide a way of accounting for the way arguments move and develop.

Discourse in education – the principal research context within which the Middlesex project operates – is more a means to an end, a process by which positions are changed or reinforced. Argumentation is one particular aspect of discourse (i.e. utterances, parole) in this respect. We are continually escaping from a rule-governed, systematic (*langue*) approach to its analysis in an attempt to be clear about the particular disciplinary constraints and influences on student practice.

Argument in the everyday sense

The research projects on which this book is based have always acknowledged that 'argument' is a term that covers a wide variety of discourses in everyday life. In *Teaching and Learning Argument* (Andrews, 1995), I began with such an acknowledgement, and analysed a dispute between Paul and Clara in *Sons and Lovers*. The fact that a literary exemplum was chosen, however, reveals the lack of research material about rows, differences of opinion and disputes in personal, domestic, social and political life – or my own inability to find them.

Nevertheless, it is possible to identify some of the characteristics of argument in the everyday sense and to note the differences between this kind of argument and argument in educational contexts, which is the focus of our research. Everyday arguments are almost always adversarial; if not, they tend not to be called 'arguments' at all, but rather 'discussions' or some other term, which does nor imply conflict. They tend to be heated. They are associated more with passion and the expression of intense feeling than with reasoning. Often the real position in the argument is revealed through a process of attrition or by degrees: 'what are you really saying here?' or 'are you saying that ...?' are common questions in the course of such an argument. What appears to be the source of the dispute is often only the catalyst for the real argument, or for one party to want to raise an important issue. The argument has a partially cathartic and clarifying function: it 'clears the air'. In most cases, if the argument develops at all beyond sterile claim and counter-claim, it leads to resolution (and perhaps action as a result) or to an agreement to differ (a crucial facility in a democracy, where the acceptance of difference is essential to the continuance of the democratic equilibrium). In less common cases, it leads to violence or separation, when words fail to bring about a resolution of any kind.

What must also be acknowledged is that the complex process of discovering a position through everyday argument is important in the formation of identity. Particularly in adolescence but also throughout people's lives in Western culture, argument is a means by which to assert a position (either verbally and/or through clothes, choice of music, allegiance to a football team or allegiance to a set of ideas or values). Indeed, 'identity' might be conceived as the finding of a position in relation to others in domestic, social, political and cultural ways. Argument is one of the means by which such a position – or number of positions – is negotiated.

It is particularly interesting that assertions of identity through argument at their height, perhaps, in the years from 12 to 25, take place at the same time that school and higher education are making demands upon students to learn practices of spoken and written argument, both generically and specifically. These take place generically in the teaching and learning of the skills of debate, written argument, formal discussion and so on in English lessons in school, and also in core skills elements in communication in the 16–19 phase; and specifically in the complex positioning that students learn as they induct themselves into the discourse practices of particular disciplines (which was the focus of the Leverhulme-funded research at Middlesex University). Research is required to find out how students relate their studies to their emerging sense of self.

A new (working) definition of argument?

Any 'new' definition of argument is offered here with two caveats: first, the definition is a 'working definition' for the purposes of the research project on improving the quality of argument in higher education; it does not claim to be a comprehensive dictionary definition. Second, it is a paradox of research that there is a need to define terms clearly at the outset, but it is more than likely that the research itself will require redefinition of the parameters of the field.

What is offered here, then, is a reflection on the current state of argument research in the light of work to date and from the perspectives discussed above. At the end of the current project, we may need to refine the definition further.

The core of the original definition still stands with a focus on argumentation, located in educational and more specifically, institutional contexts in which disciplinary constraints play a major part in shaping its nature. These disciplinary influences are distinctive, confirming a hypothesis which emerged from the 1990–94 (projects two and three) research, viz. that a discipline was often constituted not only around a field of interest (e.g. the geophysical world and its relation to human culture in geography) but also around *a way of seeing and arguing about that field*. Because all four projects as a whole are located within Education and are therefore concerned with development, the emphasis is primarily on process rather than product. Secondarily, the nature of products ('arguments' in various forms) is of interest, but only insofar as their analysis sheds light on the process of argumentation. This means that the linguistic dimension to the research contributes to the overall aim of the research, which is educational.

But it is precisely in the linguistic dimension that the definition needs refinement. In the original 1990–94 definition, the phrase 'a connected series of statements' covered a range of possibilities in the manifestation of argument. It now appears that 'statements' seems too nebulous a term to account for the elements of an argument.

Consider the metaphor of the town square as one that might help clarify the ways in which argument works. A town square is a public meeting place. People enter it from the surrounding streets, each with their own preoccupations, values and points of view. Interactions take place in the square: these might be conflicting, consensual or otherwise. An individual might meet a group. Or the interactions might be one-to-one or group to group. If the metaphor of the town square is to be of any use in the attempt to reconceive argument, it can be so in respect of the relationship between positions and 'moves'. 'Statement' is too static, too final, to warrant its further use in the definition as a whole. Rather, the discrete 'moves' (we will use that term for the time being) that make up an argument need to acknowledge the dynamic nature of an argumentative exchange. Furthermore, any such 'move' in an argument is relative to the context (Which particular town square am I in? What journey am I taking? Where have I come from and where am I going? How do I need to negotiate this town square in order to continue my journey?) as well as to the agent (person, book etc.) who is providing me with alternatives to my present assumptions. In short, the process of argumentation is more than the stringing together of a 'connected series of statements'; it is the deploying of verbal, visual and physical 'moves' in order to negotiate a new position, always in relation to others (accepting, of course, that the 'other' position(s) may be generated from within one's own head or from one's own feelings/intuition). The process is essentially dialogic and optionally multimodal.

The third element in the 1990–94 definition was concerned with the function of argument: 'intended to establish a position'. We might, with hindsight, call this an immediate function, with the broader functions of argument – to persuade, to win, to clarify, to explore and assert identity, to resolve, etc. (see Andrews, 1995, pp. 150–1) – part of a wider social picture. 'Position' is still a useful term for a number of reasons, not least that it suggests that the speaker/writer/author (rhetoricians would use the generic term 'rhetor') needs to define a position in relation to others engaged in the argument. Refinement of the phrase is required, however, as far as the word 'establish' goes. The process of argumentation is concerned not only with the establishment of a position, but with the business of changing position. Establishment suggests the staking out of ground and the reinforcement of that position with supporting evidence and strengthening complementary propositions. Changing position is more concerned with understanding how positions are established and reinforced, but also how they are moved.

The final element in the original definition holds true to the dialogic (Bakhtinian) principle: that every argumentative move implies response to another (or more than one) position(s).

A new working definition of argument for the purposes of the current project would thus be: *a series of linguistic, visual and/or physical propositions in engagement with one or more other points of reference in order to change or assert a position.* This provisional definition of the territory for exploration might be seen as a *broad* definition for argument as opposed to the *narrower* definitions with which this article started. The openness of the definition is deliberate, too, in the first stages of a project in order not to close down potential avenues for researching and discovering new conceptions of argument.

Metaphors underpinning this new conception are further away from those of war and battle than they were in 1990; instead, the metaphors of journey, exchange and dance – captured in the unifying metaphor of the town square with its associations of barter, conversation and redirection – have gained in power and centrality. The metaphorical shift (and the metaphors are only there to enable orientation to the field of argument) does not imply a weakening of the power of argument. On the contrary, the changing emphasis from a simple adversarial model of argument to argument for a range of purposes and in a number of different forms indicates diversification, and the potential power of argument to influence social action. Fights may still occur in the square, but they will be occasional skirmishes rather than the *sine qua non* of argument: a means to an end, rather than the end itself.

But metaphors are *aide-memoires* and levers to activate an understanding of a field, rather than boundary lines. The boundaries have shifted somewhat in our research on argument, acknowledging the rhetorical nature of the enterprise and, as a consequence, the multimodal potential of studies in argument.

Furthermore, analytical rigour has been increased with the consideration of Toulmin et al.'s approach to judging the internal coherence of arguments; and the everyday sense of argument has reminded us that the sources of argument are social, dynamic and infused with feeling and passion as well as reason (and not always in opposition). Finally, the dialogic dimension of argument has not only reinforced the rhetorical backing; it has also supported the notion that argument cannot really take place unless the participants accept that – whatever the power relations between them – there is room for a change of position on either side. Without such agreement – tacit or otherwise – individuals, institutions and larger social and political groupings are prone to authoritarianism and fossilisation, and the bolstering of untenable ideologies. Part of the function of argument is to try to ensure that the relationship between ideas and action, and the possibility of the exchange of ideas, remain alive.

CHAPTER FOUR

ARGUMENT IN SCHOOLS: THE VALUE OF A GENERIC APPROACH [*]

Richard Andrews

The modes that have particularly interested me during the last five years (i.e. 1988–1993) are narrative and argument, or narration and argumentation in an educational context. In this chapter it is argumentation that is going to be my main focus, though the first third of it will describe – in narrative mode – how I come to be at this position. In the latter part of the chapter, I will focus on the place of genre in schooling and on two research projects currently running in 20 schools and colleges in collaboration with The University of Hull.

The story starts in Hong Kong. As English Department Chair in an international school there, I was seconded for one day per week in 1986–87 to look at 'language across the curriculum'. I interpreted this as 'discourses across the curriculum', and soon found that as an English teacher I had more in common with historians and mathematicians than I had imagined. A historian talked about the relationship between narrative and argument in history, and a mathematician, having analysed a story I told in an assembly in terms of the Fibonacci series, talked about the syntax of sentences in his subject. He described argument as 'the angle, arc or other mathematical quantity from which another required quantity may be deducted, or on which its calculation depends'.

I then started to read research of the late seventies and first half of the eighties on the place and nature of argument in English (e.g. Freedman and Pringle, 1984; Dixon and Stratta, 1986a and b; Medway, 1986; and others in this field). The general picture was as follows:

- very little revision was going on above the level of the sentence in the writing of school students;
- 'argument' took up a small or very small proportion of the work in English (figures varying from 4.8 per cent to about 12 per cent, according to the definition of argument);
- concern was expressed at the inability of students in secondary or high schools to argue well, either in speech or in writing;

[*] This chapter is a version of a paper given at a research colloquium, 'Redefining genre', held at Carleton University, Ottawa, in April 1992 and published as Andrews, R. 1993. 'Argument in schools: the value of a generic approach', *Cambridge Journal of Education* 23 (2): 277–85.

• students were being constrained by the genre of the school 'essay' at secondary level, and hardly given the chance to use argument in school at elementary level.

Various suggestions were made to remedy the problem, however, and these included the provision of models, drawing on speech genres, reading more argument, infusing argument with expressive 'voice', and so on.

My own approach was to generate a hypothesis that command of narrative structures might well help students to write better arguments. I dreamed up the notion of an alchemical transformational grammar, transposed from the syntactical level to the discourse level, in which command of and facility with narrative patterning would somehow open up argumentative discourse to students in secondary and high schools, and perhaps even in elementary schools. My approach was principally through structure: I was interested in the arrangement of different discourses, and how one might form the foundation for the other in the development of a wider repertoire of discourses (see Andrews, 1992a).

In order to test my hypothesis, I set up a study with 150 year 8 students in a town which had three high schools. I took a representative sample of the students in that year – more than a third of the total population in that age group – and gave them each two pieces of writing to do: one in narrative mode, which in generic terms might be said to be a school 'short story' ('school' in its context as a genre, not in its subject matter) and one in argumentative mode, which in generic terms might be called an 'opinion essay'. To specify the genre even more sharply, each piece of writing took one hour of class time. The resultant stories and essays were thus highly conventional and highly artificial. 'Closure', for example, was brought about by the bell rather than by any intrinsic momentum in the writing of narrative.

The criteria I developed in order to analyse the 150 stories were based on the work of Stein and Glenn (1979) on story structure (which in turn had developed from the work of Rumelhart (1975), Mandler and Johnson (1977) and others). In brief, I was analysing the stories in terms of settings and event structures. The event structures were broken down into relationships between the components of the stories (which, following van Dijk (1981), I called 'episodes') which could be characterised as AND, THEN and CAUSE relationships. The essays were analysed in terms of statements and proofs, and the proofs by a series of criteria based on various sources: classical rhetoric, simple description of the function of the component in the argument, and surface indicators of movement in argument like 'therefore' and 'nevertheless'.

Surprisingly, only two of the 300 compositions I analysed could be said to have the same structure, the same arrangement. These were two narratives. All the arguments and 99 per cent of the narratives had different structures. There was, therefore, little chance of any transformational formulae for moving from narrative to argument. I now see, however, that structure is a much more variable and flexible phenomenon than I had assumed. Not only that, it is hardly simple. Any story might be said to include a number of different structures;

different viewpoints might reveal different structures, and one of the fascinating prospects would be to look at the interplay between these different structures in any composition. I suspect we might find that the structure of children's writing was fugued, or at least as complex as the structures of quartet music.

Nevertheless, there was much to salvage from the largely negative results of this small-scale research – and I am going to narrow my focus here to the argumentative writing, the 'opinion essays' that were produced by the 150 year 8 students in my sample.

Firstly, the nature of planning in the argumentative writing was different from that in the narrative writing. Almost a third of the plans for the stories were, in fact, first drafts, whereas only 10 per cent of the plans for the essays were drafts. Rather than agree with what Burtis and others concluded in their 1983 paper, however – namely, that 'planning in narrative lags behind planning for argument' – I would say that the planning for the two modes of writing is very different. Narratives seem to be written by accretion, with planning going on during the act of composing; with arguments, the planning tends to go before the scripting of the argument. In this sample, most of the argument plans were in the form of spider diagrams, numbered notes (implying a sequence) or connected boxes. Only 2 per cent took polar form, i.e. the 'for-and-against' model that is often taught in schools as the way to construct arguments.

Secondly, given a free choice on the topics for argument, the students showed considerable invention: 'Why birds should not be allowed on the ground', 'Should fleas wear protective clothing?', 'Why sheep should not be air stewards', as well as the more predictable arguments on animal rights and the more immediate arguments for changes in school life.

Thirdly, 62 per cent of the sample were ready to change the sequence of their arguments, whereas only 26 per cent could envisage such changes in their narratives. Of those who could see possible changes in their essays, only 5 per cent claimed that there were only limited changes possible. By far the majority saw the order of their argumentative writing as being flexible.

Fourthly, one surprising result was that although, as expected, half the students found narrative the 'easier' mode to work in, with 35 per cent preferring argument (a result that is nowhere near as conclusive as earlier research might have suggested), the only low-banded/setted class in the sample found argument more conducive to expression, more personal and more enjoyable. Perhaps this class had more to argue about.

That last point can act as one from which the second part of my argument can proceed – or to use the language of mathematics and astronomy, a point from which another required angle can be deduced.

In a sense, what I am leading towards is not only to do with 'genre'. The term 'genre' has been a meeting place – I use the metaphor carefully – for many interests, but to extend the metaphor, this public square, this forum is itself part of a city. In order to get a clearer sense of the nature of genre and its relationship with other ways of organising language, I feel the need to get beyond this public space into the rest of the city, or to rise above the square and take a birds' eye view to get the whole into perspective.[1]

While we are still on the ground, however, we can identify sub-categories of genre that are more fixed, more subject to analysis of their structure and shape than genres. These can be called 'forms' or 'text-types'. An example of such a form is the sonnet, which in general is a sub-category of the genre 'lyric poem'. Most people know that the sonnet is a 14-line poem, which itself can come in various shapes: the Petrarchan, the Shakespearean, the Miltonic, the Robert Lowellian and so on. You can even split the 14 lines into two groups of seven and still call it a sonnet.

Above the level of genre, and certainly a broader-based category, is what I would call 'mode'. A mode is a 'way' rather than a genre ('type') or form ('shape'). Narrative seems to be a mode, as does argumentation. These can be conceived as umbrella terms, themselves subject to social variation, but providing a more general and collective term for ways of organising discourse. There are other modes, of course, and none of them is watertight.

A possible relationship between functions, modes, genres and forms is depicted in Figure 1.

Figure 1

A Map of Argument

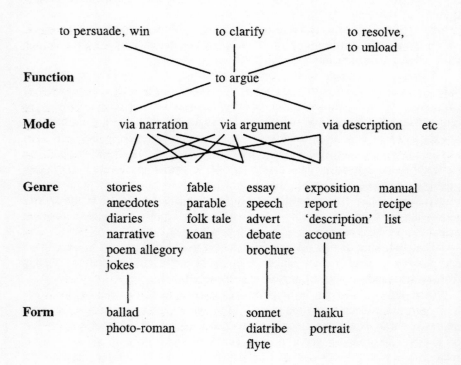

I want to make seven brief points about this model:

1. Functions are not only multi-levelled but can be multiple, for example, you can argue to persuade, clarify *and* resolve.
2. You can fulfil a function in various ways – not only in any of the ways depicted here, but visually, in dialogue and so on.
3. What is the relationship between such levels of analysis and levels of abstraction? I would suggest there is no clear correlation between the two.
4. Which of the kinds of language listed above are genres? How does the notion of genre as social action affect this model? Some would argue that narrative is a genre and that the photo-roman is also a genre. That is true if we take 'genre' to be a very elastic term, but such elasticity becomes of little use. I would prefer to maintain a distinction between the levels for purposes of clarity.
5. Is such an arrangement useful? Yes, in so far as it enables us as writers and teachers to be aware of the rhetorical route we are taking, but also to be aware of other possibilities and thus to fit the form of our expression to its purpose.
6. What is the possibility of mixed genres? There is clearly huge scope here for combinations of genres in the same communicative act, as well as for blends (see Fitzgerald, 1992).
7. How might a model like this help teachers and students to fit form to function? Does this model help us define the ground rules for speech and writing in school?

Perhaps the students mentioned earlier who preferred argument as a mode of expression in school were partly rebelling against the 'ground rules' of the school and, in particular, of the English lessons within the school. They certainly had a lot to argue against in the school, and they found narrative more difficult and less pleasurable because it was more taxing ('having to make things up') and more peripheral than argument. They eschewed the 'what if?' mode that is a given in most school situations.

The notion of 'ground rules' I owe to a book by Yanina Sheeran and Douglas Barnes, *School Writing* (1991). They make it clear that they do not see ground rules as genres as such, but as more broadly based unstated laws by which writing is shaped and evaluated within schools:

> our argument in this book is that writing in school requires the writer to take over both new conceptual structures and (at the same time) to manage sets of ground rules, some general to the school as a whole, some related to the curricular subject, and some specific to a particular occasion and teacher. (p. 14)

Indeed, adherence to a particular genre – like the school essay – can be restrictive. This is why Sheeran and Barnes – and I think they are right – reject the narrower version of the term 'genre', especially if such genres are arrayed as a teaching programme based on genres identified by their surface features.

The definition of genre is obviously crucial to the present debate. If, as the research cited so far suggests, genres cannot be fully accounted for by 'surface features' or by distinctive structures, it makes sense not to devise programmes of identifiable genres arrayed in sequences or otherwise (cf. Moffett, 1981 and 1986; Christie, 1984). On the other hand, we ought to be able to deconstruct metaphors of 'surface' and 'depth' which anyone can use to discredit an opposition and strengthen his or her own position.

Perhaps 'mode' is a better level at which to solve the problem of argumentative genres than the level of genre itself. To refer back to the metaphor of the city square – a metaphor, by the way, that rhetoricians would concur with – the place of genre within it can be better seen from a higher level, a level from which maps would be conceived. It follows that in order to conceive of alternatives to the genre in which you are composing and, therefore, not to be bound or constricted by genre, you need to distance yourself from the convention or from the most obvious form of expression for the ideas you want to convey, and consider other possibilities. You can only do this by moving up a level, as it were: by being conscious of the genre within which you are working, and/or by looking at the possible formal shapes you can use in order to say what you want to say. This point introduces the final part of my article.

With colleagues at Hull, I am currently trying to do just this in two research projects. One is an action-research project running in 20 schools in East Yorkshire and Lincolnshire, which is designed to improve the quality of argument for students aged 7 through 16. The aim of the other project is to examine the nature of argument in the 16–19 age group and in higher education (i.e. university level) across the curriculum.

In the 7–16 project, some of the work is quite conventional – like work on debating or on the kinds of argument that appear in newspapers (like leader editorials, advertisements and so on) – but it has to be remembered that the schools are defining their own research goals here with the help of the university. If moving into debating and newspaper work is an advance for a school, then that is quite within the aims of the project as a whole. However, most of the approaches to improving the quality and range of argumentation are more innovative in a wider sense. Several secondary/high schools are working on the relationship between gender and argument, trying to answer questions like: do particular genres suit girls rather than boys and vice versa? What happens to group discussion when groups that are usually mixed split into single-sex groups? What kinds of argumentation are preferred by the two sexes?

One school has been exploring the interface between spoken and written argument, and has come up with a form that I have not seen in schools before: the symposium. Students discuss an issue or a text in a small group, then write up their discussion, not in monologic form, but using the several voices that constituted the discussion in the first place. So the final written work looks more like a playscript (with appended commentary) than the conventional 'essay'. Another school has a year 8 class making a promotional video for the headteacher in order to sell the virtues of the school to the community. Such a project opens up the function of argumentation for students in that the audience is a real one, though the context is still within the school. Yet another project is getting involved in a local political issue: whether or not to build a bypass round a village near the school; others are using multi-voiced argument.

At elementary school level, the research is, if anything, more interesting, largely because others have assumed that children of elementary school age can't argue. Our emerging thinking on this issue is as follows: we don't believe that importing a repertoire of narrowly conceived genres from the high school phase is necessarily the right way to go about giving younger children access to argument. We are not in accord with the pedagogical approaches of Lipman and his school. Nor do we hold with the James Moffett notion that 'narrative must do for all' with such children. However, we are finding that, given more control over the subject matter and the shape that arguments take in the classroom, children of this age will argue readily.

I can offer two examples to illustrate my point: first, a school in which I observed a session built around a problem formulated by one of the children. The child, Henry, had a real personal problem. His mum had told him not to buy sweets with his pocket money. He took this very seriously, but on the other hand couldn't resist buying some. The problem was that he had entered the competition on the wrapper, and won two tickets to EuroDisney. What should he do? The class discussed the problem in groups and then as a class, and so resolved it. Not a difficult one to resolve, with EuroDisney having more of a hold than parental dictat, but it did have the effect of children arguing an issue about which they felt passionately.

Another elementary school has taken the notion of argument in school a stage further. The headteacher reports that children had said to her that she was trying to resolve their differences too quickly. A dispute would emerge on the playground. The two children involved would be presented to the headteacher. With a combination of headteacherly fiat and sheer lack of time, she would resolve the problem for them. However, she found it did not work. Now she is using a range of strategies to encourage children to increase self-respect and self-esteem, to argue their cases, to engage feeling with argument. This partly operates through a formal school council, and also in the way teachers relate to children and children to each other. What she is aiming for, then, is the transformation of discourses within an institution.

There are many more examples I could cite of ways of reconsidering what argument might mean in a school context. One probably under-researched aspect of this whole question is the relationship between forms of discourse outside school – both domestically and in public – and what goes on in school. In argument, this is particularly interesting. Teachers I worked with in London recently wanted to talk about nothing more than the personal arguments they had recently had and what the functions of those arguments were. When I finally diverted them from the domestic and professional levels, they generated some wonderfully witty and imaginative ways of putting cases forward – like a complaint about holes in London's roads by two cyclists who used their two voices to create a glorified whinge.

In the 16-university project, it is emerging that some school subjects are more overtly argumentative than others (e.g. sociology and politics at one end of the spectrum, biology at the other); secondly, we are examining the nature of sequences of questions in the classroom, going beyond the work of Barnes (Barnes et al., 1989) in this field (see chapter 11 in the present book).

In summary, it can be said that:

1. Attempts to define the structures of school stories or essays are fraught with difficulty. Although my initial research failed to identify correspondences between narrative and argumentative modes, I cannot fully give up the idea that rhythmic relations in texts, or syntagmatic relationships at the discourse level, are still worth pursuing, both in poetic texts and in other texts.

2. Students at year 8 level show considerable ingenuity and flexibility when it comes to playing with the arrangement of their essays at the discourse level; they are not bound by Aristotelian or Ciceronian notions of structure, nor do they conceive of argument in the 'for-and-against' frame.

3. Their knowledge about narrative and argumentative modes is more sophisticated than might be assumed. It may be that children are more sensitive to differences in genres than they are to distinction at the level of the sentence or below.

Questions I want to continue to pursue include:

·   If breaking from the conventional school essay has been like 'breaking the pentameter' ('that was the first heave', according to Pound), what is the range of forms and genres possible in schools at different ages (right up to university level)?

·   Are there other forms like the symposium which might enliven writing with shapes borrowed from speech?

·   Is there a language to describe differences between modes, genres and forms that might help teachers (and students) to clarify for themselves what they are doing or trying to do with language?

·   How do changes in the contexts of school speech and writing affect the products that are created?

Note

1. The town square metaphor might be read alongside the metaphor that describes genres as areas which hold several forces in a kind of balance or tension. In this latter description, vectors such as 'content', 'social context', and 'process' can act as descriptors of elements or aspects of genres. The town square metaphor appears to be more static until you see it in terms of people and interactions (verbal or otherwise). For a fuller discussion of the metaphor and its relevance for argumentation and rhetoric, see previous chapter.

CHAPTER FIVE

QUALITY IN ARGUMENT: WHY WE SHOULD SPELL OUT THE GROUND RULES *

Sally Mitchell and Jeff Mason

This piece was part of a colloquium in which teaching colleagues were invited to engage dialogically with a number of positions put forward on the issue of improving the quality of student argument in higher education. Here, Jeff Mason, a philosopher, intervenes to question and extend the position that Sally Mitchell is developing.

SM: There are two major players in the educational game: students and staff. Though subjects evolve and the practical conditions change, for staff the teaching experience is one of relative stability and control. For students the experience is more complex and shifting, as they move between sets and, more locally, between modules and individual tutors. Each move involves a new beginning at some level, a new set of 'ground rules' to be oriented towards. As far as writing is concerned, the activity occurs so rarely and then as the dominant form of assessment (often summative), that each written offering is as much a gamble with the unknown as a building block in an overall educational progression. Students can find the instructions they are given opaque: 'This time it says to write a report. How is that different from an essay?' and it's the same with the feedback they receive: 'You have an unusual writing style'.

JM: Yes, we do need ways to make the various 'languages' spoken in the university more accessible to students and becoming aware of their use of arguments is a useful approach. The ground rules need to be spelled out more. Students need to be told what it is to write a report as opposed to an essay, or a critical essay from exegesis. They need to know that arguments do not have to be personal, but a means to explore a topic with others. There are sides to take, but these are like parts to be played. Argument in the humanities is supposed to widen horizons, not to narrow them.

SM: On top of this, issues of identity and self expression are felt, perhaps particularly in regard to argument – often thought of in terms of conviction and

---

* First published in Riddle, M. (ed). 1997. *The Quality of Argument: a colloquium on issues of teaching and learning in higher education.* London: Middlesex University, School of Lifelong Learning and Education.

personal point of view and though clearly valued in academic writing, seemingly at odds with its other 'rules'. A student put it to me recently: 'There are two essays – the one you write and hand in, and the one you don't write – which is yours'. 'And even then', her companion added, 'the one you write still isn't the right one'.

JM: I would add to this that the one you didn't write is still not right either. Unless a student can express herself in words, it is unclear what the contents of the unwritten essay might be. Improvements can be made with practice.

SM: The difficulty for staff, even where they are aware of and concerned about these issues, is that they may have 'practical' but not 'discursive consciousness' (Giddens, 1986) of what they rate highly within their discipline and their students' contributions to it.

JM: That's because staff are at the disadvantage of tending to forget what it was like before they learned their own academic language and adopted the conventions of their discipline.

SM: As Giltrow and Valiquette (1994) point out, there is not an easy relationship between these two types of knowledge: 'much tacit knowledge is not directly accessible to discursive consciousness; practical consciousness is not exhaustively constituted by propositional beliefs'. Nonetheless, without attempts to articulate what it is that makes up practical consciousness (of say, 'expert' staff and 'novice' student), there is little possibility of improving – improving the way students experience and make sense of their learning, as well as their ability to write the 'right' essay.

JM: I wonder about this. Isn't the way for students to improve their sense of learning for them to feel that they are making progress in the subject, whatever it may be? Do we want them to become more 'competent'? Or do we want them to improve, to enjoy it more and to do it better?

SM: It's these issues and the difficulties they raise that the Middlesex Argument Project is attempting to grapple with, by thinking about what might constitute useful links across the diversity of disciplines, sets and modules, and about how both staff and students might begin to develop accessible understandings of what they value and effective strategies to carry these through into practice. At the core of the Middlesex project is an attempt to articulate a general conception of argumentation as an arena where the inhabitants of differing disciplinary worlds can meet. Argument is seen as having the potential to bring disparate groups together because it represents both a basic social activity and a highly valued cognitive operation. It articulates relations between different levels of the concrete and abstract and is an important way in which we know things about the world and know how to act to change or sustain that world. The enterprise of bringing disparate parts of the university together around argument is not unproblematic however. Where different disciplines have already well developed vocabularies and ideas about argument, the difficulties of matching or comparing understandings across boundaries become apparent. To provide some common ground the project has adopted and is adapting[1], a model of argument (Toulmin et al., 1984) which does not have a clear disciplinary home – philosophy and linguistics would be obvious places to look for alternatives. The advantage of Toulmin et al.'s model is that it is to some degree social, acknowledging that successful argument is judged by effectiveness within situations rather than by necessary recourse to the validity of logic. At the same time, the model is abstract enough to remain relatively stable across and between contexts.

JM: We've argued around this point quite a lot and I still wonder if the notion of the stability of argument has come from analogy with logic. A philosopher might try to distinguish effective argument or soundness of argument from whether it is true. Presumably, one could have a successful argument with a selected audience that was nonetheless false, as for example that which argues the Holocaust didn't happen. Nevertheless, I see the Argument Project as part of a wider project to reconsider the place of rhetoric in higher education. Argument, after all, was considered part of dialectic and dialectic part of rhetoric as a whole. In the last three or four hundred years, however, dialectic has been taken away from rhetoric and made into logic, which also was part of dialectic in the systems of ancient rhetoric. The essay form is, as you rightly point out, the prime rhetorical form which students confront. It is conventional and it demands following the rules. This can be frustrating for the student.

SM: It is not the case that identifying a model such as Toulmin's is a simple solution to the problem of disciplinary-countries not communicating and students being lost amongst them. The model, like all models, does not leap off the page and attach itself effortlessly to practices around the university. Like many models it oscillates between description and prescription and bringing it together with the local practice is something to be worked at, perhaps rather self consciously. In Design, for example, where we have been examining the critical interactions which occur between staff and students, we have been thinking of the 'claim' as constituted by an object (design solution) arrived at by working through a series of 'grounds' and 'grounds as claims' (the design brief). In actual staff/student exchanges, recognising what is being said as elements in the model is not easy. But when used in a slowed down simulated situation, access to the model can expose questions that are not being asked and assumptions that are left implicit. The model, that is, can act to raise awareness.

The same is, I think, true for students. In particular, the idea of warrants and backing opens up for examination the idea that different rules and assumptions

---

[1] See Riddle (2000) and Mitchell and Riddle (2000) for accounts of the model which the Middlesex project eventually developed.

underpin their various courses. It begins to explain for them why in essays more than 'what I think' is required, why not all arguments are equal in all situations and why attending to and referencing a body of literature might be an important way of getting your own voice heard. As these examples suggest, though, to become better arguers the abstract model is not all the students have to learn; they have, for instance, to operationalise the elements of argument in textual form (see Coirier, 1996). The essay is sometimes thought of as the perfect form for developing argument because it requires such explicitness about the moves that are made (e.g. Olson, 1977). As a leader of a module looking directly at argument, I know that this kind of knowledge is greeted by students with a mixture of interest and anger. They welcome insights into how they might argue better but they also resist the conventions that dictate how they should express themselves. In many ways they are right; in the real world argument is infinitely more things than an essay. Moreover, the essay can also be seen as the most unargumentative of forms: you're not really trying to persuade your (both very specific and rather generalised) reader of your point of view so much as your ability to represent your thinking in a conventionalised way.

JM: What you're overlooking here is that an essay is more than argument. And besides, there are many kinds of essay and other criteria of evaluation than its argumentativeness. Many 2ii students typically go through the motions in their writing. First class students always try to persuade you of their point of view.

SM: Merely to consider the most conventionally 'perfect' argument as the best argument, ignores an important dimension of learning to argue that arguments – effective arguments – come in all shapes and sizes with various degrees of explicit and implicitness, disinterestedness and passion. Persuasion does not occur through the exercise of reason alone and language is not a transparent window on thought.

Richard Lanham (1993) makes an observation which I think is central in thinking about learning to argue. He notes that a tension (a useful, creative 'bi-stability') has always existed between looking THROUGH language 'to the Eternal Truth which we all, at the end of the day, hope we have somehow served' and looking AT 'its stylistic surface and rhetorical strategy'. On the whole Toulmin's model offers a way of looking through language, emphasising the relations between propositions rather than the way in which they are expressed. (In the idealised view of the essay, the expression and the thought should, of course, be interchangeable.) But arguments occur in language and so in learning to argue we need to pay attention to the actual forms and situations in which arguments appear: discussions, essays, presentations, newspaper headlines, advertising billboards. Embodied in such forms argument becomes richer and more complex. We see how language is used persuasively, how claims can be expanded into many words or encapsulated in just a few, how warrants may not be supplied by the speaker but instead filled in by the hearer who shares the same social/conceptual backdrop, how reason alone may not be enough to drive an argument and convince, how different discourses speak or fail to speak to one another, how some arguments never get heard, how others, in order to be heard, must wear the right tone of detachment. Students may still be expected to express arguments in the standard form of the essay, but this expectation should be accompanied by an understanding about its appropriateness to the situation. In coming to that understanding, questions will be raised about alternative forms and alternative situations.

Knowing what to say and how to say it comes from understanding the situation in which one is called upon to say something. Such a dramatic sense of oneself is as important to the practice of argument as being able to grasp its abstract configuration of elements. It is also as important for students of Engineering as of the Humanities; it is as vocational as it is academic. Staff who on the whole have well developed practical consciousness in these matters, owe it to their students to find some degree of discursive consciousness so that they can pass on their expertise to students whether explicitly or by devising new learning approaches.

JM: It is also true that argument has often been seen as a part of rhetoric and the ability to persuade an audience. As a philosopher, however, I feel a sort of proprietary interest in argument, since it is our stock in trade. I do see how a critical give and take between students, teachers and their discipline cannot fail to benefit all three, and that argument in this sense should be encouraged throughout the University. But there are two dangers as I see it. One is of over dramatisation. It could be argued that, in analytic philosophy at least, a dramatic sense of argument is not only not required, but that it is superfluous. The other is of an undue fascination with the mechanics of persuasion. As with any branch of rhetoric, fascination can make you lose sight of subject matter and take off on your own. As long as the analysis and appreciation of argument is carried out first with a primary reference to content, all will be well.

CHAPTER SIX

*ARGUMENT, RHETORIC AND ENGLISH STUDIES**

Richard Andrews

'English' is a vast, amoebic subject that has a prime place in the curriculum in schools, not only in England but around the world. In England, the subject is considered part of the 'core' curriculum and is thus assured of its place; currently, it gets between 12 and 15 per cent of curriculum time in a typical week. If you go into any school or university department of English, you are likely to find that the principal basis of the practice of teaching is literary, and that 'we teach English through literature' or 'we teach language through literature'. There is a self-perpetuating circular logic about this situation: most English teachers are graduates of English Literature, not of Linguistics or Language study. 'English' as a subject is heavily saturated in literature, even though there is a separate subject that students can take at 16 or 18 called 'English Literature'. Successive British governments have been very keen that this tradition continues. They see literature teaching as part of the continuance and inculcation of 'heritage' – a heritage it sees as mythically 'English' rather than European, rather than international, rather than Scottish, Welsh or Irish.

I can demonstrate this obsession with literary heritage as the main plank of the government's backward-looking vision of the future of the subject by listing some of the texts it suggests 7–16 year olds should read. These include:

John Masefield's *Sea Fever*
Longfellow's *The Wreck of the Hesperus*
Edward Lear's *The Jumblies*
Arthur Ransome's *Swallows and Amazons*
(note that all these have a maritime flavour and at least two have to do with sinking)
Alfred Noyes (a minor poet whose favourite topics were the sea and fairyland and whose best-known poem is 'Drake')
R.B. Sheridan (who was also treasurer of the Navy from 1806–07).

---

* Keynote address to the Australian Association for the Teaching of English conference, Adelaide, July 19
and first published as Andrews, R. 1993. 'The future of English: reclaiming the territory', *English Australia*, 106, December 1993, pp. 41–54 (also published in *English in Aotearoa*, 22, May 1994, pp. 34–45

For a number of reasons, I find this conception of English anachronistic and inappropriate to present-day needs:

- it is based around an insular notion of literature, assuming that immersion in these texts will create a national identity;
- it ignores the boundary-crossing nature of contemporary literature that we find in, say, the novels of Amy Tan, Thomas Keneally or Doris Lessing;
- it sees the world of discourse as divided neatly into fiction and non-fiction by which it means 'factual' material such as information to be gathered from computer technology, travel writing, etc.;
- it pays scant regard to argumentative approaches to language and literature. Argument is either subsumed under the category of 'exposition', in which case it is seen as expounding received ideas; or it is seen in narrow terms of the 'literary essay' – a form that only the best students get access to and which itself is all too often a ritualistic way of assessing response to literature.

In short, the English curriculum up to 18 – in the period of compulsory and post-compulsory schooling – busies itself with description and with interpretation, but not with criticism, not even with seeing literary texts as propositions to argue with. We have found in research at The University of Hull that literature is approached, to use Ricoeur's terms, with a 'vow of obedience' (i.e. passively) rather than with a critical or 'suspicious' eye (see Mitchell, 1992a and 1994e).

Such a literary conception of the subject affects not only what is studied but how it is studied. Because literature is conventionally seen as text-based, the emphasis on dialogue and criticism has been subsidiary to the elucidation of the text. Argument and study of argument has not been a major component in the subject, perhaps because of its public nature, its association with politics (through rhetoric) and its roots in speech rather than writing. Argument does appear in this conventional English syllabus, but tends to be confined to the form with which students have a love–hate relationship: the literary essay.

Let us now turn to the question of how argument is represented in the National Curriculum.

Argument in the National Curriculum[1]

The National Curriculum in English is divided into three main profile components: speaking and listening; reading; and writing. I will look at each of these in turn, and then consider other aspects of the curriculum that come under the umbrella of English, such as drama, media studies and information technology. I necessarily give an exhaustive account of argument as it is represented in the National Curriculum[2] – in order to complete my argument in this chapter, but also to provide a record of the state of play in the English education system at the time of writing, June 1994.

Speaking and listening

The current programmes of study for key stage 1 include the following. Planned situations and activities should cover:

> development of speaking and listening skills, both when role-playing and otherwise – when expressing opinions

> development by informal means and in the course of purposeful activities, of pupils' powers of concentration, grasp of turn-taking, ability to gain and hold the attention of their listeners, and ability to voice disagreement courteously with an opposing point of view. (1.3)

All activities should:

> help to develop in pupils' speaking and listening their grasp of sequence, cause and effect, reasoning, sense of consistency, clarity of argument, appreciation of relevance and irrelevance. (1.4)

When we come on to key stages 2 to 4, the general provisions determine that pupils should be given the opportunity to learn how to:

> express and justify feelings, opinions and viewpoints with increasing sophistication

> discuss increasingly complex issues

> assess and interpret arguments and opinions with increasing precision and discrimination

> ask increasingly precise or detailed questions

> respond to increasingly complex instructions and questions

> discriminate between fact and opinion and between relevance and irrelevance, and recognise bias

> discuss issues in small and large groups, taking account of the views of others, and negotiating a consensus

> engage in prediction, speculation and hypothesis in the course of group activity. (1.6)

More specifically, in order to achieve level 4,

> Pupils should be encouraged to express their opinions and to argue a point of view; to be receptive to the contributions of others and make their own contributions effectively

and in order to achieve level 5,

> pupils should be helped to make more extended contributions to group or class discussions and to informal or formal presentations ... They should be helped to make their questions more probing, and contributions to discussions more reasoned. (1.14)

There is no specific mention of argumentative skills in order to achieve level 6, but at level 7,

> the topics for discussion should vary widely and involve the development and probing of argument and evidence. It should also require the presentation of the main issues. Literary texts (including drama scripts), the use of language, responses to the media, pupils' own written work and the use of information technology might furnish many of the materials and topics for discussion for which planned outcomes, *e.g. in written work or presentations,* might emerge. (1.18)

At level 8 the 'increased opportunities for undertaking individual, responsible and formal roles' might include

> some debating activities within a formal structure, opportunities to give talks on a topic of individual interest or expertise (1.19),

and at levels 9 and 10, while greater fluency is the general principle, pupils will be required to:

> take leading and discerning roles in discussion, to encourage others to make contributions and respond to them with understanding and appreciation ... to be rigorous in argument and the use of evidence, and to take effective account of audience and context. (ibid.)

and should be helped to recognise that speech ranges from intimate or casual spontaneous conversation through discussion, commentary and debate to more formal forms.

Reading

There is no such extensive reference to argument in the programmes of study which support the attainment target for reading at key stage 1.

At key stage 2, however, pupils are expected to:

> learn how to find information in books and databases, sometimes drawing on more than one source, and how to pursue an independent line of enquiry. (2.10)

and in order to achieve level 5, pupils:

> should be shown how to distinguish between fact and opinion. (2.13)

It is not until level 7 that the non-literary texts suggested include persuasive writing. Up to that level, 'non-literary' means largely referential writing. Examples given at level 7 are advertisements, leader columns from newspapers, and campaign literature from pressure groups.

At level 8, pupils should be taught how to:

> Recognise the author's viewpoint and – where relevant – persuasive or rhetorical techniques in a range of texts

but nowhere else in the programme of study for reading is there specific reference to the reading of argumentative texts.

Writing

Again, there is no reference to argument at key stage 1 in the programme of study for writing, though there is a general requirement that pupils should undertake a range of 'non-chronological' writing.

At key stage 2, pupils should:

> read good examples of descriptions, explanations, opinions, etc., and be helped to plan and produce these types of writing by being given purposeful opportunities to write their own.

It is not until levels 3 and 4 that pupils should be made aware of a range of functions of writing:

> for communicating meaning to others: reporting, narrating, persuading, arguing ...

for thinking and learning: recollecting, organising thoughts, reconstructing, reviewing, hypothesising. (3.24)

It is at these stages that pupils should have the opportunities to write in a range of forms (e.g. pamphlets, book reviews, advertisements), be able to express a point of view in writing, and use writing to facilitate their own thinking and learning. More specifically, in order to achieve level 8, pupils should:

> be helped to recognise the patterns of organisation of formal expository writing: *e.g. the introduction, development and conclusion of the academic essay; the use of illustrations and examples in persuasive writing and of comparison and contrast in argument. (3.30)*

In the general provisions for key stage 4, the forms that students should be given the opportunity to write in are extended to include essays and reviews of books, television programmes and films or plays; and the 'wider range of communicative purposes' include:

> expressing a point of view, persuading, comparing and contrasting ideas, arguing or different points of view. (3.31)

In May 1994, at the time of writing this chapter, the School Curriculum and Assessment Auhority (SCAA) issued a further set of proposals for English (1994) that were intended to act as a basis for the curriculum for five years from September 1995. They were a result of the 'slimming down' of the curriculum in the wake of The Dearing Report (1994). Changes from the 1993 proposals were minimal, though the fact that argument retained some space within a slimmed down curriculum was heartening. As in the previous orders and proposals, the main location for argumentative work was seen to be in Speaking and Listening, with significant elements of arguments embedded in the curriculum for key stages 1, 3 and 4 (in key stage 2, the emphasis seemed to shift to passivity in the face of 'information'). In the programmes of study for Reading, there was more emphasis on reading 'arguments of non-fiction texts' at levels 1–3, though again the world of discourse appeared to divide into 'literature' and 'information', or 'fiction' and 'non-fiction'. Such a binary distinction tends to sideline argument. The same is true of the programme of study for Writing. The National Curriculum for English assumes that argument is a sub-category of non-fictional, informative communication.

It is clear from the above summary of the place of argument in the National Curriculum for English that it is in speaking and listening that the principal work in argument is expected to take place. Argumentation is seen as beginning earlier in speech in that there is no reference to argument in writing or reading at key stage 1. The general provision for key stages 2 to 4 provides plenty of opportunity for spoken argument, but little in the way of written or read argument until key stage 3.

Indeed, it is in the programme of study for writing that we find the only reference to 'good examples of descriptions, explanations, opinions, etc.' as models to read and follow; in the programme of study for reading, there is a requirement for pupils to be shown how to distinguish between fact and opinion.

When it comes to key stages 3 and 4, the movement in writing seems to be towards the formal academic essay. There is little scope for alternative forms of argument or inventiveness. It seems as though the conception of argumentative writing is limited by the chronological/non-chronological distinction referred to earlier. This distinction is an unhelpful one in thinking about language modes such as narrative and argument, and is the subject of a critique by Gibson and Andrews (1993 – see chapter 8 of the present book).

Argument in other subjects of the curriculum

Though not mentioned extensively in the orders for English, drama is given a chapter in the Cox Report (DES, 1989), and it is clear that it could provide many different kinds of opportunity for the exploration of argument both at primary and secondary school level. Such possibilities are indicated in the report as helping pupils to 'develop the logic of different situations' (8.15) and providing opportunities for pupils to:

argue, discuss, defend and justify a point of view;

persuade, negotiate, mediate;

come to conclusions, sum up. (8.11)

Although television shows relatively little argument *per se* there is scope for exploring its presentation both here and on the radio; newspapers also provide a resource for the study of argument (in leaders, features, etc.).

It has been suggested (see Snyder, 1992) that word-processing provides a suitable medium for learning to write argument, because of its ability to move around sections of text – a technique more suited to argument than to narrative, according to her research.

A survey of other subjects in the National Curriculum reveals a mixed picture as far as argument is concerned.

In the orders for geography, for example, the verbs used in the attainment targets to describe the activity required range from 'describe', 'give an account of' and 'identify' at one end of the spectrum to 'consider', 'explain' and 'analyse' at the other. Only at level 10 do the terms 'appraise', 'evaluate' and 'discuss' appear. The general development seems to be from description and identification through explanation and analysis to evaluation. Exceptions to this trend in the orders are the suggestions to 'look at and talk about pictures', 'ask questions' and 'give reasons why people make journeys of different lengths' at level 2 in the human geography attainment target (no. 4) and 'express personal likes and dislikes' about features of the local area (at level 1) and 'plan and take part in the development of a school garden' at level 2 in the environmental geography attainment target (no. 5). In general, however, geography doesn't become controversial until level 10, a level that most schoolchildren will not attain.

History seems a more argumentative subject. In its three attainment targets – Knowledge and understanding (AT1), Interpretation (AT2), and Use of historical sources (AT3) – there is a wider range of approaches suggested and a less clear movement from description to evaluation. Pupils are asked to 'give reasons' at level 1 (AT1) and 'make deductions from sources' at level 3 in AT3. There is a movement back and forth between description, evaluation and analysis throughout the orders – more so, perhaps, than in English where one would expect such a 'spiral' or recursive – rather than linear – curriculum.

But as Mitchell points out in *Questions and Schooling* (1992b), history, politics and sociology – subjects constituted around argument – make English look a relatively conservative discipline, even outside the National Curriculum. It is conservative because it doesn't admit argument as much as we like to think it does.

A rhetorical perspective

If you look at the subject 'English' (to use that term for the time being) from a rhetorical perspective, however, things begin to look different. Instead of seeing fictional literature at the core of this new subject, you see texts – everything from Shakespeare plays and short stories by Chinese writers to bus tickets, reports and everyday arguments in speech and writing of mixed in with visuals as on television or in multimedia texts.

You see that world of texts sitting alongside each other, blending with each other and always within contexts, both social and political. To use Terry Eagleton's phrase, literary criticism becomes 'political criticism', his version of rhetoric.

Not only does the subject move beyond the narrowly literary and narrowly conceived notion of a national literature, but it also becomes dialogic or 'multi-voiced' rather than monologic. That shift, brought about by Bakhtin and by the influence of spoken conceptions of language on written modes, has the following consequences:

- Any text is seen as part of an ongoing dialogue. It is brought into the classroom or seminar room as 'another voice' to take its place in relation to the voices that are already there and which will arise from it. In teaching and learning classrooms and seminar rooms, the pedagogic possibilities are enormous. Learning in relation to texts is seen as transformational rather than transmissive. It is *what happens* in such rooms with texts that matters, because what happens socially is what is learnt (cf. Britton, 1987).

- 'Literature' or more broadly speaking, 'fiction' no longer has pre-eminent place. Part of its pre-eminence has been due to the fact that classrooms have been seen as places in which simulations have taken place. Because fiction presents possible worlds, these have been – and are – ideal for consideration in the sealed-off world of classrooms where symbolising is the predominant activity.

- When I say 'what happens' in classrooms, I am thinking not only of what happens in terms of speech acts, but also what actually happens as a result of the deployment of language. In other words, I am suggesting that it is not only social talk that provides the interaction that is taken on board as 'thought' and transformation of existing models in the head, but that experience of using language in different situations affects – *informs* – the way we think with language. For example, the group of children or students who research, discuss and write a commissioned report for a librarian on the use of periodicals in the library are engaging in language that makes things happen.

These pointers, already rooted in practice in certain quarters, suggest that the notion of 'English' based on a narrow canon of 'English Literature' is no longer adequate to the needs of language users and learners. They point to a model of language learning that is rhetorical, dialogic, geared towards action and in which literature plays a part – a very important part – but not a central part.

One of the reasons that rhetoric has renewed itself in the second half of the twentieth century is that, as Bakhtin has observed, there has been an emergent understanding through the development of linguistics to discourse analysis that large-scale structures in discourse – the mediation of social relations through language – are a good point at which to enter the study of language and its effects. Rhetoric embraces function (why am I/why are we saying this?) within particular social contexts (who is our audience, and what are the social relations between us? what other contextual or contingent factors bear upon us?) in considering mode (what is the best way to conduct the transaction?) and form (in which written and/or visual form is the message best couched?) Those rhetorical decisions necessarily influence particular registers (i.e. selections of diction) syntaxes and tones. In other words, every level of language is part of the domain of rhetoric, and rhetoric goes further than linguistics because it also takes into account the social context and at its best, is a flexible and powerfully practical art.

Because argument is one of the principal tools of rhetoric, argumentation is highlighted within this new conception of English studies. Students are likely to 'argue with' texts, devise arguments to link texts and to highlight their differences, find their own positions on issues that are framed in language via argument, and thus assert identity in relation to the existing culture through argumentation.

Freed from narrowly based ideas about the relationship between language, nationhood and identity, 'English' becomes increasingly inappropriate as the name for the social, interactive and intellectual activity that goes on around language in the classroom and seminar room. I can't see the subject being renamed 'Argumentation' but I can perhaps see, using telescopic sights, our adopting a title like 'Language Arts' or more specifically – because of its association with rhetoric and argumentation – 'Discourse Arts' as the name for the activity we are all engaged in and through which we are inducted into an increasingly international, multimedia culture. After all, this common interest – both in education and in our everyday lives outside the classroom – goes beyond the boundaries of different languages; it is an interest and preoccupation for French speakers, Dutch speakers and speakers of Mandarin or Hindi.

From the perspective I've been outlining – that of a rhetorically informed view that privileges argumentation over transmission, dialogue over monologue – literature has its place. The place of narrative literature may be, as Hesse (1992) suggests, as 'rhetoric's fourth mode' – a kind of persuasive mode that stands in argumentative relation to the assumed world in which most of us operate. Essentially, it is the means by which possible worlds are explored, hypotheses tested, inductive arguments generated (and sometimes deductive ones, as in Kundera's *The Unbearable Lightness of Being)* at various distances from the 'real world'. To narrow those possible worlds to ones that have been conceived within the shores of a particular country, and exclusively in the past, is an abnegation of the very function of literature and a closing down of thought itself.

Conclusion

Although, in the short term, governments might be trying to contain the literary canon in order to promote a particular view of 'Englishness', such a highly ideological project – despite the fact it claims to be immune from ideology – is doomed to failure. The tide is running against such a project in at least two ways. First, in the increasing internationalisation and cross-cultural nature of the literary world; and second – the more important reason as far as the present book is concerned – because of the increasing awareness that texts are constituted in an argumentative framework. This framework is a rhetorical one, assuming that discourse is interactive, social and productive.

But at the same time, the coming of age of argumentation in the English curriculum is threatened by the current prevailing view that information technology privileges *information* rather than argumentation or thought. It is at this moment that argument has to stake its claim to a central pillar of the English curriculum if it is not to be marginalised by a view that sees literature on the one hand, and non-fiction on the other as the twin pillars of discourse in education.

Notes

1.   The National Curriculum was implemented in England and Wales in the early 1990s as a result of the 1988 Education Act. It divided schooling into four 'key stages', covering ages +7, 8–11, 11–14 and 14–16. The National Curriculum for English, drawn up by a working group chaired by Professor Brian Cox, consisted of three main 'profile components' – reading, writing, and speaking and listening. Each profile component consisted of 'attainment targets' and in English the first two happen to be the same as the first two profile components. The third fourth and fifth attainment targets – 'Writing', 'Spelling' and 'Handwriting' came under the umbrella of the third profile component, 'Writing'. Each attainment target had ten levels of attainment, described by the 'statements of attainment'. Broadly speaking, students were expected, on average, to attain level 4 by the time they finished at primary/elementary school, and level 7 or 8 at the end of compulsory schooling. In the summer of 1992, the Secretary of State called for proposals for a revision and 'simplification' of the National Curriculum for English. A set of proposals was published in April 1993 and another in May 1994. At the time of writing, these latter proposals were still under review, pending further consultation on the National Curriculum in the wake of The Dearing Report (Dearing, 1994).

2.   The curriculum as described in this section of the chapter is that enshrined in DES (1990), i.e. one which was being implemented in schools in England and Wales between 1990 and 1994.

CHAPTER SEVEN

NARRATIVE, ARGUMENT AND RHETORIC[*]

Richard Andrews

When I reflect on narrative and its place in my reading and teaching, it is the dislocations to expected narrative pattern that have excited the children I have taught and myself as a teacher and reader. They have made me more aware of narrative and what it can do. Take the passage in Kurt Vonnegut's *Slaughterhouse Five*, for instance, in which Billy Pilgrim imagines the war running backwards, like a film running backwards before his eyes; or Pinter's *Betrayal*, Kunert's 'Film Put in Backwards' or Ian Seraillier's backwards fairytale. Running narrative backwards makes you much more aware of how the sequence is constructed forwards, and what its constituent parts are.

There is no shortage of literature on how stories are constructed, but it tends to be a critical account of how existing texts are constructed. Barthes's (1966) 'Introduction to the structural analysis of narratives' was seminal, but there were other seeds germinating in 1966 and before: Booth (1961), Propp (1968), Bremond (1973) and others.

Another strand of story analysis is that in which Bartlett's work on memory in the 1930s is looked to as a foundation. The work of Rumelhart (1975), Mandler and Johnson (1977), Johnson and Mandler (1980), Stein and Glenn (1979) and others focuses on story structure, but again we are dealing with minimal stories, analysed within a syntactic paradigm, and via their retention and comprehension. Yet another strand is the ethnographic and social linguistic, characterised in the work by Labov and others (e.g. Labov and Waletsky, 1967) on naturally occurring oral narrative.

The description of the construction of an existing narrative is no guide to the composition of narrative. There is no neat formula to translate reception into production, though of course what we read and hear must have a connection to what we write and can write. There are guides on how to write a story, but only Mills & Boon hopefuls take them seriously.

This lack of understanding of how children compose narratives (and other modes of writing) prompted me to try to devise ways of getting inside that process. My focus was on structure and arrangement, not on drafting or any of the other more organic aspects of writing. I was interested in the routes taken by writers in the very act of composing; not in any rules for the conduct of the

---

[*] This chapter first appeared in Andrews, R. (ed). 1992. *Rebirth of Rhetoric: Essays in Language, Culture and Education*. London: Routledge.

journey, but in the split-second decisions that are made to take a story one way rather than another.

What I devised was an instrument based on the filmic principle of putting one image alongside another. Working with 150 year 8 pupils in the three comprehensive schools in Beverley, I gave each pupil a set of seven photographs. I asked them to compose (literally!) a narrative, using any number of the photos in the series, and arranging them in any order. I had two sets so that students sitting next to each other would not be affected by the choices of their neighbours.

What happened was that only two students in my sample came up with the same structural sequence. Most of the stories were different, and no doubt would have been even if the sequences of photographs had been the same. Here is an example of one of the stories, generated from two photographs in a set:

Revenge of the killer kippers

Deep in the sea some herrings were thinking of a way to get back at humans because they were smoking them then eating them. So they formed an air force of flying fish and set out to smoke and eat humans! They flew out of the water of the flying fish and attacked! The guns on the port wall started shooting them but they kept on coming and eventually wiped out the inhabitants of the village and had smoked humans for tea.

Nine months later, all England is ruled by kippers except for one town – Beverley – where Iain Norman was keeping the kippers at bay with fishmongers. So all the kippers in the land attacked the fish, and we all had smoked kippers for tea and the reign of the kippers was over.

Pedagogically, these photographs were a success. I've yet to come across a child who cannot use them to generate a told or written story. The sample covered young people with a wide range of capabilities, including a semi-paralysed child in a wheelchair who composed a story half in words and half in pictures. But that is not the point. What did they tell me about the structure of the stories and the ways in which those structures were produced?

I used Van Dijk's term 'episode' to describe the units of narrative discourse, preferring it to 'narreme'. My analysis is one level 'higher' in the linguistic scale than that at which the 'narreme' operates. An overall term to describe the units of narrative and argumentative discourse I have been looking at is 'stage' – that way, a setting or an opening proposition in argument can be seen as stages rather than as 'episodes' or 'points'.

Iain's story can be analysed as consisting of five episodes: the setting ('Deep in the sea ...'), a 'then' episode ('they flew out of the water ...'), another 'then' episode ('Nine months later ...'), a 'cause' episode ('So all the kippers in the land attacked Beverley ...') and a resolution ('... and we all had smoked kippers for tea and the reign of the kippers was over'). But it could equally be analysed as consisting of seven, if we took each sentence as an episode and the last one as two episodes. As a principle, I have looked for larger structural units in the stories.

The average number of episodes per story was 7.9. Almost all these stories began with a setting of some kind: 98.6 per cent of the total sample. The exceptions might be considered to have the function of settings, even if they did not actually set the scene, giving the reader a glimpse of action from the middle of the narrative. The sample as a whole ranged from stories with three episodes to one with 17. Only two structures were alike. In terms of form, there were stories within stories, stories purely in dialogue, stories as letters, picaresque structures, stories from different points of view, stories in the present tense – and combinations of these.

As an example of the variety of structures evidenced in the sample, here are the structures of the six stories that took a three-part structure:

Kelly Sheepwash – *in media res* (a rumour) + narrator tells story which itself has six subsections + resolution
June Robinson – setting + event (then) + event (then) – abrupt ending
Nicola Hastings – setting + event (and) + event (and)
Simon Davidson – setting (long) + event (then) + event (resolution)
Fergus Whinham – setting + event (dialogue) + event (resolution)
Paul Ramsay – setting + event (cause) + event (then) – incomplete

What was particularly striking was that, when asked whether they could envisage a rearrangement of the basic structures of the stories without affecting the nature of the stories, only 26.45 per cent of the sample said that they could. This compares with 62.16 per cent who could envisage a similar change in their arguments – more on which later. Only two students in the whole sample could envisage complete flexibility of order. Of those who could envisage some change (only one-quarter of the sample, remember) most envisaged just one change to the original order of their story.

I felt it important to pursue this question because, as Pringle and Freedman (1985) had reported on their research in Ottawa in the early 1980s, very little revision goes on above the level of the sentence in schools, despite the facilities offered by word-processors. I am not surprised by that, because of the history of 'marking' in English teaching and also because computer monitors are not generally big enough to enable writers to see the whole text at once.

Let us return for a moment to the beginnings of the students' work on the narratives. I made planning – on paper that is – optional; 49 per cent took up this option. Of this 49 per cent, the majority (70 per cent) did not plan in the conventional sense of that term. That is to say, they did not map out the whole story before they began to write/transcribe it. Most of these plans were drafts of the beginning of the story; they were foundations from which the story might be built – first attempts to get started.

The number of stages in the plans did not always correspond to the number of photographs chosen, and in turn the final stories did not always correspond to the plans. This is very different from what happens in the composition of argument. It appears that each stage of planning in the composition of narrative acts as a springboard to the next stage. Each stage in the process supersedes and jettisons the previous one. As teachers of writing, we probably need to be aware of the different compositional processes involved in different types of writing. Certainly, the imposition of drafting for every type of writing would be, from this point of view, a mistake.

Here are some of the students' comments made about the process of writing narrative by the students in the research sample. I took a 12.5 per cent sub-sample to interview: in effect, three students from each of the six classes I worked with. The three were selected on the following basis: one who said they could change the order of their narrative but not of their argument; one who could change the argument but not the narrative: and one who could envisage changing both. Apart from that, selection was random.

> I quite often change my plans in narrative. I add things but don't change the order much. In argument I add things and rearrange things. (Emma)

> I think writing narrative is difficult for the same reason as having a bath is difficult; the hardest part is actually getting in. (Philippe)

> Q: What is it like being in the middle of a story?
> A: It's like going into a series of caverns.

> The ending could be considered to be the most important part because everything has been brought together for an actual final countdown to a closure, and everything is then falling into place ... like a jigsaw. (Simon)

Any research in this field throws up more questions than it can answer. If you move above the level of the sentence, not only in trying to find ways of helping students to play with their writing – to revise, to rethink at the 'macro-level' – but also in simply trying to define what the units of composition are, you run into difficulty. The analysis of the structures of narrative is more complicated than that of the structure of arguments. Conventionally, argument is more subject to division, categorisation and logic than narrative. I used the Stein and Glenn taxonomy, applying the 'then', 'and' and 'cause' categories to the story as a whole. I had to use a range of determinants to define the narrative units:

- paragraphs (where they existed – and of course they did not always correspond to shifts in the narrative when they did);
- textual markers, like 'then', 'so', 'after a few years', 'suddenly', 'in the end', and so on;
- introduction of new characters or settings;

- spaces in the text, indicating a shift of perspective or time;
- shifts of tense;
- the introduction of chunks of dialogue (a difficult one).

What about argument? First, there is no doubt that it is important and pervasive, and that considering the modes of discourse is part of our business.

My second observation rests on the work of Fox (1989 and 1990), Wilkinson (1989 and 1990), Wilkinson et al. (1990) and others, and it is this: argument starts early, much earlier than is recognised in the National Curriculum for English. Fox has indicated, in a series of papers on the stories told by four-, five- and six-year-olds, how many of the rhetorical devices of argument are embedded in their narratives. Wilkinson's chapters in *Spoken English Illuminated* ('Our first great conversationalists', 'Homemade argument' and 'Primary acts of mind'), and two articles published in *English in Education* argue for our recognition of the presence of argument in the first discourses of pre-schoolchildren.

Third, what is argument? A brief look at the OED reveals three strands, strands that are there in the Latin *arguer*, meaning (i) to show, to make clear; (ii) to assert, to prove; and, as part of a legal process or as dialogue, (iii) to accuse, to blame. Translate those through the centuries, and you get a range of meanings from the narrowly logical (e.g. in astronomy and mathematics, 'the angle, or other mathematical quantity from which another required quantity may be deduced') to 'a connected series of statements or reasons intended to establish a position; a process of reasoning; argumentation', that is, both the product (argument) and the process (argumentation). You also get some interesting peripheral definitions, like 'the subject-matter of discussion or discourse in speech or writing; theme, subject' and one that is close to narrative, 'the summary or abstract of the subject-matter of a book; a syllabus; the contents'. It is as though the function of argument is to move one step beyond the present state, both in the sense of moving 'up' a level in terms of abstraction and exposition, and in the sense of taking a position that will move things 'on'.

But if you presented these definitions to a child or, for that matter, almost anyone, they would point out that there is a huge dimension of argument missing. Indeed, the first thing most of us probably think of when we hear the term 'argument' is a row, a tiff, a barney, an argy-bargy, a squabble, a ding-dong, a good shouting match, a set-to, a spat, a difference of opinion. Reason hardly comes into it, sometimes. These encounters are often driven by passion and feeling.

To see argument as merely 'a connected series of statements or reasons intended to establish a position' and to limit its expression to the written essay – a form that gained prominence in the Renaissance and now maintains a stranglehold on much of education from about age 15 or 16 upwards – is to narrow the possibilities of expression. It has been notoriously difficult to teach, and I think only now are we beginning to look seriously again at ways of making it accessible to all children and students. The difficulties were outlined by Clarke (1984) and by Freedman and Pringle (1984). The APU surveys (Gorman et al., 1988) between 1979 and 1983 (not fully published until 1988) pin-pointed argument as one of the areas in which 11- and 15-year-olds had trouble, and several of the researchers published independently, expressing their concern about this. Meanwhile, Dixon and Stratta (1982) were carrying out inductive research for the Southern Regional Examining Board (as it was then) and publishing their findings in small pamphlets. Some of these findings and meditations were collected in two publications in 1986: *Writing Narrative – and Beyond* and *The Writing of Writing*. Among others, I want to add the name of Deborah Berrill (1990a and b; see also Wilkinson et al., 1990), whose work adds a great deal to our understanding of how teenagers compose argument, and especially to the difference between exposition and argument.

Recently my own focus has been on the difference between narrative and argument. Before I present my findings from the study on the composition of argument I would like to address the distinction between narrative and argument made by Kress (1989) in the collection *Narrative and Argument* (Andrews, 1989). This distinction has not been without controversy. Kress suggests that narrative and argument are two very different modes of organising verbal or visual text. Although both aim to handle difference in a culture, argument 'provides the means for bringing difference into existence' while narrative, as a textual form, 'provides means of resolution of difference in an uncontentious mode'. So argument is a progressive cultural form in that it is an agent of change; narrative is conservative in that the closure comes from within. When closure takes place in argument, it is imposed from without.

There seems to have been some misunderstanding of the application of this distinction. Kress is not saying here that narrative is an inferior cultural form to argument (though conventionally argumentative forms have been privileged over narrative forms like 'anecdote' and 'tale'). On the contrary, the suggestion is that critical awareness of these two modes of expression enables us to free narrative from such a position. Elsewhere in his chapter, Kress is at pains to point out that he does not accept the view that sees narrative as the vehicle and argument as the tenor of expression.

The distinction is worth further debate. At least it is clear from Kress's work that narrative and argument are modes of organisation, operating at more general level than genres or forms. It is at this point we can return to the study.

The same sample of 150 12–13-year-olds in the three comprehensive schools in Beverley wrote arguments. They had completely free choice as to topic, some of which were:

It is wrong that first years get to lunch first
It is wrong that girls are treated differently
We should play football in school time
There should be more dinner ladies [sic]

It is wrong to have to go to school

What good does war do?
There's too much violence on TV
Using animals in experiments is wrong

Birds should not be allowed to live on the earth
Koala bears should wear climbing gear
Lightning should not be allowed to strike in the same place
'I think sheep should not be air hostesses'

Candy is brill

More central to my own concerns, however, was arrangement. I deliberately limited the range of argumentative forms so that I could make a reasonable comparison between the essays, and between them and the narratives written in the same week by the same children. Most of the children wrote what tends to be called a 'discursive essay'. Not all. Here is an example of one child's work. It takes the form of Socratic dialogue but then seems to move into a report of the proceedings of a meeting.

Should fleas wear protective clothing and helmets?

'I think they should because they are always flying into walls and hurting themselves and getting bruised and falling to the floor, what a torture.'
'How do you think we could supply every flea with 50p worth of gear? How do you think we could afford all that?'

After further to-ing and fro-ing, the argument ends:

Chairman: The votes follow like this For: 42; Against: 20
So fleas will wear protective clothes.

In this research the approach is one of aiming at the heart of the problem in argumentative writing: the essay. I use this term to mean a sustained piece of writing that puts over a point of view or argues a case, as in the John Gross (1991) collection *The Oxford Book of Essays*.

All the students wrote plans for their essays, though only 2 per cent of these were in the 'for and against' pattern that is often taught. Ten per cent of them took the form of drafts, rather like the majority of the plans for narrative. The rest consisted of a combination of spider diagrams, lists and points in the order that the writer was going to make them.

There is a major difference between narrative and argument in the relationship of the plans to the final written pieces. Despite the artificial context I had provided for the students, with planning optional for the narrative and compulsory for the argument, students reported in a questionnaire and in interviews that they would usually plan for argument but not for narrative. I have already mentioned the function of planning in narrative. In argument the student is much more likely to 'stick to the plan'; he or she may rearrange it or add to it, but the additions are adjustments, embellishments and so on within the structure mapped out in the plan.

The average number of stages in the arguments written in this study was 6.1, compared to the 7.9 I have mentioned as the average for the narratives. Those figures may or may not be significant. It might be simply a matter of length (though students had the same amount of time to write each piece); it may be something to do with the additive nature of composition in narrative; it may be that the six-stage argument corresponds closely to the Aristotelian six-part oration. These questions still have to be resolved, but I can say from analysing the arguments that hardly any follow the Aristotelian six-part pattern. I shall return to Aristotle in a moment.

As with narratives, we can look at a manageable number of structures. Unlike narrative, it is possible to compose two-part structures (basically statement and proof) but again I have chosen those compositions which took a three-part structure. There were seven in all:

> Paul Ramsey – statement + 'nevertheless' + 'on the other hand'
> Malcolm Spencer – statement + reason + expression of opinion
> Philip Ashby – statement + reason + 'when' (instance)
> Stephen Spivey – supposition ('if') + example + example
> Kathryn Pengilly – statement + credo + anti-credo ('I don't think')
> Melanie Wright – statement + reason + statement
> Sarah Pelham – example + example + example

A general point first: most of these (and indeed 86.2 per cent of the total sample) take the 'statement + proof' shape. The two that do not fit the pattern begin 'If people keep killing whales, there won't be any whales left in the world' (Stephen Spivey) and, in an essay entitled 'Murder in our homes and streets', 'I have nothing against London, but I just decided to use it as an example. London, especially East, is a main drug area' (Sarah Pelham). The others in the total sample that do not fit the basic pattern begin with exordia, examples (in the form of micro-stories) and a setting.

More specifically, what seems to me to be striking is the variety of sequence and strategy evident in these seven structures. No two essay structures are alike in the whole sample. I find that heartening. But not only is there variety. As I reported earlier, 62 per cent of the students in the sample felt that they could rearrange the order of their arguments. Of these, 26.6 per cent could envisage their same essay in any order; the rest suggested specific changes. For many of these, 'the first point has to come first' – but not for all.

What do the students themselves say about argument? One mentioned the importance of the voice in argument:

> I think that voice has a lot to do with how good your argument is. You can use your voice like plasticine: you can mould it into the argument, bringing your voice high and then letting it drop down.

Another talked about the construction of the different parts of an argument:

> I tried to fit the different rail tracks together so that they'd fix up so that one would lead to another, which is quite hard to do.

And another talked about different ways he might approach the writing of argument:

> I could then do it the other way round: put the less important first and build up to a climax if you like, where the importance really wants coming out; or you could do it another way. You could put the middle ones first as a taster, build up to a climax and then go down again. What I usually do is to do it in my own style, which is to build right up to a climax.

It is the flexibility on the part of the students, their willingness to play with the structures of argument, their experimentation, their personal imprint (and, by the way, many of them see argument as more personal than narrative) that seem to me to be some of the outcomes of this relatively small-scale research. I find it particularly interesting to look at statements and suggestions from classical rhetoric about the construction of arguments alongside the structures generated by the students. These are from Aristotle (1926) and the author of the Roman *Ad Herennium* (Cicero, 1954), and they focus on the aspect of composition with which I am concerned here, namely *dispositio* or arrangement. From Aristotle:

> A speech has two parts. It is necessary to state the subject, and then to prove it.

and

> at most the parts are four in number: exordium, statement, proof, epilogue.

though 'statement' might be divided into 'narrative' and 'division', and a refutation might be added to make a six-part oration. From the *Ad Herennium*:

> The most complete and perfect argument, then, is that which is comprised of [sic] five parts: the Proposition, the Reason, the Proof of the Reason, the Embellishment and the Resumé.

> The fullest argument is fivefold, the briefest threefold [without the last two parts] and the mean fourfold, lacking either the Embellishment or the Resumé. (pp. 107, 113)

Compare these with the rather crude formulae we have come down to, such as 'A good essay must have an introduction, a development and a conclusion' or the equivalent for narrative, 'a beginning, middle and an end'. Or even worse, 'First say what you are going to say, then say it, and then say what you've just said'. And compare these formulaic approaches to the teaching and learning of writing with the actual practice of these students, even under artificially tight conditions. Furthermore, how much do our students 'know about language' at the level of discourse? On the evidence of the 18 students I interviewed, quite a lot. Not only do they know about the nature of language forms but also about appropriateness, that much-vaunted and, as Harold Rosen has pointed out, dangerously loaded word in the National Curriculum. But they also know how to subvert propriety, and by subverting, dislocating and rearranging, they make their own marks and learn a great deal more at the same time about themselves, about their audience, about their subject-matter and about language. There is also a lot of humour to be had in inappropriateness, incongruity, dislocation – humour that children and adolescents enjoy.

To summarise some of the points made so far:

- The arrangements of narratives and arguments are not fixed. There are general formulae which we can apply after the event of composing, but in the middle of the act of composing, they are not much help. We need a theory of writing in which process and the possibilities of product are interrelated. We need to be able to account for the speed at which the mind chooses to take this route rather than that.

- It may be that in a particular context a certain genre will suggest itself. This does not mean that we have to accept this genre wholesale. For example, if we have to make a funeral oration or speech, or, more informally, say a few words about someone who has died, we can – as a friend of mine did recently – tell the story of someone's life backwards, from death to birth. There is a kind of hopefulness about that approach.

- The process involved in composing narrative is different from that involved in composing argument.

- Children know more about language at the discourse level than might be imagined, but the National Curriculum in English does not reflect this.

- Children can argue from an early age. The assumption that narrative precedes argument in learning should be looked at critically.

- Narrative and argument might be separate rhetorical categories of mode, but they need not be polarised; there can be narrative in argument and, looking at it at a different level, narratives argue.
- There is much to be done to liberate argument for pupils in school and students in colleges and universities, right across the curriculum.

Questions of narrative and argument are concerned with rhetoric, in the best sense of that word. In the Library of Congress classification of the *Narrative and Argument* (Andrews, 1989), 'rhetoric' appears in brackets after both 'narrative' and 'argument'. What rhetoric can offer is an overview of the relationship between speaker/writer, audience, subject-matter and text or utterance. This theoretical perspective, like all good theory, suggests possibilities and alternatives – the kinds of alternative explored by 12–13-year-olds in the research reported here. It's indubitably creative and imaginative. Perhaps as a term, it should still remain in parentheses? On the other hand, perhaps those brackets now need to come off.

CHAPTER EIGHT

A CRITIQUE OF THE 'CHRONOLOGICAL/NON-CHRONOLOGICAL' DISTINCTION IN THE NATIONAL CURRICULUM FOR ENGLISH[*]

Howard Gibson and Richard Andrews

Introduction

Anyone interested in the development of children's writing must, we think, have at least questioned the 'chronological/non-chronological' distinction that has found its way into the statements of attainment for Writing in the English National Curriculum orders. In this article we have developed such questions into a critique.

The distinction manifests itself in the Statements of Attainment for levels 2, 3 and 4 in AT (Attainment Target) 3 and is 'supported' by the Programmes of Study for Key Stages 1 and 2 (e.g. 9, 18) which indicate that pupils 'should undertake a range of chronological writing [and] a range of non-chronological writing'. Pupils should also be:

> ... helped to understand that non-chronological types of writing can be organised in a variety of ways and so, generally, require careful planning; this might include the presentation of information or imaginative prose. (DES, 1990, p. 37)

The distinction then disappears, to be transformed by the 'imaginative/ transactional' dichotomy at level 7, for example, and yet again recast into the 'imaginative' and 'factual' writing of Key Stage 4. There is no mention of the distinction in the Programmes of Study for Key Stages 3 and 4, and no mention of it in the Statements of Attainment or the Programmes of Study for Speaking and Listening or Reading.

In this article we first examine the history of the 'chronological/non-chronological' distinction, then look in more detail at the way it has been absorbed into the National Curriculum for English. We note that others have had problems with the distinction, reconsider it in relation to alternative theoretical work on narrative and discourse, and then summarise our position.

---

[*] First published under this title as Gibson, H. and Andrews, R. 1993 in *Educational Review* 45 (3): 239ff.

History of 'chronological/non-chronological' dichotomy

The notion that chronology was useful in examining discourses was established prior to its adoption by educational linguists. One early exponent outside the field of education was Robert Longacre (Longacre and Levinson, 1978). Longacre maintained that a principal distinction between discourses was to be found in the way they employed cohesive devices, that cohesion served to cement random ideas and provide coherence and was indicative of 'deep' organisational differences in textual structures. There was, as he saw it, a primary distinction to be made between temporally or chronologically linked discourses on the one hand, and those that were non-chronologically or conceptually-logically bonded on the other:

> It is assumed that anywhere where minus chronological linkage is indicated, it is replaced by conceptual linkage in the discourse in question, i.e. the assumption is made that the very sort of discourse has some principle of cohesion whether it be chronological or conceptual-logical. (1978, p. 204)

Chronological linkage was said to be a characteristic of *narrative* and *procedural* discourses – the distinction between these two temporal forms rested with the presence, or absence, of 'agent orientation' (1978) or what Longacre later called 'participant reference' (1983) – while *behavioural* and *expository* discourses were said to be structured conceptual–logically rather than temporally. Despite digressions into descriptions of setting, background or collateral material (1978, p. 107), strands of temporal cohesion in narratives could be discovered in an 'event-line', in an 'agent-line', or even in a 'repartee-line'. An event-line, for example, would reveal successive events, successive times, or successive places, or a combination of these three. Thus for Longacre 'the fairy tale and myth, the short story, the short short story, the novel and various varieties of novels such as historical novels, gothic novels, detective mystery stories' as well as 'first person accounts, newspaper reporting, and historiography which ... makes pretensions to factuality' were all examples of temporally organised narratives; 'recipes', 'how-to-do it books' and 'instructions' were said to be examples of procedural discourses. (1983, p. 9])

Linguists more closely wedded to educational issues than Longacre were spurred to investigate chronology by a desire to question the prevailing assumptions that had come to underpin children's writing in school in the 1970s and early 1980s. For Harris and Kay (1981) in *Writing Developments: suggestions for a policy 8–13 years* and Harris (1986a,b) one needed to challenge the orthodox and 'simplistic' distinction between creative and factual writing that would 'sanction the practice of only a narrow range of writing at primary level'. (1986a, p. 50) For Perera in *Children's Writing and Reading* (1984) it was the absence of hard linguistic evidence that seemed to undermine the value of Britton's then fashionable model of writing development giving its categories mere 'subjective' appeal. For Perera this was manifest in the fact that

Britton's anecdotal typology revealed little in the way of evidence regarding the psycholinguistic demands that different types of writing might make upon the young writer, a criticism that Britton now seems to accept (1990, p. 6). The observation that there existed a link between temporality and the degree of difficulty young writers might experience in constructing various texts seemed to provide an insight of crucial importance. Linguistic evidence to support this notion was readily available in children's writing:

> ... there is a broad division between texts that are organised chronologically and those that are not ... In a chronologically ordered text (which can loosely be called *narrative*) the sequence of events in time structures the material: in a non-chronologically ordered text, the relationships between the parts are not temporal but logical, e.g. comparison, contrast, similarity, whole–part, cause–effect, and so on. Linguistically, a chronological text can be identified by its high use of verbs that describe actions or events and by the fact that sentences which contain verbs can generally be joined by connectives like *then, next, after that*. (1984, p. 217)

Harris and Kay, and Perera concurred that whereas chronological texts required the writer to perform the relatively straightforward task of arranging events in a time sequence, non-chronological discourses followed more abstract principles of organisation. Non-chronological writing was more difficult because of the need to pre-plan: 'such a plan has to be determined from the outset and the end kept in mind from the beginning of the act of writing. If children are unable to create and hold in mind such a plan it will be difficult for them to construct a coherent piece of writing,' (Harris, 1986a, p. 52) On the other hand, because temporal forms of writing were said to be constructed by establishing 'what happens next?' they were more easy to construct:

> stories, and many other types of writing are, like the party story-game, organised on a *time-related* basis. To make up, or determine upon, the next bit, the writer has to ask 'what happened next?' The principle of time-related organisation is very powerful and holds good whether we are dealing with a story deriving from the imagination, an account of a visit, of a biological process (such as germination) or a history essay retelling, say, the events of a battle. In fact, much of the writing in the middle years of schooling will be found to be organised on a time-related basis. However, as children progress to top junior stage and beyond they will increasingly be required to tackle writing that is not organised in this way. Writing that involves making comparisons, presenting arguments or interpreting evidence is organised on different bases [*viz* non-time related]. (1986, pp. 51–2)

Having concurred with Harris and Kay that young children found chronological writing easier, Perera could conceive of principles for the provision of appropriate contexts in which primary-aged children's writing might best be approached: 'if a chronological plan of organisation is not possible, then perhaps the writing can be in a personal style; conversely, if a personal style is inappropriate, then maybe the facts can be presented in the form of a narrative'. (1984, p. 223) Similarly, Harris and Kay concluded with 'helpful' suggestions for approaching non-chronological writing with children; teachers must prepare them for the 'sort of pre-planning involved in non-time-related writing', and also draw attention to the problems of '*sentence linkage*' (1981, our italics).

'Chronological/Non-Chronological' in National Curriculum English

Table 1

Chronological	Non-chronological
Narratives	Description (e.g. of a person or place)
Reports (e.g. accounts of tasks they have done and of personal experiences)	Explanations (e.g. of a scientific process)
Diaries	Arguments (e.g. for a point of view)
Explanations	Opinion (e.g. as a news report)
Letters	Lists (collating and ordering mathematical data)
Accounts (e.g. records of observations they have made - in a science or design activity; of a family occasion; of a personal experience)	Captions
	Labels
Instruction (e.g. recipes) for carrying out a task	Invitations
	Greeting cards
	Notices
	Posters
	Letters
	Notes for an activity (e.g. in science or designing and making)

A compilation from the NCC and DES documentation

Despite this apparent lack of clarity, the notion of temporality was subsequently appropriated uncritically by bodies such as the Schools Examination and Assessment Council (SEAC). In *Children's Work Assessed: Key Stage 1* (1990/91) for example, SEAC make the observation that Sarah's writing, resulting from her work on candles, contains both a 'list' and an 'account'.

1. *What I used*

   Three candles
   Three glass jars
   A metal tray
   A box of matches
   Two sand timers

2. *What I did*

   First we used the matches to light the candles
   then put the jars over the candles
   and then turned over sand timers
   the candle in the little jar went out
   the one in the middle jar and
   last of all the one in the big jar went out

Elements within the organisation of the latter part of Sarah's writing indicating temporality are evident – 'First we', 'then' 'and last of all' – and yet, curiously, the work is classified by SEAC as an example of 'non-chronological writing' (p. 38). Now this sits awkwardly with the classification of Christine's writing three pages later (p. 42) for it is *just* these temporal connectives – 'First of all', 'Next cut out', 'Then last of all' – that are said to provide clear evidence of her writing being of 'chronological' construction. In fact both these pieces of children's writing are similarly constructed; both contain a 'list' – non-chronological? – and both follow with a chronological 'explanation' of what the children found out, and yet they are given different temporal tags. And so, even working *within* the parameters set by the National Curriculum both children's work might more accurately be described as containing a blend of both chronological *and* non-chronological elements. That temporality may be said to be 'clear-cut' and 'absolute' is, in this light, at best suspect.

Indeed, that writing can cut across the chronological/non-chronological divide and contain blends is convincingly documented outside the National Curriculum. While playing a key role in developing the notion Harris himself refers us to the mixture of temporal and non-temporal elements contained in one child's piece of writing on reflex actions: 'The first part is organised on a non-time related basis, the second part is basically time-related in that the principle for determining the content of any subsequent sentence is 'what does the nervous impulse do next?' (1986b, p. 103). Tann makes a related observation, that in encouraging a written response to a construction task in technology, primary teachers are quite likely to see aspects of chronological and of non-chronological organisation – a 'list' of materials used, a 'description' of the task, an 'explanation' of why a particular approach was chosen, a 'recount' of procedures, an 'evaluation' of outcomes, an 'argument' for more model-making or for less, and so on (1991, pp. 224–5). Again, Stratta and Dixon (1922, p. 19) have drawn attention to Kress's observation that a 'generic mix, or blend [is] something not at all unusual in … texts produced by competent writers and speakers', and see this as a move away from the entrenched position of Martin, Christie and Rothery (see Stratta and Dixon, 1992).

With specific regard to narratives we have already observed Longacre's reference to 'digressions' from a line of temporal succession to descriptions and the like. Roger Beard too, having drawn his reader's attention to various modes of writing, notes that they 'are rarely used in isolation, but selectively and eclectically according to the task undertaken and basic aim of writing. For instance, a typical short story is likely to be dominated by the use of the narrative mode, but is also likely to contain descriptions of settings, classifications of characters and evaluations of themes which run through it' (1986, p. 175). In this regard LINC (1992) actually 'cautions' us against the National Curriculum:

> However, a final word of caution is necessary. The NC statement suggests there is a polarity between chronological and non-chronological. In practice, the distinction is more in the nature of a continuum and in many texts some parts may be time-sequenced (chronological) and other parts sequenced on another basis (non-chronological). Even in narrative which may appear to be the most straightforward time-sequences, there are likely to be, perhaps as a mark of increasing sophistication in exploring the possibilities of the form, manipulations of chronology (flash-backs, for instance); the handling of simultaneous action; and passages of reflection or argument that stand outside the main sequence (p. 334) … narrative cuts across the chronological and non-chronological distinction also made in the NC. Indeed, narrative consists of a succession of related events (often organised in a cause–effect relationship …) In this sense, they work on a time-related or chronological basis. However, some aspects of story telling may contain non-chronological elements, e.g. descriptions of setting, place character and situation; or observations and comments. (p. 347)

Again, Fox (1989 and 1990) has written persuasively on the nature of 'discursive argumentation' within children's narratives, as when characters in stories discuss problems and their possible solutions: 'Questions, problems, hypotheses and explanations are the tools of argumentative discourse; they are part of the structure of the story' (1989a). Her research has clearly demonstrated that within their narratives 'children show some understanding that an argument is not a conflict of assertion/counter assertion, nor an expression of anger, but a verbal construct whose proposition must be supported by explanations, reasons and evidence of various kinds' (1990).

A discourse distinction?

We think it is clear from the history of the distinction and its absorption into the National Curriculum that this binary distinction between 'chronological' and 'non-chronological' writing is derived from syntax-based linguistics rather than from discourse theory. The answer to the question in the sub-heading for this section must therefore be 'no'. It is a distinction that tries to describe the ways in which utterances or sentences are linked *within* a discourse or text; one that aims to account for the cohesion of particular texts (see Halliday and Hasan, 1976), or the way that one part of a text leads on to another. There are several problems arising from the misapplication of this syntax-based distinction to children's writing and to the orders for English. First, notions like 'chronological' do not translate easily to the discourse/text level, where relationships between parts of a composition are more complex. Second, units of composition in the various kinds of writing are not always defined by sentences, paragraphs and other 'surface markers'. Third, writers of any age do not compose with reference to a 'chronological/non-chronological' distinction. It is an unhelpful distinction as far as the processes or acts of writing go.

The best hope for an understanding of the large scale structures of stories and other kinds of writing is via the theory of 'episodes'. Van Dijk (1981) has attempted to free himself from the syntax-bound notions of cohesion and try to account for the 'macrostructures' of written discourse. These inhabit a level that is between that of the sentence and that of 'meaning' and intention (the semantic and rhetorical dimensions of communication). Episodes are hard to pin down, however. They do not conform only to sentences or paragraphs or any other 'surface markers' in written discourse. They have to be defined by a combination of methods. Van Dijk characterises episodes as:

> coherent sequences of sentences in a discourse, linguistically marked for beginning and/or end, and further defined in terms of some kind of 'thematic unity' – for instance, in terms of identical participants, time location or global event or action. (p. 177)

Definition of 'thematic unity' – of the 'macropropositions' of a text – can be difficult and quite subjective. It is possible to read several different structures into a single piece of writing. The 'markers' or grammatical signals that help to indicate the beginnings of episodes include pauses, paragraph indentation, time change markers (e.g. 'in the meantime', 'the previous day', etc. – neither of these are chronological!), place change markers (e.g. 'in Amsterdam', 'in the other room'), the introduction of new characters, changing predicates ('tell', 'believe', etc.) and changes of perspective. But even these are insufficient to identify all the episodes in a story or other text, let alone the relationship between the episodes. These relationships can be accounted for in several ways. One way is to describe the relationship of one episode to the previous one in terms of whether it is chronological ('then'), casual/logical ('so', 'because') or synchronic 'and'. It must be stressed, though, that these relationships do not always coincide with the use of these particular connectives between clauses or sentences.

In short, the field of accounting for large-scale structures in writing is a rich and complex one. What is certain is that simple dichotomies like 'chronological' and 'non-chronological' come nowhere near accounting for the products or, more importantly for learning to write, the *processes* of writing in school. Further support for our position comes from the work of Paul Ricoeur. As Ricoeur (1981, p. 180) notes, an analysis of narrative writing that only takes into account 'the linear succession of episodes' is impoverished. As well as the syntagmatic dimension, there is the paradigmatic to take into account. He criticises Propp's formulations for the description of relations in Russian folk tales by accusing them of unidimensionality, and then goes on to emphasise the importance of repetition in any account of narrative patterning. Already we see that a simple distinction like 'chronological/non-chronological' is too crude to account for even the most straightforward of folk tales or children's writing, because there is a third element in the equation: repetition. This element is central to the production of aesthetically pleasing works in writing and music because it is the principle on which rhythm and rhythmic variation is founded. As Ricoeur suggests, repetition 'deepens' and complicates – but also makes more memorable – chronology. And as Octavio Paz (1974) says:

> Rhythm is the original metaphor and encompasses all the others. It says: succession is repetition, time is nontime ... The instant dissolves in the succession of other nameless instants. In order to *save* it we must *convert it* into a rhythm. (p. 65)

We take the songs, poems and stories of children in primary school – as well as their jokes, lists, explanations and other discourses – as *conversions* , rather than as 'read-offs' from 'reality'. Indeed, to see them as anything less than conversions, and to reduce the significance of the shaping energies of children's language is to impoverish the curriculum. At one point in his argument, Ricoeur uses the very terms we are considering in this article, but in a way that undermines their use in the National Curriculum:

> Every narrative combines two dimensions in various proportions, one chronological and the other non-chronological. The first may be called the episodic dimension, which characterises the story as made out of events. The second is the configurational dimension, according to which the plot construes significant wholes out of scattered events.

Because narrative is both chronological and non-chronological, the two dimensions cannot be characterised as different types of writing. Ricoeur's argument is summed up thus:

> In a word, the correlation between thought and plot supersedes the 'then' and 'and then' of mere succession.
> But [he adds] it would be a complete mistake to consider thought as a-chronological. (p. 175)

Conclusion

Our own research (e.g. Andrews, 1992a) and that of others (e.g. Wilkinson, 1990) would suggest that the chronological/non-chronological distinction is inaccurate, over-simple and misleading. The research has looked at whole texts, whether they be oral and written accounts by pre- and early-schoolchildren or the written work of older pupils. Much of this recent work questions Moffett's (1968) formulations based on the equation 'chronologic=narrative' and the attendant model in which narrative is the 'logic of lowest verbal abstraction ... because it conforms most closely to the temporal and spatial order in which phenomena occur' (p. 34).

It is clear that many narratives are non-chronological and that many narratives contain non-chronological elements such as description and argument: that reports can be both chronological and non-chronological; that diaries, told stories and letters can all play with chronological sequence; that a Sainsbury's shopping-list may well be constructed temporally to reflect a knowledge of the store's layout and one's anticipated passage around it, just as an itemised till-receipt may reflect one's decision to group frozen items, tins, or whatever, together; that a list can form the backbone of a narrative as in Michael Rosen's *Today I Ate* (1983, pp. 121-3) where eating a list of rich foods in chronological sequence – and, later, the list's strict temporal invention – is crucial for humorous effect. (See also Lobel, 1973; Hutchins, 1976; Burningham, 1983.) Indeed, of narrative it could be said that one of its distinguishing features is that it plays with time (see Andrews and Fisher, 1991), often subverting chronological sequence for particular effect. At the very least, such narratives read as 'redescriptions' of the world. Insights into the narrative structure of stories as well as a good deal of fun and/or emotional insight are to be had from such subversions, as in this piece by a year 7 pupil:

> As the wheel comes rolling out of the ditch and the bonnet goes down, the glass of the headlights gets sucked into position and a person somersaults back through the windscreen which starts to form. The fear on their faces changes to happiness, and the dents in the front of the car wrinkle out like screwed-up paper unwinding ... (See also Vonnegut, 1983)

Similarly, the so-called 'non-chronological' *genres* like descriptions, arguments, lists, invitations, notes for an activity, and so on can either be completely organised on a chronological basis or contain elements of chronological sequence.

Before we summarise our objections to the chronological/non-chronological distinction, we want to welcome the expansion in the kinds of writing that the distinction offers. What the 'non-chronological' category tries to chart are the largely non-fictional *genres* and forms such as argument, explanations, letters, notes and news reports. We are pleased to see such a widening of the range of discourses made available to young children, but we feel the distinction that has been the subject of our critique is unhelpful for several reasons.

- We think that sequences of kinds of discourse (like 'chronological' before 'non-chronological') need to be questioned. The conventional notion that 'chronological' or narrative forms must come first (one that is represented in the progymnasmata of classical rhetoric e.g. Matsen et al. (1990, p. 277 ff) or in the work of Moffett) raises questions about the order in which children gain command of different kinds of discourse.

- We do not think that the chronological/non-chronological polarity is helpful in determining degrees of difficulty, a principle on which the statements of attainment in the National Curriculum have been built.

- Because the distinction attempts to account for a product (writing) it does not necessarily apply to the *process* of writing in different modes, *genres* and forms; it is therefore not helpful to teachers and children in the act of writing.

- The distinction is culturally narrow. What counts as chronology in one culture does not necessarily signify in the same way in another. The chronological/non-chronological distinction is fallaciously attributed an 'absolute' and 'clear-cut' nature.

- Following on from the previous point, the assumed simplicity of the distinction is misleading. 'Chronological' structures are more limited than 'time-related' ones, and these in turn are more limited than narrative structures. Similarly, 'non-chronological' structures are more limited than 'non-time-related' ones, and these are more limited than narrative structures. Similarly, 'non-chronological' structures are more limited than 'non-time-related' ones, and these are more limited than the possibilities open to exposition, argumentation and so on. What we are offered in the distinction is a cramping of the possibilities open to young children as they compose.

- There is no mention of such a distinction in the attainment target for reading, nor any consideration of how 'chronological' or 'non-chronological' texts are read; and yet we assume a close and complex relationship between writing and reading, as between speaking and listening.

- In any binary distinction the first element is usually the dominant one. 'Chronological' and 'non-chronological' are like the terms 'fiction' and 'non-fiction' in this respect, reducing the status of the second term.
- The distinction is not helpful in categorising, interpreting or assessing children's writing at Key Stages 1 and 2.

We intend to look at children's writing in a more empirical study in the near future. In the meantime, we hope that primary schoolchildren are not being directed along these narrow channels in their writing development in order to satisfy ill-conceived assessment categories.

CHAPTER NINE

DEMOCRACY AND THE TEACHING OF ARGUMENT [*]

Richard Andrews

Over the last four or five years I have been working on projects that are to do with arguing (see Andrews, 1992a; Andrews and Costello, 1992; Mitchell, 1992a). This might seem odd, and when I explain to children in particular that I am interested in argument, they think it's even odder. They think, of course, that I am about to start quarrelling with them, or rowing, or having a tiff, a spat, or to engage in what, with typical British understatement, is often described as 'having words' with them. Put another way, they see argument as a natural part of discourse and are bemused by anyone wanting to study it. As a definition of argument for working on the projects, I've used the broad-based 'connected series of statements or reasons intended to establish a position' and for argumentation, 'a process of reasoning; exchange of views'. Those definitions seem to embrace the personal and domestic as well as the public and formal dimensions of argument.

The everyday nature and functions of argument – disputes in the kitchen, differences of opinion on the playground, altercations at the office – if you like, the arguments of the *demos*, of the people – are indeed partly what I'm interested in. For too long, the discourses that are natural to us as we go about our lives have been seen to be cut off from the so-called 'higher' discourses of schools and the academic life. Take the essay for instance, which although it takes different forms according to disciplinary or geographical context, is a fairly standard way of representing material and/or opinions for assessment on academic courses. This is a well-recognised form for presenting knowledge in the humanities; it is the staple form in education from 16 to university level; it has a stranglehold on assessment and expression at these levels; and it often presents difficulties for learner-writers.

But it is a long way from forms of writing that are, perhaps, more popular. Part of my research has been to build bridges between the vernacular forms of writing and speech and the 'high' forms; and also to transform those high forms to make them more accessible as well as diversifying the forms that are available to writers as they attempt to shape what they have to say. In short, my aim has been to invest those high academic forms with energy and feeling and

[*] First published as Andrews, R. 1994.'Democracy and the teaching of argument', *English Journal* 83 (6): 62–9; and winner of the Edwin M. Hopkins Award, received in Chicago, November 1996.

personality as well as with intellectual clarity; to close the gap between the vernacular, 'natural' forms and the forms prescribed by the academy.

The functions of argument

To stick with the vernacular forms of argument for the moment, though, it's interesting and revealing to ask the question, 'Why do we argue?' Here are some of the answers that teachers and students have come up with over the last years, and I want to compare this list with the reasons for argument, the *functions* of argument in schooling. We argue, then, in order to:

Clarify, as when issues and positions are clearer after they have been argued out. The clarification may be public, or it may be on the part of the audience (in which case persuasion will have come into it) or it may be on the part of the thinker/speaker. Clarification can also take written form. As Vygotsky (1962), Billig (1987), Rogoff (1990) and others have testified, clarification via argument is akin to critical thinking. The argument can give dialogue shape to half-formed thoughts and feelings, thus sharpening them for consideration – as in philosophical method.

Persuade, as when we want someone to do or feel or think something different from what they currently do, feel or think. Argumentative persuasion can take many forms, from book reviews and the arguing of particular points of view (e.g. against vivisection) to persuading someone to lend you money or not to leave home. It is often thought that all argument is persuasive – a scan of the present list makes it clear that this is not necessarily so.

Win, a more extreme form of persuasion. While persuasive argument may be working towards a compromise of some sort, arguments that aim to win and to defeat the other party are more absolute in nature. The metaphor of battle is more appropriate to this kind of argument, predicated as it is upon destroying the other point of view, 'shooting down' others' argument and 'establishing the supremacy' of one's own position. The other side of the coin from winning, of course, is defending your position against those who would like you to change your mind and/or your actions. *Defending* is thus another important function of argument.

Entertain, as in the letters of Groucho Marx to Warner Brothers, for instance (see Clarke and Sinker, 1992). While we don't consider the primary *initial* function of these letters having been to entertain (Groucho's case against Warner Brothers over the use of 'Casablanca' in the film *A Night in Casablanca* having been a bonafide one that he wanted to win), the subsequent function has been primarily to entertain. Some arguments – like Punch and Judy shows, dialogues between comedians and even formal disputations between monks – have entertainment as their primary function.

Unload, as in a domestic row when the ostensible reason for the dispute is not the real reason for continuing the argument. This is interesting psychological territory. Suggestions have been made that arguments can be deliberately (or perhaps unconsciously) triggered in order to release pent-up and unresolved emotion. This release of tension is often brought about between two people who know that each will forgive the other, thus people argue with close family or intimate friends in ways in which they would not even consider with professional or more distant associates.

Resolve, or come to a consensus. Argument is not always combative or adversarial; rather than metaphors of war and·battle, it can be conceived in terms of dance or negotiation of some sort. Naturally, this kind of argument requires the parties involved to move their positions to accommodate others' points of view. Without such listening and preparedness to move one's own position, resolution cannot take place. To draw on Gunther Kress's (1989) formulation and to move beyond it; argument both creates difference and is able to resolve it.

Find identity, as when adolescents argue against a position taken by their parents in order to assert their own position. I consider this to be an important function of argument, linking the process of argumentation to expressiveness, group identities and power. Although argument has often been assumed to be rational, distanced, and public, my view is that its function for the maturing individual is also to create space, to assert a position, to define oneself in relation to others.

There are no doubt other functions that argument fulfils in society. But even those listed here are more extensive than is usually assumed to be the case. Many of the above functions can be combined in a particular situation. Someone might be arguing to clarify, persuade *and* to find identity at the same time; sometimes one of these functions may be primary and the others secondary. At the very least, I hope in this list to have opened up the notion that argument can have multiple functions in society, and that the functions it does fulfil are important ones for the health of society and of the individuals within it. Compare this range with the function of argument in schools, which is largely to display competence in argument, and to offer up such display of competence in argument for judgement by the teacher. Less often used are arguing to win, defend, clarify, and persuade. Rarely is argument used to entertain, resolve or unload – within the formal curriculum, that is.

This is where the notion of democracy comes in, and where conventional school and university practice really does narrow what is possible with students. I would like to establish some key points in this argument: first, such a range of functions of argument is essential in a democracy; second, hitherto the range available in schools and colleges has been much narrower than what has been offered here, so that students are in effect disenfranchised from their own education; third, if we are to do anything about this situation, we must both extend the range of writing (and talk) in our classrooms; and fourth, such an extension might well have implications for class management, the structure of relationships within schools and colleges, and the relationship between schools and the 'outside world'.

The range of discourses in a democracy

If different points of view are to be listened to, debated, used to reach a consensus, or argued out until one point of view gains ascendancy, then argument is the principal means by which decision are reached and democratic processes are seen to work. It is no good just 'telling our story'. Personal or group narratives may be effective ways of persuading another party that our case is one that should be taken into account, but without dialogue or comeback, they cannot hope to hold much sway. (Narrative isn't essentially monologic, but is often used that way by groups in weak positions and also as a power tool.)

Representative democracies are, on the whole, bureaucratic. As the *Oxford Companion to Classical Literature* (1989) notes, 'It was a feature of Athenian democracy that considerable power to influence decisions was wielded by skilful orators who held no official position and exercised this power with varying degrees of responsibility' (p. 178). Hence the importance of rhetoric in a democracy: being able to use language to persuade and convince and argue one's position as well as to be critical about other people's use of language to persuade and control (especially the language of those in power). The range of discourses needed in a representative democracy is great if: a) people are to express themselves, b) the machinery of democracy is to work, c) people are able to defend themselves against sophisticated techniques of persuasion, and d) there is to be any commerce between what the people want to say and the system that represents them. This last point is an important one, because we are seeing ostensible democracies in the West, like that in Britain, for example, suffering tension between notions of direct democracy (the voice or voices of the people) and representative democracy.

Let me illustrate the point about how discourses are closed down in decadent or emergent democracies by citing two examples. An example of an emergent democracy might be contemporary Russia, with Yeltsin temporarily closing down some papers because they represent the voice of the old parliament, the old order. An example of a decadent democracy might be Britain.

The Liberal Democrats, who occupy a position in British politics just to the left of centre, as it were, see the present structures of British politics as outmoded. 'Above all also', they declare in their recent policy document, *Facing up to the Future*, 'we want to build a *reinvented democracy* ... which provides government which is open, accountable and participatory – which belongs, in short, to its people' (Liberal Democrats, 1993, p. 3). Of course, each party says it will do something like that, because the diction of democracy has become essential to making its views palatable to the general populace and to the press. The terms differ slightly: the Conservatives use 'choice' and 'freedom' as their buzz words; Labour use 'community' and 'responsibility'. The caricatured problems presented by these two main parties – the Conservatives on the right and Labour on the left, are clear:

> Although the Conservatives have used the rhetoric of individual freedom, they have in reality constructed a state that is more powerful and authoritarian, and less participatory and democratic, than at almost any time in peacetime history. (p. 4)

And Labour is accused of putting the demands of society before those of individuals. The Liberal Democrat solution is to go for a form of government which is, in their terms, enabling, decentralised, reinvented and participatory.

What has all this got to do with what goes on in classrooms? More than you might imagine. The Conservative government has brought in a National Curriculum over the last few years, not without some major hiccups. One of the problems of the curriculum is that it sees children and their learning in terms of product, performance, grade levels and output – in other words, the language of business and industry, not that of choice or participation. In prescribing the levels of attainment in each subject, its implications are that material will be *taught* so that it can be readily *assessed* and then tabulated in league tables. There's nothing very democratic about it, and it implies teaching by transmission rather than interpretation or negotiation.

The range of argumentative discourses in schools and colleges

By the same token, the range of writing prescribed to test the levels of attainment or competences of students in schools and colleges is narrow. There is very heavy emphasis on the essay at the higher levels, as if all writing lower down was contributory to it. There is even heavier emphasis at university level, where with some exceptions, we in Great Britain have found lecturers to be very conservative about the forms in which they ask their students to write. The essay is accepted uncritically as *the* form for the expression and testing of knowledge in the Humanities. The form is understood as a vehicle for the disciplined free expression of thought, but rarely considered in terms of the thought it suppresses or excludes. Real argument, as Ricoeur has pointed out, on the other hand, is characterised by 'a willingness to suspect' (1970, p. 27). It is critical, sceptical and is thus able to get behind apparent completeness. It can question an ideology.

The purpose of my research has not been to denigrate the essay – it is, after all, a potentially wonderful form when infused with imagination and energy, and I can think of many examples ranging from essays by Joan Didion to one by a 14 year old student in Leeds writing about travel and working in a bar.

I am interested, however, in trying to rediscover the essay by looking for ways to improve access to it and so to improve the quality of essay-writing in schools and universities, but also to find alternatives to it.

Alternatives to the conventional forms of argument

If there are alternatives to the argumentative essay, what are they? Let me give two examples. A thirteen year old group of students has read Terry Pratchett's novel *Equal Rites* with its teacher, and she now writes to them in the role of one of the characters in the book, a wizard who argues against girls gaining access to a university of wizardry. The girls have to argue back, persuading that they are just as well qualified as boys. The advantage of this in role writing exchange is that the teacher can take up particular points in the argument and ask the pupils to answer them by providing better arguments – which indeed they do, as each letter displays better and better argumentative skills.

The notion of exchange is also evident in the letters a 17-year-old advanced level English student has used to convey her response to *Les Liaisons Dangereuses*. She writes in the role of Madame de Tourvel to express her implicit understanding of this character's role in the play, instead of submitting the more conventional essay.

You can probably easily call to mind now other forms which are argumentative: poems, particularly those driven by some political motive; fables and parables; plays, certainly (think of Brecht); leading articles in newspapers; advertisements; campaign literature, etc. And these are only the written forms. There are many more visual and oral forms to consider, and many that use the visual, written *and* oral forms in their delivery. In contemporary culture, such mixed media forms are increasingly prevalent.

Thus, in general, the element that all these have in common – though some more obviously than others – is *dialogue*, or a number of voices coming together to explore an issue. This seems to me an important question in language arts and English at the moment, coming as it does in the wake of Bakhtin. Let's consider why dialogue and argument go together and why a recognition of their importance has implications for the classroom.

If we see the learning of a wide range of language forms from a dialogue (rhetorical) perspective, it is no longer fixed generic forms that are the principal focus of attention in curriculum planning, but rather how children and young people interact with others in using those forms. The interaction might well obscure the forms themselves as the contingencies of the communicative/social situation take over. It's clear now that it is through dialogue and interaction that we learn language, not by reciting texts or learning grammars of the sentence or of discourses – in short, with other people and not on our own – though of course an individual can provide his or her own audience in talking to him/herself, thinking aloud, doing as Gorky does in his diaries which is to ask himself questions and then answer them, or by demonstrating the process of reaching agreement through taking disagreement into account. In dialogue we use the discipline of others' responses to move forward.

So there are two stages to move: the first is to explore the argumentative, dialogue forms like Socratic dialogue, symposia, play scripts, dialogue in stories, stories with more than one narrator, poems that take question-and-answer format, interviews, conversations. If we look outside Anglo-American culture, we'll find more of these. The second is to create contexts for this kind of writing and talk. This brings me on to the fourth point – each a turning point in my argument – and in many ways the most difficult area, *viz* the implications for the classroom of such a view of writing and communication in general.

Implications for classrooms

There are certain principles of this dialogue approach which remind us that writing must have a relatively more specific audience than has been the case in the past; there must be scope for dialogue and hence real communication. What does this mean for the classroom? It means that there will be clear *purposes* for writing. I stress purposes to pick up what I said earlier about the multiple functions of arguing. Although in the past student teachers and perhaps even conscientious experienced teachers have outlined the purposes of a writing assignment to themselves, they have rarely communicated these purposes to the students who are actually carrying out the assignment. 'Why are we doing this?' is often met by 'Because you have to' at worst, and at best, 'Because it will help you to apply for a job' or 'Because it is the best way to write if you want to pass the exam'. In other words, there is an element of coercion and simulation about the whole enterprise, and of deferred pleasure. It's not real communication, but you do have to do it. It's good for you.

So whereas in the 1970s, thinkers about the range of writing in schools like James Britton and others were urging real audiences for *some* of the writing taking place, what I'm urging is real audiences for most of the writing that goes on in school. Those real audiences include public organisations, parents, industries of all kinds and, of course, the teacher and students in the class, as well as the other teachers, secretarial and support staff and other children in the school.

A good example of a classroom transformed by attention to real audiences is one in Oldham, Lancashire (in the north-west of England). I witnessed, over a six-week period, the class teacher, Helen Lennie, set up a project for year 10 students and then gradually withdraw as the project gained momentum. The brief given to the students was to write a report for the school librarian 'which will contain your recommendations on how she should spend the library capitation which she has for newspapers and magazines.' In other words, this was a real commission for the class. The work involved devising and administering questionnaires for all the students in the school as to their reading habits and preferences; and meetings to discuss the progress of the research and the writing of the report, with minutes being taken and circulated, memos being sent to each other, and in the end the presentation of a 64-page report to the librarian. There was nothing simulated about this project. The librarian acted upon the recommendations of the report, and you won't be surprised to know that use of the library increased after its implementation.

To quote from the report on this and other projects:

> The students thought that this kind of work was more difficult than conventional group work which they enjoyed and were used to. One student explained that in literature groups there was the text before them and if someone came up with a reasonable idea then it was likely the rest would go along with it. But when groups formed for this kind of research they had nothing to start with except their aims. In class discussion, this type of group work was identified as being different because the students had to begin to collaborate on questions and procedures, searching for methods of working which would produce results. Often they did not feel any sense of achievement until something practical had occurred, such as the undertaking of interviews. (Brown et al., 1990, p. 57)

Whereas students would be inclined to agree with each other, often for the sake of getting through an 'exercise', now they were arguing with each other in order to reach a consensus and thus put their collective resolution into action.

You might be interested in how the present British government in 1994 views such developments in the teaching of English, particularly as a National Curriculum is on the agenda in the United States and in other English-speaking countries, such as Australia and New Zealand. The simple answer is that our government is not interested in dialogue and certainly not in helping children to argue well in order to take a reasonable and positive role in a modern democracy. Let me use a time-honoured mode-narrative – to tell you about this situation and to argue, relatively implicitly, for the importance of teaching argument in schools.

Recent undemocratic reforms to English in England

In 1988 the Education Reform Act, among other initiatives, ushered in the National Curriculum. A working party was set up to draft 'attainment targets' and 'programmes of study' for each subject in a fairly Victorian curriculum. 'English' was assured of a central place in the curriculum, identified as a 'core' subject along with maths and science. The time allocated to it in a typical week in school was, however, reduced, because there was so much else to cram into the curriculum.

The working party for English put its proposals to the Secretary of State, and these were broadly accepted, with two exceptions: the government wanted more emphasis on teaching grammar and less on speaking and listening. More emphasis on teaching grammar because of a misplaced belief that teaching sentence grammar would improve writing quality, and because of a connection in the government's mind between grammar and personal hygiene, cricket and the health of the nation. Less emphasis on speaking and listening because that wasn't real English, even though English teachers and people from business and industry had formed an unholy alliance to argue for the equal status of speaking and listening in the English curriculum. In 1990, when this particular debate was going on, English teachers and business people won. Since then, the story has been different.

You'll have made the connection between the importance of speaking and listening and the place of argument in the curriculum: much argument takes place in speech; the dialogue nature of argument has its roots in speech; and written forms are increasingly reflecting that debt to speech. But the British government isn't interested in that kind of dialogue taking place. Subsequent to the decision to give speaking and listening 'equal status' with a third of English curriculum time (which still isn't equal in my view, as 'Writing' and 'Reading' have a third each even though they are as reciprocal as speaking and listening), the government, by *fiat* – in other words, undemocratically, without consultation – reduced the proportion to 20 per cent.

References to argumentation in the National Curriculum for English are few and far between. It is in speaking and listening that the principal work in argument is to take place, with argument getting very scant provision in reading and writing in the elementary school, and formal, conventional provision in the secondary, i.e. the writing of essays, pupils understanding the difference between fact and opinion, and the promoting of the 'for-and-against' model of argument. Nowhere is there reference to the connection between imagination, expression or personal conviction and argument; elementary students are assumed not to be able to read or write it; there is no scope for alternative forms of argument; there is no understanding that narratives can contribute to arguments or, indeed, *be* arguments.

Furthermore, the whole English curriculum is framed in monologic terms: individuals compete against others in the classrooms, classes (and their teachers) compete for rankings in school, schools compete both locally, regionally and nationally and are represented in league tables. There is no sense that learning is a dialogic, negotiated activity. Rather, learning is seen to be the direct result of teaching and can be measured in 'performance' or 'output'. You can see how contrary this set-up is to the spirit of inquiry ('No, we haven't time to discuss that fossil you brought into the classroom this morning, because we've got to concentrate on the National Curriculum') and how it reduces argument to safe, conventional forms that are more to do with control and regulation from above than with the genuine exploration of ideas in language, with understanding a multiplicity of positions, with resolution, with the exploration and acceptance of difference.

In effect, what we have in the present government in England is a hegemonic, ideologically-driven situation in which successive Secretaries of State have been influenced more by government 'think tanks' – small, ill-informed groups of extremists – than by the testimonies of teachers or anyone who knows anything about education. Indeed, it has been the express intention of the government to eradicate anyone with a knowledge of language or language education from these committees, guided by the principle that if you don't know anything about a field, you are in the best position to advise on it. Anyone who does know is branded as prejudiced or 'liberal' and treated with suspicion by the government.

Things came to a head early in 1993 after government-appointed agencies announced the format of tests for students at 14 (the government wants national tests at 7, 11, 14 and 16). Teachers and students of this age group had been preparing for a part coursework, part exam assessment in July after three years of working to the requirements of the National Curriculum in English. In the final year of this preparation, and in some cases only a few months before the end of the course, the government announced that one of three Shakespeare plays was to be compulsory; that an anthology of poems and passages – all by white dead Anglo-Saxon males with a few taken exceptions, and almost all of them contributing to an idea of England as a kind of bucolic paradise – would be set for all pupils; and that there was to be greater emphasis on the final exam and less on teacher assessment than had previously been the case. These announcements, coupled with the high-handed way in which they were made, seemed anathema to most English teachers for a number of reasons, among them: 1) the over-emphasis on Shakespeare was denying other dramatists space; 2) the narrowing of the canon seemed to be undoing 10 or 15 years of expansion in which writing from different cultures was being celebrated and explored by children and students from age 5 to 16 and beyond; and 3) the move away from coursework undermined teachers' self-esteem and the documented rise in standards that had taken place in England since the introduction of coursework in the late 1970s. With characteristic 'logic', the government calls this rise in standards a 'lowering of standards', because more people are doing well.

What happened? English teachers, led by the London Association for the Teaching of English, wrote letters to parents, governors of schools, their headteachers and of course to the government, and gradually got parents and governing bodies on their side. Fellow teachers in science, maths and other subjects, also appalled by the *dictat* of a democratically elected government in their own subjects, put their weight behind English teachers; and crucially, unions backed their case too. This varied and strong alliance refused to co-operate with the government's legal requirements that the exams should be sat in the week beginning 9 June, and despite threats from government to sack teachers, dock pay, bring in outside agencies to administer and mark the tests and so on, the boycott held firm and in the end, fewer than 15 schools in the entire country undertook to supervise the tests. In a sense, direct democracy had swung into action.

There is much more to tell, of course, both of what led up to this situation and what has happened since June. My point in relating the bare bones of the story from the autumn of 1992 to mid-June 1993 in England has been two-fold; first, to inform you of what has been happening in the longest continuously-running democracy in the West, and second to suggest that in a working democracy, proper consultation, collaboration, and argument as to the best course of action are essential – they are not just embellishments to a democracy, a kind of writing or talk that can be simulated or seen as a nice form for the most able to practice on the way to university – they are absolutely essential, and of the very nature of democracy itself.

Conclusion

It is not enough for everyone to 'have their own voice', nor for us to 'tell our own stories'. You can see that there is a rhetoric of such expressiveness and narrative that has been current in our field for some years. It is a wonderfully rich and varied vein that we must tap and celebrate, but if such a line is played too exclusively, it can lead right into the powerbrokers' hands. At national levels, some things are allowed, and some are not. It is important to look at the wider context when considering what can and cannot be argued. Democracies in which power is wielded by the few on behalf of the many, but in which that power is abused to impose upon the many forms of English which are neither enlightened nor ultimately usable and practically that they don't take children's oracy and literacy needs into account – these democracies don't deserve the name of 'democracy.' Such governments and societies are quite pleased if individuals and groups of individuals are content to 'tell their own stories' because however powerful story is as a mode, it doesn't threaten or challenge the stories that the hegemonic powers tell. It is allowing people small spaces in which to operate, while denying them access to larger public space.

What is needed as well as narrative is argument: argument between individuals that will accept or resolve difference; argument to arrive at a consensus; argument to clarify, expose, unload – as I tried to make clear earlier – as well as argument for expressive purposes. This might mean forming groups to argue a case, and it certainly means that governments who claim to be standard-bearers of democracy, not only in their own country but to the rest of the world, must reach decisions by fair and open argument, at local, regional, and national levels. Schools are microcosms of that larger society, and the classrooms in which we teach are even smaller versions of society at large. That is why the encouragement of argument in the classroom, not only in English but in other subjects as well, is something we should celebrate and shape to the positive. It's essential to thinking as well as to social harmony, and it is one small way in which our classrooms, and the lives of our students that are partly shaped there, can contribute to a healthy, active, and real democracy in our own countries, and in the wider world that surrounds them.

CHAPTER TEN

KEEPING ARGUMENT ALIVE: MORALITY, YOUNG PEOPLE AND THE LANGUAGE ARTS CURRICULUM[*]

Richard Andrews

I want in this chapter to address the question of how to keep argument alive in the classroom by looking at three sub-topics: the political nature of the classroom, the literature that is studied there, and the nature and range of writing that is produced in what we call the 'English' classroom. My principal experience is of English – or language discourse arts – in English and Chinese classrooms, but I have observed classes in Canada, the USA and more recently in Australia and I think the issues – though not necessarily the practices – have much common ground. I will draw on a number of research projects conducted since 1987 to illustrate my points.

First, what is the political nature of the classroom – or to put it in Charles Bazerman's words 'Where is the classroom?' (Bazerman, 1994). In his essay, Bazerman brings to our awareness what any teacher would know intuitively or subconsciously: that the writing act in the classroom is framed by the institutional dynamics of schooling, the teacher's 'own imaginative construct of the meaning of the course' (ibid, p. 27) and by the students' interpretation of the situation – in short, by the rhetorical context for the act of writing. We might add to these three frames to the writing act two larger ones that surround them: one is the status of writing in the political life of the nation in which the writing is taking place; and the second, larger still, is the tradition and history of writing and the teaching of writing. In the first part of this paper, I'm going to concentrate on the third and fourth frames from the centre, *viz* the institutional dynamics of schooling and their national, political context, in so far as they bear on writing practice and pedagogy; and on the possibilities of argument.

I became acutely aware of the framing of the writing act in the classroom recently when I collaborated with an architect and colleagues in the School of Education in which I work in London. Our aim was to design a new primary/elementary school for an architectural competition. As soon as you begin to imagine an ideal space for young people to learn to write, you see the

---

[*] Previously unpublished paper delivered at National Council of Teachers of English annual convention, Cobo Convention Center, Detroit, 21 November 1997.

limitations of the *status quo*. In our imagined, ideal school, young writers (it doesn't matter what age) would be able to:

• come together in large groups to perform writing, e.g. in plays, large-scale readings, to hear writers etc., i.e. the currently fairly widespread school hall – the big room;

• work in groups of 25–40 to receive commissions and also perform – the conventional class-size.

So far, this describes what we already have in most schools: a hall or big room and a number of smaller rooms ('classrooms') in which educational activity takes place. I suppose you could say that this late nineteenth/early twentieth-century model for the education of young people is supplemented by the space that young people have at home to complete, continue or prepare for writing in the larger, more public spaces of the school. The home space, where homework is done, is ideally a quiet space with a desk or table. But we know that such space is not afforded every child, and that there are inequalities in such provision.

In our design for a new school, however, we wanted further space, for three principal reasons:

• for young people to work together, in small groups (i.e. three to six people) on collaborative writing projects, e.g. the scripting of a play, the writing of a joint report, the discussion of a piece of writing, and making of notes for a larger discussion forum.

• for work on computers. One of the huge benefits that writing collaboratively on-screen has brought is the talk about writing that ensues.

• for young people to work individually.

In design terms, then, this means a school with spaces (not necessarily rooms *per se*), for activities of varying sizes, from whole-school presentations to standard classroom-size spaces to small group spaces to spaces for individuals to concentrate. The rhetorical space is political within the school institution: in the new spaces which I've laid out, young people are more in control of the language that fills that space. They may be preparing material for presentation in a larger, more teacher-dominated space of the classroom, but at least they will have some of their own space in which to make their contribution.

The colonisation of space within a school is important because the bigger spaces are weighted against the student not only in terms of the authority they have or don't have, but more pointedly as far as the present paper goes in terms of the discourses that are sanctioned within those spaces. My experience and my observation is that in the larger spaces (in which I include the standard classroom) the emphasis is on narrative and information *genres*, rather than on argumentative and (more generally) dialogic ones. The central role of narrative in English work is well documented and, at times, has taken on the feel of a 'movement', particularly in its relation to fiction, the emergent self and group identity. The information *genres* have more subtly taken centre stage recently, supported by digital technology, but are the subject of critique in Andrews and Clarke (1996) and elsewhere. Still relatively neglected are the argumentative *genres* – debate, discussion, the essay, Socratic dialogue, persuasive, audience-focused writing – writing that is intended to change people's minds, stake out and defend positions, achieve consensus and so on. I would argue that the relative underplaying of the argumentative *genres* in schooling, and even in some cases, at university level, is partly a result of the lack of space for such discourse in nationally prescribed curricula and in the more immediate confines of the classroom and school. There is an uneasy approval of argument happening in school by teachers and headteachers: uneasy because although they want their students to be able to argue well, they are reluctant to give them the space and opportunity to do so.

Before I move on in my argument to how more discoursal space can be created within the conventional classroom, I want to mention briefly the potential of work that goes beyond the confines of the classroom or school altogether. My example, cited elsewhere, is a class of 14-year-olds which was commissioned by the school librarian to undertake a survey of magazine and journal use by students in the school. The 30 or so students split themselves into working groups of four to six and undertook the project by issuing a questionnaire to fellow students, interviewing others, visiting the local public library to check the range of magazines and journals available and surveying the actual use of the school library. Classes took the form of meetings between the various project groups, with minutes being taken to track and monitor progress. The class finally submitted a persuasive 64-page report to the School Librarian, who acted upon it, discontinuing some journal subscriptions and starting up others. Use of the library increased considerably.

What has this to do with morality, young people and keeping argument alive? The key factor in its success as a project (see Brown et al., 1990) was its empowerment of students at the core of the learning enterprise. They were commissioned in a real project that took them outside the classroom and the school. They had a stake in the outcome as learners but also as users of the library and the school. The curriculum was democratised by the project. They learnt responsibility, the importance of deadlines, the importance of their own and their fellow students' views. Argument was deployed, acted upon, with tangible gains for them and others to see. The discoursal spaces of the school were used differently, and of course the teacher's role was a supportive, challenging one rather than a managing, directing one. A sense of moral worth and responsibility was learnt rather than taught. As one of the students I interviewed said, 'it was the best thing that had ever happened in school, that'.

Now for a different approach.

My second section is concerned with the range and deployment of literature in the classroom, particularly with my overarching theme of 'keeping argument alive' in mind. Note that 'fiction' is the subject for the classroom *par excellence*. You can read it, study it, write about it without leaving the classroom. What it provides is, to borrow Pavel's title from his 1985 book, 'fictional worlds' or spaces beyond the classroom without anyone actually having to travel anywhere. And yet the sense of exploration is diminished if the literature chosen is not from a range of cultures. I am also aware that students – particularly older ones – like political literature that moves away from the 'emotion recollected in tranquility' tradition; which moves beyond the confines of its own literariness – like moving beyond the classroom – into political debate, action.

Last year, at the NCTE conference in Chicago, I went to see a production of *Hamlet* by the Shakespeare Repertory Company. It was terrific: athletic, youthful, complex. It had the scariest ghost I've ever seen (except for the one that sat in Jonathan Pryce's stomach in a Royal Court production in London in 1980). The Chicago ghost appeared in a shaft of ethereal light – on stage, in the audience, underneath the stage – to the sound of thunder. In short, this was a wonderful production, but it lacked a political dimension. Hamlet himself seemed to operate as an individual without anything more than a family context: the wider societal and political dimensions were largely absent. You could argue for a production of the play in which Hamlet is unaware of the political implications of his actions and inactions, until the very end, when Fortinbras assumes the kingship of Denmark – but in the Chicago production, the last lines, when Fortinbras, the Norwegian, arrives to see the carnage of Denmark, were cut. The play ended with the death of Hamlet.

Without wanting to labour the point, there's a lot of politics in *Hamlet*: the relationship between Denmark and Norway is a reference point throughout, and on his return from England, Hamlet sees Fortinbras leading his army across Danish soil to settle an issue in Poland; 'the state is out of joint', 'Denmark's a prison' – there are many references to the state throughout, and the fact that Hamlet is a prince, with royal and political responsibility as well as privilege, can't be ignored. And we know from Shakespeare's other plays, from the context within which he wrote, that – like any dramatist – his work is a commentary on the state in England or anywhere, as well as on Denmark.

The political as well as so-called 'universal' dimension of Shakespeare was very much on my mind when I was in Australia this summer. As part of a lecture/workshop tour, I was asked to work in a school in Sydney for a morning on *Hamlet*, Yeats and the Nobel prize winner and Professor at Harvard, Seamus Heaney. The first thing I did was try to find some common element around which I could weave the morning: density and richness of language was the first thing that came to me, but that seemed to me too conventional in literature teaching terms, too much in the tradition of treating a text as if it were free-standing, in a vacuum. The next idea I tried was to think of the political: each writer, each text, had politics at the heart. *Hamlet* I've already discussed; Yeats' writing was overtly political from about 1911 and he acted as a statesmen in the 1920s; Heaney's writing is set against those continuing troubles in Northern Ireland, and orients itself in relation to the political conflict, through the lens of Viking and Irish history and mythology, and in particular through the filter of the bog people – the massacres, atrocities of Denmark. But there is also the direct Heaney: 'This morning from the dewy motorway/I saw the new camp for the internees ...' Or 'When the fuck are you going to write something for us ...?'

My next task, having done the literary–political work, was to think about the pedagogic challenge ahead of me. I visited a number of schools in Australia, but this one was a fairly privileged independent boys' school in the eastern suburbs; I don't think my approach would have been much different in the school I taught at in London's East End. What interest do the politics of sixteenth-century Denmark/England, or twentieth-century Britain, in particular Northern Ireland, have for 16/17-year-olds in Sydney? The answer I came up with was 'land rights'. There have been two cases in the last five years or so that have acted like a geological fault or tremor for Caucasian–Australian consciousness: Mabo and Wick. Essentially, these cases have been about Aboriginal rights to land; land on which the colonisers have assumed possession, but which Aboriginal people have reclaimed. No matter that Mabo was a small island off the north-east coast of Queensland. The principle is clear: if Mabo is Aboriginal land, it follows that the land on which the cities are built, the land on which the huge suburbs are built, the land under your feet is sacred Aboriginal land. This current political time-bomb is exactly one of the main issues that underpin *Hamlet*, and it's central to the work of Heaney and Yeats. Once we'd dug to that level, and found common ground to explore in our own lives and in the texts we were studying for the morning, things went with such momentum. I should add that my own ethnic and political positioning – Romano-Celtic, but living as I've done for most of my life on the eastern (Viking, Anglo-Saxon) side of England close to the place from where Captain Cook and the *Endeavour* set sail to chart the southern Pacific – had to be taken into account too.

To come back to my theme: young people seem to enjoy literature that has a political function. Often the texts that fulfil that function most explicitly speak with an uncluttered clarity and directness that is disarming. As well as Neruda, think of Brecht or other Eastern European writing; of Octavio Paz, Maya Angelou or Solzhenitsyn. Theirs is a writing that argues, that takes positions, that moves people physically into action as well as moving their feelings; writing rather than that emanating from 'emotion recollected in tranquility' (Wordsworth), from a purely internal impulse, instead is deployed in the public realm, and acts to motivate or inspire, to express with no less passion or energy, the individual voice within a political context. I don't know if there is a similar publication here, but the poet Tom Paulin's *Faber Book of Political Verse* is a model of that kind of writing in English literature, tracing an often neglected tradition from Milton to the present. If it doesn't include Hamlet, it should have done: it's a play that's full of arguments, from the quibbling of Hamlet with Rosencrantz and Guildenstern through the altercations with Ophelia to the matters of political significance – and beyond that to academic and centrally personal arguments about the nature of death in relation to life.

And to return a step further to the overall theme of this paper, keeping argument alive through literature seems to me an important element in the literature curriculum, but also important to young people's emerging political sensibilities and sense of identity. I have a strong sense that you can't *teach* morality; rather you have to live it, and learn from experience. Part of that learning is trying to understand and accept difference, and that's where imagination and literature – the creation and exploration of 'other worlds' is so important.

The third section of my talk on keeping argument alive is concerned with what young people write in the classroom. We know that, for various reasons, the classroom is not an entirely free space for children or students to write. First, it is owned, on the whole, by the local school board or education authority; and teachers police that space. I may be overstating this factor, but young people are not only at school to learn; they are there as part of a socialisation process and as a place to be during the day. Their writing, therefore, is a product of the politics and rhetoric of the spaces they are given during the day and in homework. I've said in the first section that the kind of writing that is favoured by such a situation is narrative and information writing: writing that is composed and presented within safe walls. All the major research in the late 1970s and 1980s through to the 1990s suggests that the writing world of students in classrooms in England and Wales is still like this; it is no wonder, then, that 11- and 15-year-olds find argumentative writing difficult. Figures from research in the 1980s, for example, suggested that less than 10 per cent of writing time in a range of 12-year-old classes was devoted to argument.

When argument is practised, it is still largely through the essay, the 'default *genre* or text-type' of argument in school and college life. Despite changes to the National Curriculum as a result of pressure to celebrate argument as well as narrative and informative writing, there is still a long way to go. The prevailing view is that at elementary and high school levels, narrative and informative writing – laced with some lyrical and dialogic work – is the norm, and that argumentative writing should emerge at best between the ages of 12–16 before becoming the only form of expression from about 16 onwards in the education sector.

What has all this – the nature of the classroom as a rhetorical space, the kind of literature that is read there and the kinds of writing that do, or do not go on there – got to do with the title of my talk, 'Keeping argument alive: morality, young people and the language arts curriculum'? First, argument has to be kept alive, and the English classroom is one of the places where we can give young people the chance to try out ideas, argue for particular positions, come up against issues and explore them, encounter views very different from our own and try to understand them, and explore what George Myerson calls the 'argumentative imagination': the imagination that posits other worlds, different from our own. But we have to be realistic about our role as guardians of an argumentative culture. We may be teachers in a subject that's potentially more argumentative than geography or biology, but at the same time there are other subjects and disciplines – history, sociology, politics and maybe even mathematics – that give more scope for the handling of abstraction, of theories and hypotheses, than ours does.

Second, we can exploit the political dimension to literature and the political positioning of the student within the classroom. I have tried to give examples of how that might be done. I think this is possible at any age, but it may be in the high school years that it becomes particularly important to give students a political space in which to read and write. The formation of identity takes place, I would suggest, often through opposition to other positions and or trying out of other positions, either through fiction and imagination or in talk and action. So emergent senses of values and morality are dependent on a free flow of ideas, questions, 'possible words' and handling of conflict in verbal exchanges – through argument – rather than by resorting to fighting. In a democracy, you can generate and resolve conflict through language; we, as English teachers, are helping our students to handle the most volatile and explosive medium – words – for the common good. To quote Carol Burnett in *Four Seasons*, the Alan Alda film from the 1980s, why don't we 'fight it out' in demotic argument rather than give up and go separate ways, without communication? That's supported by the German philosopher Habermas.

Third, in the wider political – local, regional, national and international – arenas, the sense of young people's identities being connected to wider communities is essential to notions of citizenship and to the health of a democracy. Argument is enfranchising in that respect: you might lose or win the argument; you might come to a positive compromise; you will unload, find out more about your own positioning, generate some humour perhaps, and certainly find out more about other young people, by arguing. That's why it's important in the curriculum, and that's why, as teachers, we need to argue to keep it there, and use all our imagination to find ways of making it accessible and enjoyable for all our students.

Chapter Eleven

QUESTIONS AND SCHOOLING: CLASSROOM DISCOURSE ACROSS THE CURRICULUM[*]

SALLY MITCHELL

Ask yourself: what is it like to be asked a question?

Are you thinking about who's doing the asking, where, when, how, why? While the result of your reflections may be highly dependent on answers to these supplementary questions, it is perhaps possible to arrive at a general conclusion: being asked a question certainly feels like being challenged or tested in some way. Most of us feel pressure to answer: it is only politicians who have mastered the skill of evading questions without an apology or a blush.

Now ask yourself: what is it like to ask a question?

Very often it is to find yourself in a position of exercising control. At a talk, when the speaker has finished speaking, this control is, by convention, handed over to the previously passive listeners. Often the opportunity is only taken up by those who already hold power, the teachers, the experts, the adults.

But even to those in a weak position the simplest question can lend power. The question 'why have you imprisoned me here?' is the pivot which reverses the institutionalised relationship between prisoner and jailer. It empowers the speaker to change the direction of the dialogue in a way which the conversant may not have anticipated or desired. The prisoner's question suggests the possibility of an alternative reason, a dialogue (*two* logics). To the jailers, the judges and the authorities just such a simple question can be immensely threatening. When *they* ask a question it is securely monologic, designed to maintain the status quo, the structures of institutionalised justice. In discussing learning processes we tend to be on the side of the prisoner; that is to say the pupil – the analogy is easily, if unwillingly, made, since both occupy an institutionally weak position.

Questions forge relationships between people; they also determine what the relationship is. The association of questions with some kind of threat is a result of the kinds of *genres* in which questions tend to play a major structural role: interviews, inquisitions, making statements to the police. The impact of questions in these spoken *genres* is immediate upon the context. They play a significant role in shaping the social, cultural, political nature and function of

---

[*] First published as Mitchell, S. 1992. *Questions and Schooling: Classroom Discourse across the Curriculum*. Hull: University of Hull, Centre for Studies in Rhetoric Occasional Paper Series no. 1.

the occasion. What kind of role, then, do questions play in classroom situations? What do they tell us about the generic character of those situations?

Classrooms are characterised by contradictions: freedom and control, individual growth and normative assessment, self-expression and disciplinary training. These polarities exist in tension, informing one another with constantly shifting emphases, suggesting how the individual can both structure and be structured within and by the educational system. This chapter focuses on the use of questions in actual classroom situations as offering insights into the complex and shifting relations of teaching and learning, independence and conformity. The question is more than a linguistic form; it has social, disciplinary and pedagogical implications. In the majority of classroom situations far more questions are asked by teachers than by their pupils. What are the implications of this? To what ends are these questions asked? How do they both reproduce and newly produce knowledge and learning? How far do they structure the learner and how far allow her to engage in individual structuring? How can the student's own questioning role be enhanced?

The prisoner's question – 'Why have you imprisoned me here?' – opened up the possibility of an alternative to the jailer's monologue. It created a situation in which *dialogue* might take place. The implications of this shift in relations are important for education. Questions can play a major role in structuring exchanges in which difference is dialectically produced and fostered as dialogue. The chapter considers dialogue – the operation of *more than one* logic – to be essentially a questioning activity in which both speakers are engaged. Dialogue is examined both as an activity in living situations and as a concept which provides insights into learning.

The chapter also considers the ways in which enquiry and exchange are variously constituted amongst specific and particular discourses. Questions can both encourage and suppress dialogue: they can also operate to produce in learners the discourse practices which identify a subject and distinguish it from others. Since questions often occur in situations where the balance of power – the licence to question – is unequal, I argue, finally, that in practice the fostering of dialogue may mean creating situations in which the mechanisms of control and initiation – of which questions are one form – are handed to the institutionally weak as a positive means of empowerment.

Learning to question authority

At this point in the chapter I would like to explore some aspects of the questioning in which I have engaged myself, hoping thereby to reflect something of its process: a process of learning and of being taught.

At the beginning of a research project which takes a grounded theory approach – one which seems very rapidly to swamp the researcher in oceans of empirical data, a great deal of which clamours for attention and the security and orderliness of a conceptual or theoretical home – it is of great use, and a great relief, to come across a book based on similar research to one's own and whose findings and speculations give one a point of anchorage from which one can begin to formulate, question and diverge.

Language, The Learner and The School (Barnes, Britton and Torbe, 1989) is such a book, valuable because it is in a sense so general and treats that aspect of education which is ubiquitous: communication between and amongst teachers and learners. Though the research upon which the book is based was conducted in the late 1960s, to someone who has recently sat through a school lesson in the role of observer, the issues it raises are instantly recognisable. They foreground themselves as the very things which make up the substance and texture of the lesson: the teacher's questions, pupils' participation, the language of instruction, the social relationships. Each of these areas requires some attention if one is to make sense of what one has seen and heard going on.

Douglas Barnes gives an overview of these areas in the book's first chapter. He and I meet on common ground; he is the authority, I am the student and our situation is one shared by teachers and learners every day. Since his knowledge and experience and mine share points of similarity but are not, I suspect, in any way identical, how do I go about bringing the two together? This question is not, I think, irrelevant to the subject which it is the purpose of this chapter to discuss.

One of the ways in which Barnes analysed the data he and his team collected was to categorise the different forms of questions asked in class:

1. Factual ('What?' questions)
    (i) naming
    (ii) information

2. Reasoning ('How?' and 'Why?' questions)
    (i) 'closed' reasoning – recalled sequences
    (ii) 'closed' reasoning – not recalled
    (iii) 'open' reasoning
    (iv) observation

3. 'Open' questions not calling for reasoning

4. Social
    (i) control ('Won't you?' questions)
    (ii) appeal ('Aren't we?' questions)
    (iii) other

In the event the usefulness of this categorisation to my own analyses lay, paradoxically, in my inability to use it; my inability, that is, to make the categorisation work for my experience. There is a great deal in Barnes' chapter with which I agree, but it is this small section I have needed to question, and – here my point is made – found most useful.

Barnes' comments on his own model that assigning a question to a particular category was not always easy. There was sometimes a discrepancy between the linguistic structure of a question and the function that it served within the particular context of its use, as when, for example, an apparently closed reasoning question was used for the social purpose of recalling a child's attention to the class. The difficulty experienced by Barnes seems to me to be crucial rather than incidental. The divorce between the linguistic structure and the question's function is not a mere quirk but should be a central factor in any analysis. The fact that there is no easy correlation between the two gives reason to doubt the adequacy of the categories themselves. New questions need to be asked, going beyond the counting of question types to a consideration of their relations and the complex context of their production and reception. What action does the utterance perform in the context in which it occurs? (Since every turn in talk is sequentially embedded, context here includes previous utterances and those which occur subsequently.)

Barnes notes that there was a predominance of factual over reasoning questions in history, English, RE and maths and that only in science did reasoning questions predominate. It would be a mistake I believe to infer from this observation a strict correlation between identifiable 'reasoning questions' and the process of reasoning itself. Other factors, and other routes to reasoning are involved. From my limited analysis I would at least speculate that in some instances the proportion of factual to reasoning questions derives from the extent of recall that is perceived to be needed in the subject. Often, from my observations this recall is not necessarily an end in itself but is a way of knitting substantive material into a process of reasoning or argumentation. A 'closed' request that a student recall a particular aspect, even the date, of an historical situation may inferentially open a new discursive position. As the student is supplying the factually correct answer, she may (it is generally the questioner's intention that she does) consider the significance of the question within the contextual whole, asking herself, 'Why am I being asked this question?' It is inadequate to deal with such questions in isolation as if they were not part of a process, not preceded by other utterances and interpreted in a particular way.

Asking a question, as I mentioned before, makes a relation between the speaker and listener, at the same time inviting a reciprocation of that communicative gesture in a response. The understanding that is made in such an exchange is demonstrated in the response; it is this which is crucial in determining the use or function of the question. This idea is developed in the discussion of Bakhtin's notion of dialogue which concludes the chapter, but is also illustrated in the following example which shows how understanding is developed between the teacher and students through a variety of questioning forms. Overall the sequence is one of shared enquiry or reasoning, but its progression does not rely on the use of 'reasoning questions'.

The example is from an A-level history class in which the group is looking at a photograph (referred to as source 94) of women sweeping the streets in the First World War and is discussing its message in relation to the wider question of whether the war marked a turning point in the history of women:

T: What about source 94, Robert, anything different? I mean there's
    the obvious points, but anything different? What would you say
    first of all about it?

R: Well, it's like women doing a job which had previously attached
    like – men's role.

T: Yeah, had this picture been taken in 1910, had that incident have
    occurred in 1910, how would you have expected people to respond
    to it? If it had been taken in 1910?

R: Shock, horror!

T: It'd be shock wouldn't it? Women didn't sweep the streets. It was
    alright for women to sweep people's houses, but not to sweep the
    streets. Which, interestingly enough ... Can any body throw in a
    temporal perspective here on it through to modern times? [pause]
    Can anybody, given that we're trying to judge the significance of
    these photos in determining the economic effects on women?
    Source 94, as we just said if you'd seen that picture in 1910 it
    wouldn't have – actually it wouldn't have been photographed – it
    would've been impossible – women didn't do that job.

B: Even today though you don't get that many women ...

T: Exactly, yeah. Even now ...

B: But the fact that if women wanted ...

R: Yeah there was that big stink in the paper about it. The fact that
    there was that big stink in the paper about it shows – well yes it
    shows ...

T: Means that it's still an issue.

R: Yeah.

T: But even so you're right. I mean whatever reason. For whatever
    reasons you don't see on the whole women sweeping the streets. If
    you walk inside an office building you don't see men cleaning the
    office on the whole do you? You've still got now, 70 years later,
    longer, 70-

R: 6 or 7.

T: Yes 70 odd years later you've still got the same in a sense, the same division of labour to do with sweeping as you had then haven't you? So what maybe does that allow us to say?

R: That perhaps it wasn't a turning point, 'cos I mean by a temporal perspective things are still the same.

T: Yet women in the war were clearly sweeping the streets and they weren't before the war.

M: It was a short-term effect.

T. Yeah so maybe the economic effect on women wasn't sustained.

The process of reasoning here emerges from the appeal to contemporary experience as a point of comparison from which to advance the argument about the significance of the First World War photograph. The notion of a 'temporal perspective' which underlies the appeal is a disciplinary tool for the building of historical argument. The teacher's argument is embedded with appeal questions (they might also be described as rhetorical questions) which lead up to an invitation to conclude, to encapsulate the valid point: 'So what maybe does that allow us to say?' The general statements at which the students and teacher arrive are the outcomes of an argumentative process which has employed a variety of question forms, including, incidentally, statements which have functioned as questions (e.g. 'yet women in the war were clearly sweeping the streets and they weren't before the war'). In this case linguistic form is entirely subordinate to function; the statement functions to question, to challenge. The function derives from its sequential positioning after the turn it qualifies: the statement-as-question could be seen as a function of context.

Appeal questions are described by Barnes as those 'which ask pupils to agree, or share an attitude, or remember an experience' (p. 16). This example shows them to have an expository function, to help establish a common base for understanding. Analysis of written argument has indicated that exposition, or the 'exploration of underlying assumptions' – often in oral form – may be an important intermediary step towards reasoning (Berrill, 1990). Berrill identifies a relation between 'oral groundwork' (p. 84) and the subsequent production of written work, suggesting that the process of reasoning does not necessarily conclude or resolve in classroom dialogue. It seems certain that in many cases processes of reasoning are to be identified across a wider pattern of questioning strategies than Barnes' categories suggested; and that, if the written form is also considered, questioning may occupy a differently sanctioned position in the different forms through which knowledge is made and displayed.

Interestingly Barnes himself records a doubt as to the reproducibility of the categories with which he first analysed his data, saying with hindsight:

I realise now that cultural categories of this kind are created in part by the act of categorising and cannot be handed over unambiguously to another person simply by definition: I was hankering after an objectivity which the very nature of intersubjective meaning probably makes unobtainable. (1990, p. 19)

His doubt is I think very well founded. In applying a set of categories, in making a series of interpretations, especially of a living interaction (audio and even video tape only provide an incomplete message; the whole we can never know), the researcher is only doing the best she can to account for all the possible variants, the overlaps, the questions which seem to her persistently to be raised. Glaser and Strauss (1967) talk of 'emergent categories'; 'usually it takes reflection afterwards to discover what one has actually found' (p. 72) – you don't *discover* what you have found until you've applied your own thought processes to it. What you discover is also (I think Barnes' comment suggests this) always contingent, always emergent, always, that is, open to new questions. To question oneself and one's own point of view leaves one vulnerable to having all one's answers destroyed and for the work to begin again in earnest. But such 'destruction' can, I suggest, be empowering, since it puts one in command of the work and in the position to make new thought. The application of thought processes to a body of material or experience progresses through the formulation of questions. An onlooker at an event becomes a *witness* only when the question (the possibility) of significance is raised.

So in conducting one's own research – and in any process of learning – another person's categories won't always do but to use them as foils against which to test one's own emergent view is a useful focusing exercise. If we can look at existing formulations differently then we can move on. As I read through Barnes' book, gleaning what I can of it, I am happiest when I feel the need to challenge; this seems to confirm my critical reading and gives me confidence that I too will develop categories. Earlier in my own experience it was not until at least my second year at university that I became, gradually, fuzzily aware that a question or – probably it was more unformed than that – an area of doubt surfacing when I was writing an essay or attending a seminar was not a sign of my lack of understanding, a flaw in my argument to be suppressed, pushed to one side to that I could get the work done, but was in fact a cause for excitement, an opportunity to make connections (to journey) or, if that were not quite possible in such a concrete way, at least – and just as satisfyingly – to 'entertain conjecture'.

I did not experience this position as one of weakness. Rather it felt like one of strength: *I* was asking the questions. Why did it take so long to reach this position? Is there a taboo about this form of questioning? Or do we simply believe that it cannot be taught? Does the system teach us that we are successful only when we find things easy (when our learning conforms to task objectives)? Do we believe that the ability – and right – to question comes only at the point when one has achieved power, that therefore, it results from power (from one's role as a teacher, from one's proven academic prowess, from one's suitability to assess the work of others)? Why is it that in many seminar situations it is the teachers who are left to ask questions, whilst the students, the *learners*, those whom we might assume have the most to ask, remain silent? There are situations in which I still feel my ability to formulate questions is hampered by my lack of sanctioned knowledge, my lack of *authority*. My confidence to feel that the thing I don't understand – or that seems continually to block my understanding – might be the legitimate subject for a question is not great enough. Because I am not 'clever' my question is just 'silly'. Until that moment, that is, when, if I am fortunate, it is articulated by some other person; then I feel confirmed. Maybe next time I will trust to my doubt and pursue it; invest myself with some authority, believe that my failure to understand may be a weakness of the speaker and a point from which we can both learn; believe too that I can be successful by finding things difficult and by confronting that difficulty with my questions.

Questions and discourse practices

Questions come in many shapes and sizes and serve many different functions. Some questions aim to clarify, others to challenge, still others to persuade; some elicit factual information and others, reasoning. What is the logic of such questions? Is it monological, dialogical, teleological? Who asks them? Why? There are questions which require an answer (and are possible to answer) and those which stand on their own, hang in the air, carry with them the force of statement and yet in such a way that the statement itself is only a possibility, but an acceptable possibility, worth considering. In some subjects the student who merely poses such a question might well be regarded as displaying a high degree of sophistication.

Questions are difficult to categorise or classify; they exist as parts of sequences of talk and their functions are always to some extent influenced by their contexts. In the analyses that follow, however, I do categorise and name to some extent. Many of the terms I use are taken from the classification compiled by Douglas Barnes and reproduced earlier. The difficulties discussed there become clearer through the analyses themselves. They suggest the failure of such a categorisation to account for relations between questions and for their operation within contexts. My initial focus in analysing this material was on the questions themselves, but in considering their implications I came to see them as at least partial clues to the way the disciplines function, the assumptions about knowledge on which they operate.

English

The following is a snatch of talk which occurs in the English classroom early in the teaching of Graham Swift's novel, *Waterland*. The students have been discussing in pairs the general question 'What should the opening chapter of a novel do?' Here they pool their ideas about setting the scene:

T: How important ...? I mean are we all agreed that that's important? Do you need to have something, do you want to have something you can visualise inside your head? Do you think so Liz?

G: [not one addressed]: I don't know if it has to be in the first chapter, but ...

T: But it's got to be early on?

G: Yeah, you need to have some idea of the setting, but not necessarily right from the off sort of thing.

R: It's like background into the important story and stuff like that. And you need it like Greg said, you need it early on if not in the first chapter.

T: Yeah. [pause]

L: Does it depend on the style of writing though?

T. Yes.

L. Because some are really vague and jump back and forth and give you a ...

T: Yes, yes. Well, that's what I was wondering you see. Some writers really are very vague about setting scenes. I wonder whether that means that's a lack in a writer or whether it's important to have something established, a setting established, or not? Is it just to help you visualise or does it do anything for you as a reader? I mean what is the whole business of reading a story actually doing to you as a reader?

G: Makes you feel as though you're part of it, though you're reading it.

T: Yeah, yeah, that's right. I mean it's a new world isn't it? I mean when you open a book don't you hope that you're going to enter into the world of that story and be taken up in it? And unless you feel the world's created then you probably won't feel taken into it.

What has been established here? More questions seem to have been raised than answered – and as usual when looking at a transcript, interpretation is complex rather than succinct. Nothing categorical seems to have been stated. When Robert (R) restates Greg's assessment of setting in order to confirm it the teacher complies with what he has said but not with its conclusory tone: 'Yeah' she says and pauses; it is not the end of the story. And Laura (L) repays her pause with a tentative question (the question form is important in testing conclusions). The teacher complies with the questioning here but doesn't fully allow the point – it was perhaps to be about the deliberate alienation of the reader – which lies unformed behind it, to be explored. Instead the question (more than the point) is incorporated into what *she* is wondering.

The teacher's approach needs to be considered within the wider context of the literary critical discipline for the purposes of which students have to learn that they are reading a modern experimental form, that *Waterland* is a challenge to conventionally received ideas about what a novel should and should not do or be. In order to achieve a sense of its difference they must first hold some consensus view: a position against which to argue. Laura complicates this already by indicating that what they collectively decide might 'depend'. In one sense the teacher keeps Laura's idea afloat by wondering whether vagueness in setting scenes might be a lack. This seems to me one of those 'worth considering' questions, generated within the fast moving classroom situation with its predefined end point – precisely, the bell; less precisely, the teacher's agenda. Notice though that despite this *sense* of openness the teacher's questions are constructed as alternatives, choices of two. The extract ends with the teacher using appeal questions: 'I mean it's a new world isn't it?', appealing to her students' experiences of reading and at the same time, I would suggest, creating a discourse within which these experiences are formulated. That discourse may itself take the form of an appeal to experience.

Why does the English teacher use questions? She seems to have a point to make, some information to impart about the need for a scene to be set at the opening of a novel. Teaching and questioning overlap. There is a reluctance to tell or dictate. The students certainly don't feel the compulsion to write it all down. But there are traces of an agenda, an already formed view, a body of knowledge. Whether these things are open to question is difficult to decide where the talk is in the mode of persuasive appeal; appeal to the experiential, to subjective experience. At the same time that subjective experience is filtered through the discourse of the subject, the norms of what counts as Literature and Criticism. Does this mean, then, that there is only one 'subjectivity' – a collective subjectivity – in which the students' personal experiences of reading eventually become the *same* 'personal' experiences? Interviewed about work in his A-level subjects, one of the students, Jack, suggested this might be so. He commented, comparing English with history: 'There are more rights and wrongs in English ... it's the way it's discussed sort of openly, everyone ends up thinking the same thing, with the same ideas'.

Jack's perception seems to be confirmed by a close look at another sequence of talk from the A-level English class. I was originally interested in the following extract as demonstrating the role of recall and closed questions in leading to a request for reasoning: a process of establishing the evidence, then testing its significance. Analysing this process however led me to wonder whether something of the wider form of enquiry in which the students were engaged might be captured here. The discussion arises from presentations to the class by pairs of students on aspects of the book's narrator, Tom Crick, in particular here, Tom's relation with his brother, Dick. The extract is long, but the critical realisation at which the students arrive – a point about the culmination of the novel as according with historical necessity and therefore one of its major themes – is painstakingly achieved. The teacher described this lesson as rather 'suet-pudding'-like; ideas did not flow rapidly as on other occasions. Some sense of labouring is detectable in the sequence. For my purposes though this slow motion version is useful since it exposes the use of persistent questioning, of factual chipping away, of *method* in reasoning which is undetectable in the sped-up reasoning we call intuition or insight.

At the opening of the sequence the teacher gives the students a pair of alternative questions which prompt a series of responses, each developing from the other. The choice itself is an open one, but the text with which they are dealing, *Waterland*, determines the selection of one in favour of the other. Through the teacher's subsequent use of closed and factual questions members of the class become engaged in pursuit of significance, the critical point. The teacher uses the responses to direct the subsequent talk and returns to them at the end.

T: Now how is it that at the end of the book, as Peter says, we actually feel for Dick? Is it because the process that Tom is going through of gradually getting to understand his brother – is what happens to us as we're reading it? Or would you have felt as sad about Dick dying if that had been earlier in the book? [A few comments omitted]

C: You wouldn't have felt that earlier on in the book because you didn't know about Dick. All you knew was that he was a potato-head. You didn't know anything else about him.

T: Umh.

C: But because it's the end of the book, or even if it had been near the end – not at the very end, but near the end, you'd still have felt sorry for Dick because you knew more about him.

G: Yeah, you've sort o' like learnt all the things that have happened to him, but none of it was really his fault. He's a victim of circumstances.

L: That's what makes it more tragic really.

T: He's a tragic figure, Laura?

L: [laughs] Yeah well it's not really his fault is it? He's, it's people way back who've determined his fate. He's not really got anything to do with it, yet he's got a – pointless life really. A lot pointless, it's sad.

T: You see the point that Laura's making? And that Greg started off for us? That it isn't just that in narrative terms you know it makes a good end to the book. It's *got* to be the end of the book hasn't it? If you could pursue the point that you two have started. I mean what does Dick become by the end of the book? [a few comments omitted] Why is fate against him? I mean what – what do you *mean?* Spell it out for us. [pause] Why is everything against him?

L: Cos he can't change anything can he? So no matter what he does – and the more he learns, the more it hurts him – the more he learns about himself.

T: So he's caught in the grip –

L: Yeah.

T: Well, pass it back. Why is Dick like he is? – to ask a really straightforward question?

M: Ernest and Helen.

T: Because of Ernest and Helen.

M: Incestuous affair.

T: Incestuous affair. Right take it back. [pause] Why was Ernest like he was?

M: Because he was a rebel.

T: Because he was a rebel. Thank you Mark, you're on my trail. Right, take it back. Why was he a rebel? Why was Ernest a rebel?

L: Because – the village went against him because his politics was different to what – his father had been Conservative. And he changed the beer.

T: [laughs] And he changed the beer. And got his revenge, so to speak, with the Coronation Ale. Right, why is –

how, in what way is he different from his forefathers, so the generation that went before and even the generation that went before that. Why is Ernest a rebel?

F: 'Cos they ...

T: Politics I know. Go on Fiona.

F: 'Cos they all succeeded.

M: 'Cos they were all Conservatives.

T: Yeah, good. They were all Conservatives. [A few comments omitted] Carry it further back.

L: He was ...

T: Go on.

L: He was more studious wasn't he? He wanted to do something different with his life, but he had to go in the same role as his father. And he wanted to start rebuilding like his great-great-grandfather or whatever.

T: Yes.

L: Who stood in that cornfield.

T: Yes, stood in that cornfield and looked down over the plains and said what I'm going to do is *this*. Right now are you aware that here's another of those historical cycles that's there in the book as well? But the Atkinsons who started so gloriously as we have them portrayed down the ages ...

F: They become failures.

T: They become Dick, don't they? [laughs] I mean Dick is the product of all the Atkinsons. [There is a general laugh] So in a way, Gary, your point – the point that you and Laura made between you is even more significant in the context of the book. You've *got* to know about the life of the Atkinsons haven't you in order to understand in an even wider dimension why Dick is significant, why he's important and why he's a bungle? He's a bungle in a much wider way, he's sort of the twentieth-century

bungle. The rise and fall of the Atkinsons is all there in
the story of Dick.

By using the contributions offered by Greg and Laura as a starting point for the
discussion, the teacher takes on something of the role of chairperson, making
the reasoning appear not to belong to herself but as part of the collective reading
of the group. She elicits the personal responses of the students, but through her
direction of the discussion, these become homogenised into a position of
consensus. The sequence is one of directed reasoning in the sense that the
teacher asks the students first to 'spell out', then to follow her 'trail' towards the
conclusion that the book had to end in the way that it did. The questions she
asks of the students on the course of this journey require them to recall the
chains of cause and effect as they are made in the book and to construct a
reverse chronology of its characters. The sequence gathers pace as it progresses
to the point where Fiona completes the teacher's sentence for her and where the
statement 'Dick is the product of all the Atkinsons' produces a general murmur
of both humour and approval; a denouement which, as in a detective story, one
can't quite predict in advance, but which when revealed seems always to have
been anticipated, inevitable.

Scholes (1985) has described three types of approaches to texts. Each is in
some way constructive: 'reading' constructs 'texts within texts'; interpretation',
'texts upon texts'; 'criticism', 'text against texts' (p. 24). If my analysis is
correct the class is involved in reading and interpretation here. In order to
perform critical analysis they would need to develop an awareness of their own
position or interpretation as only one of a number of possible alternative
positions and correspondingly to become aware of the text as manifesting a
certain position or positions. As it is the members of the class are engaged here
in the construction of a collective and singular reading of *Waterland*. The
interpretation is largely unproblematic and uni-vocal; consensus harmoniously
arrived at, because utilising so many individual readings. Since the consensus is
predicated on these subjective experiences, it is difficult to envisage how one
might break out of or see beyond its conclusions: collective subjectivity makes
an unassailable claim on truth.

It would not be accurate, however, to see this particular sequence of
classroom discussion as characterising the practices of English A level in their
entirety; on a number of occasions, for instance, the teacher raises the
possibility of incompleteness or lack in the book and in doing so hints at a
position outside the text from which it might be debated and evaluated. In
addition, as I indicated above, there were reasons of a social nature for the
questioning strategy adopted by the teacher on this occasion; the students needed
to be motivated and stimulated into response, and the strategy was certainly
successful in this respect. Nevertheless I believe that the kind of questioning
demonstrated here – a questioning for consensus – is almost certainly indicative
of wider disciplinary practices of English, at least at this level of study.

Politics

In contrast is this extract from a politics class where the teacher and students are discussing the theories of Marx. The approach is extra-textual and questions are used rather differently. Here the function of language structures to question, to carry a questioning approach is more apparent. The movement of the discourse is far less teleological than in English. The pattern of discourse which evolves takes the form of question and answer; the form, that is, of dialogue, even where the linguistic structure of a turn may not be strictly that of a question. Whether as a conversational exchange or in the contribution of a single speaker the making of a point followed by a counterpoint is basically a questioning and dialogic activity, based as it is upon the difference of one statement from another (the difference Bakhtin – whose ideas I discuss in more detail later on – locates between speaker and listener; mutually supported in the way that the polarities in a dialectic are).

T: So Marx would say that change in society is always due to economic things – that's the key thing. Can anybody see why many people, many philosophers would say this is totally wrong, this neglects some fundamental things about human beings? What fundamental things would some people say Marx has ignored here about the reasons why society changes? And I can think of certainly one incredible factor throughout history which some people would say is vital to human development – what?

M: Self-determination.

T: Well, certainly this thing about individual ideas, that maybe every so often some incredible individual comes along who changes society, you know. Such as Hitler maybe or Jenner and the discovery of smallpox.

B: Or Stevenson.

T: Or Stevenson and the discovery of steam engines. Or Jesus Christ – how about him? Where does he fit into all this?

R: Marx's interpretation of Jesus Christ [rather mumbled]

T: Yeah well we're going to have a look at Marx's interpretation of Christianity. But if you think about it that's a problem isn't it? If you're saying that all change in society is due to economic factors, what about ideas and beliefs – that some people would say that society changes as a result of beliefs? That's the big – we'd better

M: jot that down – that's the big problem: ideas and beliefs. That some people would say society changes because of ideas: new theories, new ideas.

M: But why do we get like Communist countries and that? It's because of Marx's ideas.

T: Ah! But he would argue that those ideas are the product of the economic society which they're formed from. He's not saying that there aren't ideas, he's saying that they come out of material changes. Yeah? Whereas a non-Marxist view would be that the ideas are the things which change society in the first place. I mean certainly you know a religious response to this would be y'know that once you've got Christianity then society's going to change. That's the thing that changes society. But again we'll have to explore that in more detail later.

This extract is taken from a 'teaching lesson', that is a lesson which, according to the teacher's description, is given over largely to the presentation and comprehension of material, rather than to discussion and debate. The lesson is dominated largely by the teacher and although in this extract he invites the students' responses, through the use of questions, he nevertheless controls the scope of the discussion. As the teacher speaks the openness of his questions is reduced largely because he reveals that he has 'one incredible factor' in mind. This becomes the standard by which all the other factors, ventured by the students, are assessed.

Despite this the questions themselves indicate something of the nature of the discipline they are exploring. The teacher's opening questions could be either open or closed; the students could refer to particular 'philosophers', particular 'people' in thinking of objections to Marx's theory, but equally they could employ hypotheses, use their existing knowledge more obliquely to imagine, deduce, predict and formulate a plausible answer. How much of such an answer would be recalled and how much created would depend on the individual knowledge and experience of the student. In contrast to English the acknowledgement and exploration of an alternative opinion is always implied. The function of the phrase 'some people' is crucial here in creating an alternative viewpoint. The process and progression of the politics discourse is predicated upon this recognition and use of otherness and of difference. Otherness is not an option but is central to successful operation in the subject. The students are helped in their appreciation of otherness by the surety that it exists, that it has, in many cases, a name, either as a group – Marxist, feminist, functionalist – or as an individual writer. These names are used as the basis both for recall and for hypothetical speculation; the construction of viewpoints which others (in the plural) both would and might adhere to. (These names – and theories – might of course eventually hamper the questioning activities of students, should they come to identify their own views too closely with any one of them.)

Questions which call for hypothesis-construction are not infrequent in the 'humanities' subjects: the question in a sociology lesson, for example, 'what would Illich say in reply to that point?' does not rely on a close reading of Illich's actual words, but upon the extrapolation and application of his principal themes or theories. The movement is from the specific through abstraction and generalisation to the new specific situation. Again this is a dialogic activity: the question brings the known into contact with the unknown, creating as it does so a relation between the two. What is known about Illich is applied to a situation on which his actual views are unknown, on which he may not, indeed, have had a view. It is this kind of thinking which allows new Marxist positions to be formulated a hundred years after Marx's death.

In politics the process of enquiry does not appear to be over once one point has been made; progression occurs with the posing of a counterpoint. So in learning about Marx the aim and process is not primarily to know what he said, to follow and replicate his argument but to take a stance towards it, continually to evaluate it.

The raising of questions establishes the mode of thinking required by the discipline; in a sense the deferral of answers does so too – the important thing at this stage being that the question had been raised and closure avoided. How might this kind of enquiry be characterised? The politics teacher describes his subject as functioning as and by *argument*.   What kind of activity is this? According to one description (Kress, 1989) argument – as opposed to narrative – is a progressive (as opposed to conservative) form, tolerant of difference which it brings into existence and maintains. Argument tends towards continuance and change rather than resolution and closure. All these characteristics are identifiable in the politics lesson; relative to politics, English literature, at least at A level, appears to be a conservative activity.

Biology

The notion of conservation, the maintenance of the status quo is more straightforwardly apparent in a subject which is less 'discussion-based' than either English or politics. Each subject has a content base, but also a mode of operation. In biology the emphasis on content is very pronounced and the mode of operation apparently more transparent. That is to say the material appears less to be negotiated. The texts with which the students work are textbooks and *reading* – to use Scholes' classification – the primary activity that is performed upon them. Again an examination of the role of questions in classroom interaction leads to those broader characterisations. Unlike the subjects discussed above the biology teacher's input contains no questions. The following example contains a sustained piece of teacher-talk which is prompted by a question from a student, who is working with another boy on notes on classification:

S: Is Number 8 (a picture in the textbook), is, is that   one? A phylum or whatever?

T: Yes, yes.

S: It looks like an ear to me!

S2:   An ear!

T: Um well yes [inaudible few words] Well what you want to watch out for here is the fact that they have what is called a mantle cavity and that basically means they've got a space, a fold inside or their body, which is very very wet and its what they have their breathing apparatus in – an equivalent of gills – they call them gills but they're not like fish gills. And it's in that wet space inside the body there where they can have a gas exchange which links them into the (?) of the octopus. Because on the face of it an octopus is not anything like a slug or a snail, and it, but they do both have this mantle cavity.

S: [mumble]

T: Yeah. And because they both have that and other similarities too, they're arched in the same ...

S: That's to help with breathing?

T: Yeah absolutely. I mean in point of fact with squids and octopus they use their mantle cavity, they've changed the nature of it so they can take in a greater volume of water and the walls around them become muscularised so they can actually propel by squeezing it very quickly, force the water out and move it quick. Where of course with slugs and snails, their mantle cavity is like you said just for breathing.

The teacher is doing two main things here: he is explaining the mantle cavity – what it is and what it does – and he is drawing attention to the significance of this attribute to the process of classification. The presence of the mantle cavity means that the animal will belong to a certain class. It is this particular characteristic which means that the octopus and snail can be classified together. The joint functions of the teacher's exposition are difficult to prise apart; the abstract principle of classification lies close to its exemplification, its realisation in the predetermined classes themselves. The principle is not divorced from practice. This mode of operation was revealed in the first lesson on the topic (and the first lesson of term) where the teacher adopted various open approaches to classification (including at this stage the question 'Why classify?'). He then went through some of the models in diagram form which are used to classify and at one point invited students to give their opinions as to which of two versions they thought most useful. One student thought A, another B, each giving their reasons. Here the discussion ended, however, with the teacher informing the students of what they *should* think: B is better. The principle or rule is immutable (at least at this stage of learning biology) and the task (there is a very strong sense of task) is in selecting information which will illustrate it. This is not to say that students must know everything, rather that they should know routes to familiarity. The teacher's grasp of the subject knowledge is extensive; he is a resource which the students turn to. The student here seems to abstract from the teacher's description the essential point for his understanding: the ear shape is for breathing. The teacher is aware though that his students can find difficulty in generalising; they are anxious to 'get everything down'. This is not surprising when on the one hand there is the *idea* of relationships to be grasped and on the other the *truth* that the idea is not enough but must be exemplified. How many and how few examples mean that the idea has been grasped and how many more before that idea itself is open to challenge?

The limits of enquiry

Grasping an idea is a rather different notion from forming an opinion. The possibility of grasping an idea suggests the idea as already formed, pre-existing in some body of knowledge which is 'out there'. Forming an opinion, on the other hand, suggests active engagement, the making of something new, for oneself. Analysis of the above examples of talk suggests, however, that the two forms of learning may not be radically opposed but rather form part of a continuum. Opinions – at least in these instances – are not formed by the students of English literature without also being informed and collectively formed by the teacher-directed discussion. Similarly in politics and related Humanities subjects the alternatives amongst which the student may situate herself or use continually to resituate herself are to some extent pre-specified and named. The politics teacher wants the students to engage in dialogue, adopt an argumentative stance but there is a sense too in which he directs the interchange, hints that there might be an idea – the 'one incredible factor' – to be grasped. The difference is one of degree. It is also, as I think the example of English shows, one of how the subjects choose to present themselves. The interplay between opinion and informed/formed opinion shows itself in questioning, particularly where its appropriateness to learning as it is defined by the subject is in doubt. I recently heard a student complain that her teacher had disallowed her opinion in class discussion on the grounds that it was not how a historian would respond (or feel perhaps; I think it was a strong emotional view). The boundaries of a subject, the rules within which it is permissible and desirable to operate define the extent to which a question may be 'open' or 'closed' (Barnes' terms). How 'open' can a question be before it attracts off-the-point, irrelevant answers? A tactic – probably unconscious – I have seen many teachers use is to reformulate the – academically? – dubious response of a student in such a way as to make it conform to acceptable boundaries.

Dialogue, questions, arguments are closed to the extent that they fall within conventional and disciplinary boundaries. These may alter according to the status one has achieved within the discipline, so that when one has become an authority on some particular area one may also become a legitimate iconoclast. But the history student mentioned above was insufficiently established within the discipline to be able effectively to challenge its sanctioned practices.

It may be that the extent and forms of questions used within a discipline is an indicator of the greater or lesser visibility of its boundaries. Compare the example of politics to biology where subject knowledge and discourse (what constitutes the subject) seems to be based on questioning to understand, to assimilate, rather than questioning to construct further questions. Questions asked of the biology teacher were regarded by him as a positive sign, a sign that clarification was being sought, but once a point was clear it was not further challenged by the student. She aimed to be clear in her own mind about the knowledge presented to her by the authoritative sources. To do this she had to be able to select, note and draw again on the principal factors involved. This is not a criticism of the student nor is it to her detriment. Such involvement seemed appropriate to the style and nature of learning typical of the subject and its pedagogical conventions. The scope of relevant questioning and dialogue is clearly demarcated at this stage of learning biology and of becoming a biologist, at least. My friend, a graduate in biology, told me how a challenging questioning approach was required of her only towards the end of her degree (when the vast groundwork of the subject had been assimilated); by this stage though, her tutor complained, students had lost the ability or the confidence to argue.

It is important to notice here however that these boundaries are 'conventional'; they are neither immutable nor timeless, but are cultural constructs subject to the effects of choice and change. Dividing opinions from knowledge and facts – one suggesting that everything goes, the other that everything has already gone, propagates the classic arts–science divide. But this divide is increasingly open to question as actual practices come under scrutiny.

Theories of language

The licence to question derives from power, cleverness, authority. Might not an alternative be that the act of questioning itself creates power, is in itself a wresting of power, a taking of control? Behind these alternative views lurk theories of language. The first understands language as a *medium* through which thought is transmitted or the world described. Meaning is extra-linguistic, inside here or out there. A prior or other state is always presupposed, which must in some sense be known before it can be articulated. Many questions are predicated upon such a view. Very often the question is asked in the interests of the status quo; it is asked in order to ascertain what the person questioned knows that accords with what the questioner knows and wants to hear repeated, confirmed, reproduced. Many schooling and examination contexts employ such a view of language.

The second view suggests that meaning actually comes into being through language; an utterance is an action constitutive of the world, but a world that is always changing, so that there is never an unfailing *right* question to be asked of it. Questions (all utterances) are always contingent upon the situations in which they occur and to which they subsequently give shape. In this theory of language questions have a particular potency; they are the vehicles of potential significance. If it is right that we think only in language then questions have a vital role in realising thought which is as yet unthought, which is only potential. What Steiner (1989) says of the conjunction *if* that it 'can alter, recompose, put in radical doubt, even negate the universe as we choose to perceive it' (p. 55) can also be said of questions; the two forms are in fact often used simultaneously as part of hypothetical thought, the generating of alternative positions which resist closure.

The politics class again, appropriately discussing Utopia:

> T: Why is it that Marx felt that his society, a complex society where there was this great inequality – why did he feel that that was the perfect end society, that that itself wouldn't become part of this process of history, and that that wouldn't change to something else?

> R: Because there'd be no conflict between classes.

> T: Exactly, that's the key thing isn't it? If you take away that dialectic, that conflict, because you abolish classes, you don't have owners and workers, everyone is the same – then you've cracked it haven't you? Because society will no longer go through these processes of change. It may develop in certain ways but fundamentally you've reached the top, you've reached perfection.

> R.   That's why it's utopian isn't it?

> T: Yeah. What about that? If you remove the profit element – the idea that some people own production and some people work for their living, will you actually produce the situation where society has reached, y'know, the ultimate thing?

The teacher's first use of the if-clause allows the student to follow Marx's thought and glimpse the utopian state. The if-clause is a questioning – or bracketing – of the actual factors of a situation and allows them to be dispensed with in order to see beyond. It is a leap of imagination, here resolving in an optimistic view: 'You've cracked it haven't you?' Its outcome, what is 'seen beyond', is in a sense a celebration of that imaginative leap, that possibility. The second if-clause initiates a progression from the first. It leaves the possibility of *what would happen if*, open, by resolving in a direct question. It is the function of this question: 'will you actually produce this situation ...' to *make*, to bring into being the new territory – opened up by the if-clause.

Questions gesture towards the future, speaking, as Steiner (1989) puts it, hope:

> Above all else, language is the generator and messenger of and out of tomorrow ... I believe that this capability to say and unsay all, to construct and deconstruct space and time, to beget and speak counter-factuals – 'if Napoleon had commanded in Vietnam' – makes man of man. More especially: of all evolutionary tools towards survival, it is the ability to use future tenses of the verb – when, how did the psyche acquire this monstrous and liberating power? – which I take to beforemost. Without it men and women would be no better than 'falling stones'. (Spinoza)

> We cannot imagine being, and imagining is, immediately, a semantic move, without discursive openness, without the potentiality of questioning even death. Above the minimal vegetative plane our lives depend on our capacity to speak hope, to entrust to if-clauses and futures our active dreams of change, of progress, of deliverance. (p. 56)

Steiner makes high claims for apparently small linguistic features of language, but I do not think he overstates his case. It is through our access to and facility with these forms that our interest is stimulated, that we make connections between different areas of experience, that we tolerate and seek out difference and that we become engaged in the making of new meanings: practical, philosophical, spiritual – of all kinds and uses.

Again my thoughts here about language are furthered by Barnes. To account for the overlap between his two main descriptors, 'open' and 'closed' questions, Barnes employs a third term: 'pseudo-question' (p. 23). Pseudo-questions appear open but are in fact closed, encouraging pupils to guess what is in the teacher's head rather than actively engaging in reasoning about the issue under discussion. 'Pseudo-question' seems an odd descriptor, but it is revealing of the way Barnes finds his abstract linguistic categories continually confounded by contextual and intentional factors – do the terms 'open' and 'closed' describe functions or linguistic characteristics? Such 'pseudo-questions', I think, are closed in content and context rather than structure; rather like the questions in a quiz game to which one can reply 'correctly' and still receive the rejoinder, sympathetic but firm: 'a good answer, but not the one we were looking for'. (In school the rules of the game – and reasons for failure – are not always this explicit.) What is most interesting about the term, however, is the way it suggests that open questions are somehow more question-like than closed questions. A question is no less a question for being closed rather than open, yet there is a sense in which Barnes' preferred theory of language, knowledge and education may show through here.

What is this sense that some questions are more question-like than others, the sense that it is possible to be asked a pseudo-question which yet retains the linguistic form of a real question? Bakhtin's theory of dialogic discourse (1981) is of use here. It has the benefit both of being applicable to 'external, compositionally marked, dialogue' and of elucidating the construction of meaning in language through 'the internal dialogization of discourse' (p. 283). Bakhtin makes a distinction between 'an utterance's *neutral signification*' and 'its *actual meaning*' (p. 281). In dialogue actual meaning is constituted in the active understanding of the listener, the connections and inferences she makes, the background she can give to the words which is uniquely her own and will constitute them differently. Actual meaning is not present in the utterance, though it is potential; it awaits realisation in the thought process it triggers in the other:

> ... actual meaning is understood against the background of other concrete utterances on the same theme, a background made up of contradictory opinions, points of view and value judgements – that is, precisely that background that, as we see, complicates the path of any word towards its object. Only now this contradictory environment of alien words is present to the speaker not in the object, but rather in the consciousness of the listener, as his apperceptive background, pregnant with response and objections. (p. 281)

The speaker of the utterance is thus implicitly characterised by Bakhtin as a questioner (rather than a maker of statements). Though the speaker might anticipate the form of the listener's response, he cannot know it. He takes risks, allows his words to become detached from their referents, to operate on the alien territory of the listener's consciousness. Important though the active understanding of the listener is, the speaker must also operate with an active understanding himself: he too must listen. Unless he does so then 'nothing new can be introduced into his discourse'; he is left 'in his own context, within his own boundaries' (p. 281).

Of the listener's role, Bakhtin writes:

> To some extent primacy belongs to the response, as the activating principle: it creates the ground for understanding, it prepares the ground for an active and engaged understanding. Understanding

> only comes to fruition in the response. Understanding and response
> are dialectically merged and mutually condition one another, one is
> impossible without the other. (p. 282)

By implication here again, the listener is also the speaker, bringing understanding to fruition in a response which is already a new utterance. Understanding is both reliant on context – the particularities of the particular occasion, the particular consciousnesses involved – and is contingent: utterances which are reliant on response always having the shifting uncertain status of questions; responses no sooner uttered than breaking through 'the alien conceptual horizon of the listener' (p. 282) who was the speaker and is so now again, but differently. The roles of speaker and listener are elided; the dialogue neither begins nor ends, speaker does not precede listener nor vice versa. In this continuous exchange, dialogue is contained within the utterance itself; each utterance dialogised so that meaning is always predicated on otherness.

To return to my initial query – why do open questions seem more question-like than closed questions? – the answer is, I suspect, connected with the active and dialogic understandings by which they operate. Questions which are open imply an expectation and acceptance of difference in the consciousness of the person to whom they are directed; the questioner is as ready to be surprised by the response as to have anticipated it. The open question prompts and is open to language as new thought (rather than language as already thought) both for the respondent and the questioner, who becomes, at the point of response, the new respondent, the listener. For a question to be truly open the questioner must also possess the potential for listening, a capacity for role reversal or, better, a capacity to hold both roles in the single utterance. In this analysis an open question could not be identified by its linguistic structure alone; its openness would have to be checked against subsequent utterances and the tenor of the dialogue as a whole.

Bakhtin's description of the dialogic status of the word has implications for the conduct and objectives of schooling. A recognition of the unique apperceptive background of each individual challenges the notion that knowledge is transmitted by one speaker and understood and returned by another in unaltered form. Learning can take place in this form, but it is at a low level. Understanding the student's consciousness as 'alien territory' generates an alternative goal for teaching which exploits the change and difference brought about by bringing one consciousness (that of the teacher as transmitter of the subject's knowledge base) into contact with an alien other, in order that it may be modified, reshaped, dialogised. The student then becomes an active member of the discourse community and the discourse is itself diversified.

Questions contain within them the possibility of journeying from the past to the future, from the familiar to the unfamiliar. The idea of an open question – or rather an open questioner – suggests a journey on which the destination is not prespecified and on which the ultimate destination may never be reached. Yet in all journeys there are destinations, places passed through, however transiently.

And decisions – to linger, to discard excess baggage, to look out at the mountains rather than the sea – are made. The pattern the journey takes results from the interaction of the traveller with the otherness she encounters on the way. The analogy is with a dialogic view of language, where experience comes through exchange and change. This 'open' view does not preclude the leading question. The situation is not as simple as replacing the characterisation of the student as 'passive consumer' (the package-tour idea of a journey) with one of the student as entirely 'active producer' (the world is my untrammelled oyster); instead the idea of a dialogic relationship introduces a third possibility: the active, producing consumer. This possibility describes a two-way process and, importantly for teachers and learners, it accounts for the transmission of content and the initiation into distinctive practices and lines of enquiry.

Suggestions for practice

This is all very well as a theory, but how to put it to use? I believe that one practical suggestion might lie in conscious attempts by teachers to share the questioning role with students, to encourage their formulation of questions, unanswerable as well as answerable ones. This might mean setting aside time specifically for students to think up questions, to think up, that is to say, what has not already been thought, what they do not already know. The status of questions and the unknown or undetermined needs accordingly to be raised.

Students might be encouraged in critical listening and reading by a requirement to formulate and ask questions. This would be a deliberate reversal of the standard pattern whereby the teacher explains and then tests the students' comprehension by setting them questions. The element of compulsion (everyone must think up a question) goes beyond the cursory 'Any questions?' invitation with which explanations almost mythically conclude. Questions might then be asked not only as a sign of failure to grasp the given – 'Could you go over that part again?' – but would have embedded in them the recognition that the teacher can never give the whole story, that there are always further questions to be asked. The invitation would no longer be 'Are there any questions?' but 'What are the questions you would like to ask as a result of this?' Some teachers might see this strategy as entailing the risk of not being able to supply an answer but why should such a possibility be a risk if the status accorded to the questions themselves is as high as that sometimes accorded to answers? The questions would be valuable for their own sakes. The teacher could use the questions she was unable to answer as the basis for further investigation or speculation, in groups or individually. Difficult questions would become a valuable resource in learning. A record could be kept of the questions and returned to on a later occasion.

Where questions are not actively valued they tend to get lost. One thing I have noticed in my research so far is the disappearance of questions from written texts which students produce as a result of the discussion and reading that goes on in class. Where students in a sociology class I observed were involved in small group discussion of the advantages and disadvantages of a certain Marxist theory of the relation between capitalism and ill health, generating critical points amongst themselves, there is little evidence of this active questioning in the essays they have subsequently written on the subject. Instead one criticism of the theory is demonstrated by its juxtaposition with another which is contrary. In effect, then, the criticism, the active thinking is left to the experts and the students reveal only passive understanding. Yet this is not all they are capable of. Perhaps it is because the questions raised in class do not always result in neatly formulated answers or sustained arguments that the students resort to the argumentative answers of others in their writing? That the questions themselves might be valid or that tentativity, the expression of dissatisfaction or of one's sense of omission might constitute important and interesting features of an essay does not seem to be recognised by these writers.

In education the written form has traditionally been highly valued above that of speech. The process of recognising and valuing oral skills – as constituting outcomes as well as processes – has been slow. Written examinations emphasise answers in response to specific questions, rather than the thought processes involved in writing. Though changes have occurred both in respect of speech and examinations, reactionary, and perhaps popular, attitudes to education still prioritise the production of written answers under strictly controlled and closed conditions.

The idea of the listening speaker seems to me a crucial one for those involved in learning. It means posing a question in order really to hear its answer and this very often means asking again, requesting that the respondent say more, go on. Behind the use of such neutral questions or invitations to continue is not a search for what the addressee already knows and is not giving out, though this might be so. Instead the notion of active understanding sees understanding as yet unformed, as in process. The teacher can use questions aimed at pursuing this understanding, causing it to qualify, diversify, complicate, expand. Leading questions can also fulfil this role by providing a structure or direction for the unthought of to develop. The danger with the use of leading questions is that they are placed too much in the service of the teacher's passive understanding and are not interchanged with the desire to pursue the student's meaning. Thus if the leading question leads elsewhere than the teacher intended, the answer is wrong – as in the quiz game – or not worthy of further pursuit – judged inappropriate.

The following short extract shows the politics teacher using a short prompting question in pursuit of the student's understanding:

T: But what do you think? What did Marx see as wrong with
        capitalism? As it was operating in its own time? Come on,
        we can get a few thoughts about this: faults of capitalism.

S: That it continues the er class struggle.

T: Very much so. That's a problem, that it er, not only does it continue it, it makes it very brutal. You've got the people who own the means of production, who own the factories, the bourgeoisie and you've got the workers and they struggle don't they?

S: It makes equality even harder to achieve.

T: Yeah, why is that?

S: Well the fact that people do own like factories, so you can't ...

The student's first suggestion is accepted by the teacher and expanded by him to introduce the idea of brutality. The second suggestion is implicitly challenged as *incomplete*, in need of similar expansion. This time the teacher hands this task back to the student, indicating more fully by doing so the additional thought which is required. Without the addition of a reason 'why' his statement is only a reasonable hypothesis and this is an insufficient argumentative position. The forms of argument – challenge, counter point, dissatisfaction – embedded in dialogue render it open and ongoing.

The teacher's question 'Why is that?' is an invitation to show, different to a challenge in that it doesn't point to or contain another point of view. The question which *demands* showing must have an important role in deepening understanding, developing argument. In my observations I have not seen much evidence of this kind of question, but it seems to me that answering such a question is usually hard work. Hard work because, unlike many other questions it is not already charged with its answer and it requires the answerer to produce more words on the same thought, in other words – both literally and idiomatically – to make new or more thought. Such questions challenge in terms of the preceding thought, testing its coherence and logic, shaping and situating it. They don't so much move on as move deeper, deductively, from the clue to its implications, from what is to what is yet to be. Asking such questions can be hard work for the teacher too: it requires attentiveness and a willingness to suspend one's own pressing agenda in order to help the learner's emerge. But the effort might well prove worthwhile; even to produce surprising results.

This kind of questioning is internalised as self-questioning: 'What am I trying to say here?' 'Can I say more about that?' If dialogue is the operation of two or more logics – asking oneself this kind of question is the internalising of dialogue and the dialogising of language itself. It is a way of putting into language what has not yet been thought and of giving to absence the potentiality of presence. Queries perhaps are not theories. But I can't be too sure of this. They are uncertainty made powerful – absence (of answers) given presence (as questions).

If questions come before answers – as by convention they do – then their importance to learners should not be overlooked. The questions raised in this chapter – Who is doing the asking? Who is being asked? Why? In the interests of whom? In the furtherance of whose journey? To what end? – I hope will continue to be asked, and the powers of question form harnessed for both the greatest possible freedom and use. Self-questioning on the part of teachers, invested as they inevitably are with institutional and disciplinary power, can only be of benefit if it enhances the questioning potential of students who have so much to learn and so much power to gain.

Chapter Twelve

INSTITUTIONS, INDIVIDUALS AND TALK: THE CONSTRUCTION OF IDENTITY IN FINE ART [*]

Sally Mitchell

The following discussion is based on research into the uses and nature of argument within educational contexts, part of which was conducted in the Fine Art Department of a university. As it turned out, the focus on argument opened up wider perspectives – I came to understand fine art as a social activity through which meaning is contested and negotiated, and both objects (art works) and persons come to be recognised and have identity. I was alerted to the relations between learning, identity, institutions and individuals and to the contested and consensual ways these are worked out. My experience also raised questions about the role played by language in fine art; in particular, the use of talk in the teaching process.

My understanding of the Fine Art Department found an anchor – though not entirely an answer – in a model of integrated social and personal development adapted from the work of Rom Harré (1983) (see figure 1). In this chapter I want to consider this model in the light of what I discovered in fine art; both how the abstract representation corresponds to and illuminates my empirical observations and how it differs from, falls short of the complexity of what I observed.

The model consists of two axes: the public–private and the individual–collective which when they intersect, create four quadrants. The quadrants are traversed from the public–collective in a clockwise direction by four types of operation: appropriation, transformation, publication and conventionalisation. The model pictures as dynamic and interconnected the relations between public consensus and private difference, the given way of being and the development of distinctive identity. It suggests that the given and the new are not opposed and separate modes of existence but are constructed and developed through each other, the individual attaining distinctive identity through both appropriation from and recognition by the collective. The collective, in turn, is constantly renewed by the conventionalisation of what the private-individual publicly offers. As Harré's model depicts it, a sense of self emerges socially, rather than

[*] First published as Mitchell, S. 1996. 'Institutions, individuals and talk: the construction of identity in Fine Art', *Journal of Art and Design Education 15 (2)*; reprinted by permission of the journal (Blackwell/NSEAD).

subjectively; thus personal identity is not created independently, but rather is 'the product of appropriations and transformations of social resources' (p257).

Figure 1

Model of integrated social and personal development adapted from Harré

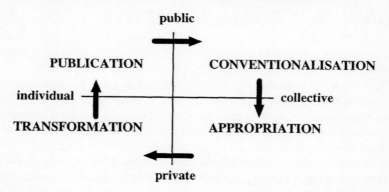

My observations in the Fine Art department brought me to see this cyclical movement between sameness and difference, points of fixity and change as driven by and at the same time constituting argument. Consider two definitions; in the first, argument is a teleological series of connecting statements through which a point is made or a position established. In the second, argument is the interaction – and clash – between positions. The first definition is about pulling together, unifying, controlling; it is about the establishment of tradition, of a narrative or rationale of consensus. The second definition breaks apart and challenges; it is about otherness and difference. These definitions are not, however, contradictory, but are mutually dependent, part of a larger process of argumentation (Harré's model suggests a cycle) in which social, cultural and intellectual norms can both identifiably exist and be open to modification. Equally in this process, persons are both formed by collective mores and can innovate or transform: they become individuals. Argument contains the central tension in achieving transformation, the point where the engaged individual begins to reciprocate, and again in publication, where that which the reciprocation has produced is opened to public assessment and so reintroduced to dialogue. Harré says of publication:

> At this point an actor stands on the threshold of radical recategorisation, since, depending on the reaction of that public, his personal innovations may earn him assessments running anywhere between 'madman' and 'genius' (p257).

What Harré calls the project of personal identity formation also describes the processes involved in learning. The student appropriates knowledge, skills and processes, internalises and adapts them, creates products or performances by which these operations are made public (assessed) and is then rewarded – or otherwise - with some kind of agreed public recognition (a certificate, entrance to a higher course etc.). It is important not to see the public–collective as a static realm – the receptacle of knowledge, wisdom and artefacts (though this is often the way learning and 'subjects' are presented to students). Rather the public–collective is constituted by dynamic processes of a conventionalised kind – what James Gee (1991, pp6-7) seems to capture in his particular definition of 'Discourse':

> Saying – (writing) – doing – being – valuing – believing combinations ... ways of being in the world ... forms of life which integrate words, acts, values, beliefs, attitudes and social identities as well as gestures, glances, body positions and clothes.

To be successful and to achieve distinctive identity within the public–collective the student has to do more than appropriate what is pre-given in a discipline; she has to become part of its discourse. More than learn *about* it, she has to participate *within* it. Transformation is the clue to achieving this status because it is here that what is learnt begins to become distinctive, made new. Publication too is decisive, for on public judgement hangs the conferment of 'insider' status: the student's learning recognised and valued within the community from which it has emerged.

My observations in the Fine Art department concentrated on third year students who, over the course of the year, were working towards the final degree show as well as writing a long essay for the theoretical component of the course. Although I had close contact with only a handful of students, my visits to the department brought me, as a matter of course, into contact with first and second year students and with a wide range of teaching in a number of different media. The main vehicle for this 'cross-communication' between levels and media was what is known in the School as 'cross-section crits'. These consisted of a small group of students, working in a range of the degree course, coming together with one or two tutors to visit the working spaces of each of the students and discuss the work found there. The focus of discussion on the work was fielded by the student who had made or was making it. Everyone was invited to take part, though in practice much of the talk took place between the tutors and the student-maker. In this chapter I want to concentrate on the 'crits' of three third-year students.

The crits offer a useful insight into the discourse of the fine art degree; they are occasions for publication in which evidence of appropriation and transformation is sought. They are focused on the art work, yet their substance consists of verbal language: talk about art and the art making process. Thus appropriation and transformation are not just of 'ways of doing' but also, to adapt Gee's phrase, about 'believing – valuing – reflecting – (and as the examples will show) analysing – situating – theorising combinations'. The course handbook for students expresses a recognition of the interplay between the creative and analytical, between doing and reflecting. The aim is to encourage a developed critical awareness whereby the creative potential of interpreting issues in ways which are analytic and interrogative is recognised and acted upon.

Whilst the crits do not constitute directly assessable evidence in the award of a degree (they are formative experiences), what they elicit of the student's making processes and responses is used to an extent as a measure for 'reading' and judging the work. Crits bind the art work together with talk about art; product and (institutionally sanctioned) process together. The eventual summative assessment (conventionalisation) of the art works in the final degree show is not separate or free from the formative legacy of the crit. Works are talked about in the same way, with the same questioning of the maker's critical awareness. The maker and/or the art work (the distinction is not always clear) must be able to indicate an understanding of, or engagement with, the relation between the perceptual and conceptual. It is in the expression of this relation that the quality of the work seems to lie: somewhere between the ideational and the physical. As an example, I was told of one student whose degree show contained two cat flaps positioned in a window of the building. Whilst the ideas and conceptual connections this generated were deemed to be highly effective, it did not warrant a first class degree. The reason for this was expressed as a question of whether, after engaging with the ideas, it was possible to go back to the work's physical presence and see that that had something about it too, that its presence had changed in a tangible significant way the space that it was in. The answer in this case was that it had not.

In the crits, language is the key to reflexivity in which the articulation and sharing of perceptions, ideas, resonances and connections in speech inform and enrich the processes of making which both precede and follow the occasion. But not all uses of language in fine art are effective and not all are recognised by the institution. Some, for instance, take place only between close confidants and still have a formative impact on making – but these uses rarely become public. Indeed, there is a great deal of ambivalence amongst students about the public language of the crits. In those crits I observed, the nature of the talk was varied; in some it appeared to model the disciplinary and pedagogical aims of the occasion, in others it was generated in opposition to or fell frustratingly short of the sharing and making of meaning. It seemed, that is, not to facilitate learning.

Example 1: Sam

In my first example, argument is taking place as the appropriation and transformation of the officially sanctioned discourse (expressed, for instance, in the Handbook aim above). It shows how a differentiated identity is based on some kind of consensus, shared conceptual perspectives, a similar fluency with ideas, vocabulary and approaches. Two tutors and four students are present around one of the students' work. Most of the discussion takes place between this student, Sam, and one of the tutors, Roy. The work is two large paintings, both in pale blue and white, made up of individually painted squares, which in combination reveal, in the first painting, sections of limbs as if from a figure painting, and in the second, a man in a white background. The second painting is unfinished.

When Sam introduces the paintings he refers to an interest in fragmentation and mass media, and discussion then develops about how computers can be used to break images up into squares. The talk is full of such analogous connections between the work and the 'world'. Identified by Sam, they act as points of return for the digressive pathways which the speakers explore. The way Sam frames the initial idea allows for this digression whilst anchoring it in the paintings themselves:

> Sam: The fragmentation idea is very much dealing with mass media techniques, in the sense that, I don't know and maybe more in these paintings at the moment – say, look at one individual square as a piece of information, sort of like here (pointing); when you look at it as a whole the space is disrupted more; it's harder to try and understand all the information put together. It's very selective ... squares are blanked out. It's like censorship or giving an image and making it difficult to see as a whole.

Sam's final comment makes it possible to see what the perceptual effects of the painting are in terms of a concept, an idea – 'censorship' – which in this case has wide political and social connotations. The nominalisation has a common currency which the painting, as a unique object, may not have. By using it he creates the possibility for the talk to extend to other abstract ideas, which are not immediately accessible in the painting, but which may nonetheless come to be found there.

Roy poses what appears a basic question: 'Is it meant to be something that is quite pleasing to look at?' Sam thinks that no, the paintings are more brutal and cruel, adding that he is not attempting figure painting, but is 'deconstructing the image of a figure'. The use of the term 'deconstruction' again signals an opportunity for the discourse to move from the particular. It triggers a generalised comment from Roy, who criticises deconstruction as a self-defeating exercise: first, it requires the support of the thing being deconstructed in order to succeed, and second, since it has to deal with things that are there, deconstruction is always reliant on something else for progress. Sam argues back to these points, saying:

> Sam: You've got to accept that things are there, haven't you? Really? I mean you're maybe reaffirming your position, if you're affirming anything. You're constantly in that problem

> or maybe the problem is your occupation as an artist. You
> have to think of ways of getting round it.

Roy pursues his point by suggesting the danger of adopting a model, perfecting it and forgetting that it is equally open to question. And Sam responds, continuing to locate the discussion not quite with the object, but with the method and intent of the artist. He does not refer precisely to himself as an artist but justifies his own practice at one remove by engaging in more abstract discourse.

> Sam: Oh totally! I mean the method, this method is not the end of
> the deconstruction of images. I don't think it's going to stand
> up for long – a year or so. After that it's got to sort of fold.
> You can't, as you say, deconstruction comes out of purely
> process, which in itself is open to deconstruction or a process
> which is open to deconstruction, so that the point where, as
> you say, it becomes a fetish as opposed to a creative process
> – a critical creative process as opposed to a fetishist way of
> treating the image.

Sam replies at length to the comment of the tutor and also attributes ideas to Roy ('as you say') which Roy did not articulate in that form. Both the length and the reinterpretation are unusual in student/teacher interaction where it is the teacher who reformulates what the student says so that it fits more comfortably with the disciplinary discourse or with the teacher's agenda. Here, in contrast, the swift rearticulation and transformation of meanings is shared: words, phrases and names have for the speakers common resonances and contexts. And this sharing of disciplinary and conceptual resources enables the speakers to differ: it is the grounds on which argumentation can take place. Sam's expansiveness also reflects his personal stake in the discussion: however abstractly, he is defending his own deconstructive activities. But the common ground which facilitates this also sets out boundaries beyond which arguments are not valid or not valued: it excludes as well as enables.

A further example from Sam's crit gives some suggestion of this, though it is less acutely apparent than for other students I will refer to later. A first-year student in the group asks about the use of colour in the paintings and Sam first replies by saying that his earlier prolific use of colour has caused him now to experiment with what happens in a picture when it is not there. Pressed to specify 'Why blue?' he talks about the night-time light which filters into his bedroom and then 'digresses' to a radio programme he had heard which was about the great rarity and expense of the blue pigment, so that its use required special permission from the church. This gives Roy an insight into the paintings:

> Roy: There is that kind of spirituality and simultaneously you're
> taking the piss, which I think is quite interesting, that. So
> you're actually doing both at once and in that you've
> succeeded, really. Using something that's got all that wide

resonance, all that, whilst doing something that like doesn't matter, you know.

Rather than refer directly to an effect of the painting, Roy attributes intention to the painter, yet it is not the intention that Sam has articulated. Sam's actual justifications for his use of colour are judged by Roy to be 'pretty limp'. His own discovered reasons (to do with his perceptual and intellectual engagement) seem more exciting and more valid, better. He suggests that Sam needs to be more convincing; a more convincing reason is, by implication, one which enables the work to be placed within the discourse (its subversion of the spiritual connotations of blue) rather than one which is autobiographical, practical or fortuitous.

Does it matter that it was not Sam but the tutor who revealed/created these cultural meanings? In an important sense probably not. Questions of origin and ownership blur where the talk – which is possible only through sharing – becomes a measure of the art work's value. Willard (1989, p11) has written that the reason we study argument is 'to explain how groups sustain intellectual stability and yet are able to change'. In its very definition, argument expresses the duality (rather than dualism) of the social and personal. Holding an opinion (an expression of individuality) is taking part in argument (a dialogic social act); as Billig (1991, p43) writes, an opinion is a 'dual expression' – both personally distinctive and an index of wider controversy, having social origins and social consequences. For Bakhtin (1981) this is the principle by which language itself operates: every use of language carries with it a history of usage in other contexts and itself constitutes a new context:

> The word in language is half someone else's. It becomes one's own, only when the speaker populates it with his own intention, his own accent, when he appropriates the word, adapting it to his own semantic and expressive intention. Prior to this moment of appropriation, the word does not exist in a neutral and impersonal language (it is not after all out of a dictionary that a speaker gets his words!), but rather it exists in other people's mouths, in other people's concrete contexts, serving other people's intentions: it is from there that one must take the word, and make it one's own (pp293-4).

Yet making the word one's own is not the end of the story: the cycle continues. The meaning of an utterance is activated not by the speaker but by the listener, who, in responding, determines how the utterance is understood. Meaning, that is, is not derived through origination, but through orientation, the relation to the other.

Example 2: Richard

The implications of this for learning and the creation of distinctive personal identity within a particular public–collective or discourse can be taken further by looking at a more negative example where the failure of speakers to orient to each other results in a kind of 'meaninglessness' for the work discussed. Richard's work is in sculpture and he has recently returned to stone-carving – his trade before becoming a student. The work he chooses to publicise in the crit is in its early stages. He introduces the work like this:

> Richard: I've no idea where it came from or why [laughter] ... What it was, um, I sort of looked at the Michelangelo tradition, where you take a piece of stone and you talk about sort of captive figures and, you know, releasing whatever it is in the piece of stone and I sat around with a piece of stone and couldn't see a bloody thing. So ['Not surprised!' laughter] I just started carving and sort of as a result of direct carving, where the um, you sort of take a lump of stone and then just the action of the chisel on the stone, you know, informed me as I'm carrying on so, er, this one was just a rough shape and I was carving away and it seemed like a sort of torso shape. It was starting to form so I followed that torso. Or there was [showing] well, it was virtually that shape so I was opening it up and trying to give it that movement ... There's all sorts of different things happening and it was just a case of carving and letting it happen.

The tutor responded:

> Roy: So, in one sense, it's a process of improvisation. So you then start thinking in terms of improvisation, of where within that area there are a certain number of things which you know you could do. [yeah] So there are things which you don't know and you discover as you are doing it [yuh] and there are things which go wrong ... So as maybe a methodology which could also be a philosophical approach which could also be to do with how it's perceived by the viewer. If during that process of making you then think you know what you're doing, then it starts becoming something, then does that go against the principle of improvisation? And revealing (?) then make the process and the thoughts with that process?

> Richard: It does, yes. It's difficult to be rigorous down one way or the other. [pause] It's disturbing.

The narrative description of process which Richard offers is quickly interpreted by Roy at a more abstract, theoretical level. At the same time it is a challenge to Richard to take on the terms and justify himself within them. Richard accepts the interpretation but doesn't develop or critique it. His concern with the process is in experimental form rather than formulated from a distance where, for instance, it is possible to talk of principles of operation and consistency of purpose. He talks about his activity as a 'defining process' in which there is a conflict between following the material and giving way to the skills of stone-masonry, which he is rediscovering. On subject-matter he is still unclear, but as he says twice he is excited by this unpredictability: 'I'm trying to solve what ultimately I should be doing'. The tutor asks 'So what informs your decision making when you are actually doing it?', but Richard cannot give a clear answer; he pauses, 'just like anything really ... it's difficult'.

Given the indeterminacy of Richard's position and the inability of the tutor to draw him into a potential space where some new insights might emerge, the discussion moves on to other artists working in the medium. The second tutor finds the sculpture conservative, tending to take itself too seriously. He compares it negatively to the 'more playful' work Richard has done before. Richard comments that for him what he is currently making are in fact 'playful objects ... It's maybe a case of actually presenting them like that'. Again, there is a mismatch between personal feeling and public effect. This is negotiated repeatedly in the discussion, but the focus does not rest long enough with the actual maker in order fully to open up his sense of the things he has made. At one level there is commonality – frequent recourse to a readymade repertoire of reference and opinion about, for instance, architectural and archaeological associations in the work – but it is not employed dynamically to make new and particular meaning in regard to the work.

Later, Richard accounted for the limitations of the crit with a notion that sculpture is under-theorised and a shared critical discourse therefore absent. The inability of the participants in the crit to construct a shared basis or to move into each other's spaces exposed the way the dominant discourse of the institution operates criteria for evaluation and predetermines or makes predictable the aspects of a work which are talked about. About which it cannot talk, it remains silent. Over time the effect of this silence was, for Richard, an increasing sense of alienation, an increasing sense in which he defined himself in opposition to the institution and its modes of validation.

According to Harré, one of the resources (theories) 'our' culture offers us is a sense of ourselves as 'active centres of experience'. This theory throws into shadow the part played by the social and collective and creates the grounds for our belief in uniqueness, originality, genius. There are distinctive institutions and practices through which we come to experience ourselves and construe our goals in this way. The Fine Art department is a particularly strong example of such an institution. Of all the subject disciplines I observed in the course of my research, it was here that the local 'person-theory' – what it was to be a student of fine art – seemed most fully to be about consciousness of oneself as an individual concerned with 'the achievement of uniqueness'. Rather than undergo an apprenticeship in each of the media available, the approach adopted in the department is for students' own objectives and sense of purpose to determine the materials they engage with. As a result, personal identity (a sense of self and of one's own purposes) is a prerequisite to being a successful student. Disciplinary work is not distinct (as it might be in, say, history) but continuous with one's individuality. Students come to see themselves less as students than as *artists*:

less apprentices to a discourse than makers in their own right. In this sense Richard's increasing sense of marginality within the institution can be seen not as a purely individual or isolated experience, but as an effect of the prevalent 'person theory'. Certainly by the time of the final degree show many of the students felt a rebellious disenchantment towards the institution. This was almost a condition of having completed the three years' course – and, for the institution, a sign of success, though a painful one, in the way that a child's flight from the parental nest is painful.

Since learning is driven by the individual, the role of tutors is to supply students with the necessary equipment to carry out and develop their ideas, in terms of both technical 'doing' skills and verbal/conceptual and contextual resources with which to talk and think about what they and others are doing. As the earlier examples of the crits suggest, however, skills and concepts are not freely available, but are filtered through particular 'ways of saying ... doing', etc.. Equally the independence positively fostered in students to the point of disillusionment with the collective is in chains to the normative assessment procedures carried out by the institution at the point of the students' departure. To award a student an average class of degree is to fly in the face of 'the achievement of uniqueness', where uniqueness is not communicated as the product of successful orientation, but rather as free-floating subjectivity.

The discourse of the Fine Art Department is complex and contradictory. The collective valuing of individual freedom, for example, was experienced by a first-year student I spoke to as an unfair compulsion. To 'loosen up!', 'be free!' was not for him an easy or satisfactory option: he wanted first to appropriate skills before he could begin to transform. Another example: the distrust of language – particularly of the public kind demanded in the crit situation – is as established within the culture of the institution as the officially stated belief in analytic engagement with creative work. Associated with the idea of the autonomy of the artist, it is a position, an instinct almost, espoused by members of the teaching staff as well as by students and gestured towards in such phrases as 'the theory/practice divide'. Personal identity, autonomy and originality on the one hand; the critical public language of the crit on the other: the potential of talk to link creativity and judgement is not, it seems, universally established or experienced.

Meanings, as I have suggested, are not all equal but rather are endorsed or passed over by the dominant critical discourse. In the crit situation some students experience a strong conflict between their private meanings (which may have been generated in a more personal intimate language) and those which are publicly demanded. One student told me she found herself only able to explain her work on a personal level and, being unable to 'intellectualise' in the formal context of the crit, her work was 'hammered' and she herself hurt. In this case the expectation that she 'appropriate' and 'transform' the public and collective discourse into a private and individual one was experienced as a kind of violence, a pushing under of what existed in the private individual area.

Example 3: Carol

My third example, Carol's crit, was an extreme example of resistance to commentary in language, and, by extension, of resistance to teaching – at least of this kind. Whilst she would tell me what she liked about the work, what amused her, Carol believed that anything can be art that is made as art and is looked at as art: a circular logic which was resistant both to challenge and to clearer definition of the parameters of art in her particular view. Instead of wanting to tackle the difficult meanings of her work, she avoided uncertainty by closing it off with a categorical statement: 'It just is art'. In the crit this avoidance made itself felt when the tutor began to question the work, to suggest alternative directions and to offer interpretations. When he noticed, for instance, a possible pattern in the way the work (a collective of telephones with random numbers on the dials) was arranged and suggested that this might indicate an overall coherence, she simply replied no, they could be arranged in any way. Whilst she talked about *playing around* with colour in two vibrant prints of telephones with rectangular dialling panels, the tutor noted that they contained a tension between the telephone shape which had perspective and the number panel which did not and suggested that she should experiment with the effect of taking the number panel away – showing, in effect, the processes of arrival. Carol resented this as unnecessary; she had worked on the images on a computer and chosen to develop the most pleasing effect.

Carol's defence of the things in themselves seemed to be a resistance to the tutor's attempts to elicit evidence of exploration and process. Eventually this led to a head-on clash. Carol mentioned some work with the technical diagrams she had found inside the phones; when she had enlarged them the straight lines became wobbly. The tutor picked up on this and wondered whether this might be explored with a medium other than glossy paints: charcoal chips, for example. This practical suggestion seemed to be a way of asking Carol to interrogate her use of colour and smoothness; to define and refine what she had done by exploring an alternative. Carol became heated and passionate: this was a waste of time, she already knew what she wanted to do. In the end, the tutor said, it comes down to honesty, whether you are following a formula or doing art. 'I am being honest!' Carol retorted.

Claiming artistic integrity, Carol founded the discussion in her fundamental purposes and sense of self. The public discourse – the generation of critical meanings for her work – and the teaching process – an attempt to elicit evidence and achieve progress through a certain kind of linguistic reflection – became impossible. Other students, less overt in their resistance than Carol also experienced the crit as a conflict and were conscious of giving a selective (and protective) account of work in order to meet the criteria of the public critical discourse. They described strategies for deflecting talk away from vulnerable areas as if putting up barriers to what was 'really' going on.

Conclusion

Harré's model does not explicitly represent such a struggle – the clash between different identities in this case fostered within the same institution. As a diagrammatic representation it suggests that the public–collective and private–individual quadrants are singular and unified, rather than themselves constituted by multiple, often competing discourses. But making the transitions between quadrants in the personal identity project is not a process of filling a blank world (as if one came to the institution not already the locus of discourse), nor does it involve appropriating something as unitary as 'skill' or even a repertoire of critical vocabulary. Instead the transitions are conflictual, sites where discourses compete for acceptance and, more than this, the domains into which the transitions give access are themselves multi-vocal, complex and contested.

In that it appears to align certain discourses with certain disciplines, Gee's definition also tends to obscure the potential for disorientation, disruption and argument. What the example of fine art adds very vividly to his definition is the insight that a discourse may itself be riven with conflict; that values, beliefs, attitudes may not be common, but in fact be in dispute, the cause of clashes, which are generated within the same institution, but which derive from different historical and ideological moments. Being within a discourse involves participating in its arguments (in the potential to change) rather than espousing any particular value, belief or meaning. At the same time, participation involves recognising the consensus on which arguments are based and the exclusions and hierarchies of value and meaning that operate. Personal identity formation may involve strategy and strategic presentation as much as belief and conviction: playing the game as much as striving for selfhood. In fine art, selfhood and disciplinary identity are brought into proximity and as a consequence individuals become part of the collective by a paradoxical process of alienation from it.

What are the implications of this discussion for the teaching and learning of art? How might we make better sense of the relations between personal and public meanings? I have given three examples of talk, a medium, Bakhtin suggests, in which meaning is made and remade through the mutual orientation of participants. In the first example, argument (as the generation of change) was based on some consensus and equality in the relationship – if not the roles – of speakers. Here, the tutor's role might be characterised as 'discourse leader'. In the second example, where the speakers seemed able only to meet on common ground unconnected with the private meanings of the student, what role might the tutor more effectively have played? Rather than assume shared perspectives and experience, he seemed here to need to forge connections, to enquire more persistently, with greater openness and with judgement perhaps suspended. Such skills in talk are not the 'expert' discourse skills of the first example, but are more educative and teacherly, drawing forth the student's meaning and carefully transforming them.

The crisis enacted in the third example sets the styles and purposes of talk in a wider context and begins to question the value of a belief system in which personal expression is central, but in which receptive, critical and aesthetic engagement are largely absent. A study by the NFER (Harland, Kinder and Hartley, 1995) suggests that 'general absence of mention of aesthetics and ... importance of expression' is characteristic of the way young people understand the arts. Carol's position in the crit might be seen as an extreme extension of such an understanding. As such it may cause us to speculate on the adequacy of a system of education in art which undervalues language (up to A level, students tend to be assessed solely on products which may be accompanied by short, static written statements) and which, perhaps as a consequence, is not adept at using it in ways which might facilitate the learning process and the development of distinctive, yet recognised identities within the discipline.

Chapter Thirteen

ARGUMENT, RHETORIC AND REASON: SOME PRACTICAL SUGGESTIONS FOR TEACHING[*]

Sally Mitchell

From two definitions, a third

Looking back on what I observed in schools, colleges and universities in the course of my research into argument, it is clear to me that whilst argument was often considered to play a role in many subject disciplines, it was rarely focused upon as a mode of operating, a strategy or technique. To succeed, students needed to do more than learn and reproduce content, they needed to transform content through argument. Yet what argument was and how to go about it were questions that were left largely unaddressed. Working out the answers for oneself – whether through practice or intuition – was, in a sense, a measure of success: the best students did so; the rest, presumably, remained unenlightened.

In the following pages I want to reverse the situations I observed and offer some suggestions for foregrounding argument in teaching and learning. The activities I suggest engage students in processes of argument. They are also opportunities for reflection on the nature of argument: What is it? What does it do? Why is it important?

To begin, then, with the question: What is argument? To complicate things immediately I have two definitions rather than one:

First, argument is a series of related ideas which substantiate a statement or point of view. It has, then, a cumulative and linear structure, an internal coherence: reasons point towards a conclusion; the conclusion gestures back to the reasons.

Second, argument is the clashing of one idea with another, the opposing of points of view. In this definition argument is produced by difference, by conflict: it breaks apart.

The two definitions seem to be at odds: one is ordered and closed; the other challenging and disruptive. One implies a singularity of purpose, a clear teleology; the other is grounded in duality, indeed multiplicity. The first seems

---

[*] First published as Mitchell, S. 1995. 'Argument, rhetoric and reason: some practical suggestions for teaching', *SELF Seminariernes Engelskloerererforening* 95 (1).

solitary; the second, social. Yet the two definitions are not incompatible and the relation between them actually produces a third, richer, more dynamic definition. The tension between relating ideas and breaking them apart is in fact the driving force of argument. Consider that the making of a coherent case is motivated by the need to exclude the possibility of dissent; that a clash of opinions need not result in war, but can give rise to a harmonious compromise position; that ideas can be related negatively – in terms of what they are not – as well as positively – in terms of what they share; that a conclusion is rarely entirely conclusive – though it may form the ground they share, or the ground for action, it (and its consequences) are generally at some stage the subject of further dialogues. The constructive and destructive definitions, brought together, result in a notion of argument that embodies both stability and change. It is these factors that make argument such an important cultural activity – and central to the linked enterprises of teaching and learning.

Speaking and writing argument

In schooling two media are generally used for the expression of argument: speech and writing. In my research I found that the medium tended to effect the kind of argument that took place: in speech it more closely resembled the second, more social, multi-directional definition; in writing, the first linear, teleological one. This was hampered rather than helped by the static formula, very common in British schools, 'one side, other side, own opinion', which suggests the need for opposition but minimises the structural opportunity for any clashes to take place.

The suggestions that follow attempt in various ways to give to both speech and writing the qualities of the third definition: in some ways this means making speech more like writing and writing more like speech.

Take speech for example. There is, we might agree, nothing better than getting a good class discussion going, but what actually happens?

some people never speak;
some people never listen;
opinions predominate over reasons;
wanting to include everyone means that nobody speaks for long;
questions are mostly asked by the teacher, who also tends to speak most;
questions tend to elicit quick information rather than processes of thought;
a written record of points raised is rarely kept except by individual note takers.

Below is one suggestion for overcoming some of these limitations in spoken argument. The suggestion is to give to speech some kind of structure. The aim is to elicit not only opinion but also the grounds for opinion and to test for awareness of alternative opinions. A secondary aim is to give teachers and students practice in asking searching neutral questions; questions, that is in which judgement is suspended. The aim is not to prevent opinions clashing, but to allow time for opinions to be explored before this takes place.

Practical suggestion 1: questions for development of argument[1]

The first task is to choose a question related to an issue which contains within it some potential for debate. This might be: What causes unemployment? What causes famine in Africa?

The class is split into pairs: A adopts the role of questioner, whilst B gives his or her opinion.

A proceeds to question with the aim of uncovering the grounds for B's opinion – or, to put it another way, the arguments which might substantiate it. For instance on the question, 'Do you believe we should have a single European currency?', A asks B:

> *Why do you believe that?
> *Can you give up to three reasons for your opinion?
> *Taking the first reason only, what evidence do you have to support it?
> *If you were asked to prove your reason, how could you do it?

> *What reasons would a person whose view is different to yours give?
> (up to three reasons)
> *What evidence could they give to support their main reason?
> *What could they do to prove their reason is correct?

A notes down the results of the enquiry and reports back to a plenary session.

The roles can be reversed at this stage. Eventually 'arguments' can be summarised on the board (using, for example, the grid suggested in Practical suggestion 4 below). Now there are more possibilities. For example:

> *discussion as a group;
> *re-pairing to allow students with different view to discuss – or argue;
> *As to offer a critique of what they have listened to and Bs to defend themselves or make concessions;
> *a review of the processes of argument themselves. Discussion, for instance, of why one person's opinion is more convincingly defended than another's; whether a single anecdote as evidence is sufficient; whether it is sufficient in some contexts, but not in others; whether

---

[1] These questions are derived from Kuhn's (1991) research into people's argumentative thinking.

inability to think of an alternative argument effects the validity of one's own.

The questions raised above suggest that the effectiveness of an argument does not depend solely on objectively determined criteria, but rather is influenced by the purposes to which it is to be put and the contexts in which it is communicated. Argument does not take place in a vacuum: argument engages, it has effects, it seeks to persuade. Rhetoric – the art of persuasion – has as much to do with argument as has reason.

As soon as we think about there being more than one point of view, this becomes the case. Each of us, in order to function in society, is a rhetorician. In different contexts we present ourselves in different ways according to the purposes we hold and the expectations we recognise others hold of us. If we want to argue successfully we draw consciously and unconsciously on all these factors. They effect not only the language we use, but the way we dress and use our bodies; or in writing, the kind of paper, format, script and so on, that we choose.

In the next practical suggestion the aim is to foreground a sense of rhetorical purpose in using language – both spoken and written – and also by using a poem as stimulus, to demonstrate how form and structure can argue as well as words.

Practical suggestion 2: different people argue differently

This exercise starts by exploring a poem which though not explicit in its arguments does nonetheless appear to be arguing something[2]. Readers may be differently persuaded as to what that something is. Here is the poem I have used:

Poem

And if it snowed and snow covered the drive.
he took a spade and tossed it to one side.
And always tucked his daughter up at night.
And slippered her the one time that she lied.

And every week he tipped up half his wage.
And what he didn't spend each week he saved.
And praised his wife for every meal she made.
And once, for laughing, punched her in the face.

And for his mum he hired a private nurse.
And every Sunday taxied her to church.

---

[2] See Mitchell and Riddle (2000) for an analysis of the poem as argument.

And he blubbed when she went from bad to worse.
And twice he lifted ten quid from her purse.

Here's how they rated him when they looked back:
sometimes he did this, sometimes he did that.

(Simon Armitage, *Kid*, 1992)

First of all, there should be some discussion of the poem, focussing on the question of whether the man described is judged as a good or bad man. Questions to consider might include:

Is there a progression throughout the poem (e.g. in the man's deeds)
How does the sonnet form suggest emphasis?
What kinds of verbs are used? What do they suggest?
Who are 'they' in the final couplet?

The students get into groups, each of which is given a rhetorical task to work on. The groups do not reveal their task to the others, because the aim is for them to be able to guess who is arguing, what and to whom.

For the poem above, the tasks could be these:

The man has died and gone to Limbo, where he is closely questioned. Write an interview between the man and his judge/interrogator in purgatory.

You are a friend of the man in the poem. Write a letter to the local council arguing that a park bench be dedicated to his name. (If time, write the council's letter of reply.)

You are the local journalist. Write an obituary for the man in the poem which paints a negative picture of his life. (If time, write a letter of complaint to the newspaper from an aggrieved relative.)

You are a social worker. Write an official report on the family in the poem arguing a need for family counselling.

Write a dialogue between two local undertakers who are preparing the man for burial. One thinks he will go to heaven; the other that he will go to hell.

Write an interview between the writer of the poem and a literary critic who is researching his work. (If time, write the first paragraph of the essay the critic goes on to write.)

Students should be encouraged to think of the extratextual aspects of their task: the social worker's report, for instance, might be set out on official paper, with a report number at the top; the obituary might be in several columns etc.

The outcomes are presented to the class either orally or in written form. The students venture suggestions as to what the situation is and what is being argued. They discuss the features of the language and presentation that helped them to interpret the piece. There may, of course, be disagreements: sometimes communication can be very ambiguous – as it is in the poem with which the exercise starts.

The tasks in this exercise have a clear sense of rhetorical purpose: they are clearly situated in social contexts. Notice that one of these – the writer and critic – is a scholarly one. This is a deliberate and important inclusion because the writing (more than speaking) that students do in academic contexts is often intended purely to demonstrate 'reasoned thought' and a 'grasp of the relevant arguments' and is not, therefore, seen to have much to do with rhetoric and role play. It is assumed, that is, to tell the whole story about a student's thinking. In fact, academic writing demands very particular rhetorical skills and its conventions constrain as much as enable the expression of thought. In Britain and America at least, structural conventions and kinds of writing 'voice' which express authority and clarity of purpose tend to be privileged. The writer sets out what she will do and her task is then to do it: doubt and deviation are not really acceptable. Argument is disinterested rather than passionate or polemical. It may contain alternative ideas but these are controlled and made subservient to the closed position the writer has indicated she will demonstrate.

Academic argument is, then, a very difficult task to do well. Meeting the rhetorical demands of the essay form can result in argument which is oversimplified and which takes no shape or substance from alternative ideas and possibilities. The following practical suggestion aims to challenge the monologic style of much academic writing, by making it part of a dialogue – giving it, that is, the insistent, challenging qualities of speech. The suggestion was devised by an American teacher of literature (Meyer 1993), who felt that her students' thinking was suffering as a result of their over-obedience to the conventions of the written form. She was frustrated by the way they adopted an all-knowing persona in their writing (what she refers to as an 'illusion of mastery'), which seemed to close down their possibilities for imaginative thought. In Double Trouble she invited them to adopt an alternative questioning persona.

Practical suggestion 3: double trouble

The following exercise is taken from Meyer (1993) and involves work based on the last lines of Shaw's *Pygmalion*. A student's response is included:

Figure 1

ASSIGNMENT: Double Trouble

Fold a piece of paper in half. On one side, tell me what you think the sentences say. Be declarative, stating your reading as though you're sure of yourself and the author's intentions. Begin your writing with a description of the text and what it "means" or represents.

Now on the other side, begin your statements with "But something bothers me". On this side be hesitant, questioning your assertions and certainties of the "right" side. Think about contradictions, about "what-ifs", about what the sentences don't say directly. Explore double meanings and alternative conclusions. Relate what is said to personal experience and to subjective responses. Don't censor the outrageous or the impossible.

> Higgins: Pickering! Nonsense: she's going to marry
> Freddy. Ha ha! Freddy! Freddy! Ha ha ha ha ha!!!! [He
> roars with laughter as the play ends]. (Pygmalion 100)

SAMPLE RESPONSE

I know that Higgins is laughing at Eliza and Freddy. Shaw shows that Higgins has not changed at all and is still scornful of others. The tone expresses his continued sense of superiority and Shaw's in relation to other human beings. He is laughing at their weaknesses, compared to his own strength.

But what if the joke is on Henry? Perhaps his laughter has a slight edge of hysteria to it. Maybe Shaw is suggesting that Henry is not the Superman he thinks he is but is vulnerable to the same emotions such as jealousy as evryone else. I'd like to believe in a more sympathetic Higgins, one who is not fully in control. But then, maybe Shaw has the "last laugh", showing me how much I want a different ending.

(Meyer 1993:60)

The exercise above breaks apart the closed propositional style of argument; the one below aims at the opposite process: the bringing together of many voices in the service of the writer's single voice. It is the combination that characterises the conventional argumentative essay: a dialogic structure governed by a monologic aim and controlling voice.

Practical suggestion 4 is a sequence of exercises designed to help students achieve this combination – frequently the biggest stumbling block in their writing. Though a written outcome is the particular aim here, there is no reason why the exercises should not also result in a spoken presentation. You may recognise in the grid the same principle of juxtaposition (bringing into contact) as in the parallel texts above.

Practical suggestion 4: using the arguments of others to argue for oneself

Students are presented with a range of views and information on the argument topic. It could be a range of written extracts, but I find that a programme like BBC Radio 4's *Any Questions?* is ideal. Here a panel of four well-known people express their views on a topic of current interest. The use of spoken, rather than written sources immediately engages students and raises a number of interesting questions for discussion about the authority and persuasiveness of the spoken word – and subsequently about the differences between speech and writing.

The students are asked to summarise each source or voice. Selection and interpretation are involved in this task and people's summaries are likely to vary accordingly. Again, there is potential for discussion here.

The next step is to tease out the common themes or points contained in the summaries. For a theme to be common, it has to be present in more than one, but not necessarily all of the summaries. A theme is a neutral category in relation to which a range of arguments may be expressed. To capture this, students might find the following grid arrangement useful. In the spaces they should note what the sources have to say in relation to the theme, paying attention to variation and nuance. For example, if the theme were 'the role of the monarchy', source 1 might say that 'the monarchy has no role; it is anachronistic'; source 2, 'it is symbolic rather than functional'; source 3, 'it is important because it creates a cohesive national identity' etc.

	Source 1	Source 2	Source 3
Common theme 1			
Common theme 2			
Common theme 3			

Students now write an account (paragraph) on each of the themes which includes the various arguments which surround it. They should be encouraged to analyse and evaluate the arguments – what are their strengths and weaknesses? – and to incorporate their own comments into the accounts.

It may be a good idea now to introduce the students to some additional sources which can be assimilated into the emerging idea structure and which will enrich and extend it.

An important step before writing the essay is to link the themes (paragraphs) into an overall structure. Are there threads/overlaps between themes? If so, the writer should try to spell these out. Spider diagrams are useful here or cutting the paragraphs up and shuffling them around on the table until a pattern emerges. The pattern should have a rationale that can be made explicit: it should, to return to my first definition, be a series of related ideas which can substantiate a point of view.

Next comes the task of writing the essay – this would be the conventional outcome of such a series of tasks in the British classroom, but it is not the only culmination possible! Students might just as well use speech to explain to each other their chain of reasoning, their understandings of the arguments of others and the position (perhaps an ambivalent one) they want to claim for themselves. Writing is, however, an important part of the process: it requires ideas to be pinned down and allows for reflection on the way material can change when it is worked on in various ways.

There is a strong notion in the above suggestion that when ideas are moved around, placed in different relation to one another, their significance can change and different meanings, new arguments emerge. In *Double Trouble*, similarly, the left-hand text might seem to give a definitive version of events until another text appeared by its side.

In my final practical suggestion, this sense that the relations between ideas are as important as the ideas themselves becomes the central activity. Once again the suggestion involves moving between speech and writing. Speech – dialogue with others – allows for fluidity and change; writing requires more 'commitment', if only as an intermediary step, ideas become fixed on paper. The exercise begins with writing, then passes through structured discussion phases in which notes are taken, to close with a return to the individual activity of writing. Here, the initial writing can be evaluated in the light of the challenges raised in discussion.

Practical suggestion 5: making patterns, developing reasons

For this exercise I have chosen as a stimulus the question 'What is art?' for two reasons: 1) most people have some kind of notion of what they think art is; 2) the principles of patterning and categorisation can be brought out more directly using visual (rather than textual) sources.

The students address the question 'What is art?' in an unstructured way, drawing on their opinions and experience. They may write a paragraph using such supplementary questions as these: What do you think art is? What are your reasons? Do you have examples? What do you think art is not? Or, what is not art? What are the criteria you are using in your definition?

In groups the students are given six postcards of paintings or other art objects, representing a variety of styles and subject matter. Each card is numbered. The group then sets about arranging the cards in the patterns suggested below. When they have decided on a configuration they should agree a rationale or an organising principle and write it down.

Figure 2

Suggested configurations:

A. (sequence)

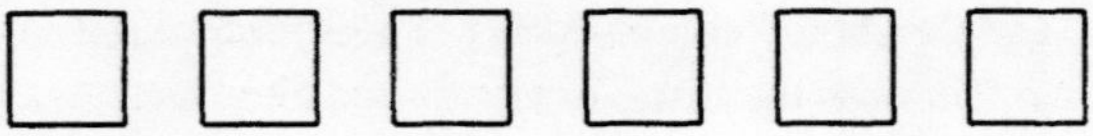

Reasons:

B. (two groups)

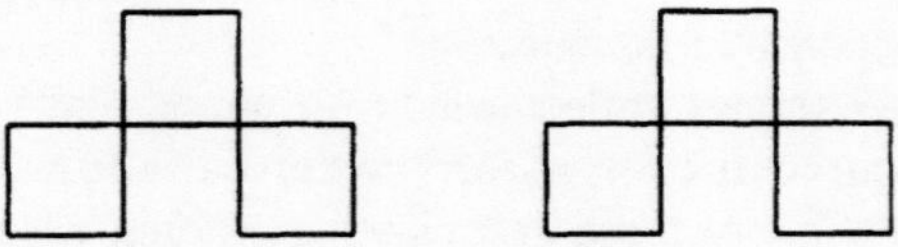

Reasons:

C. (three groups)

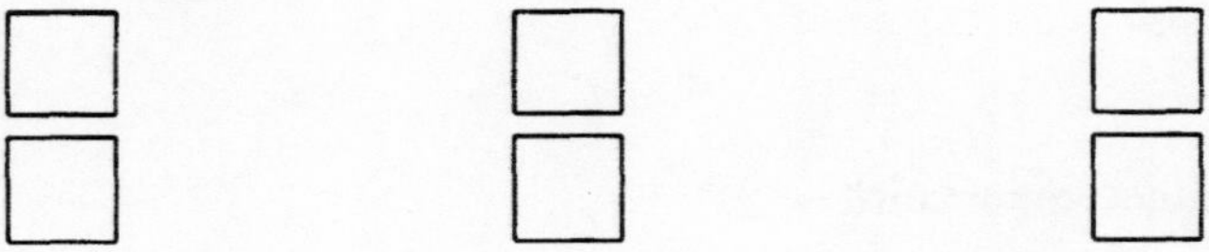

Reasons:

D. (one exception)

Reasons:

E. (hierarchy)

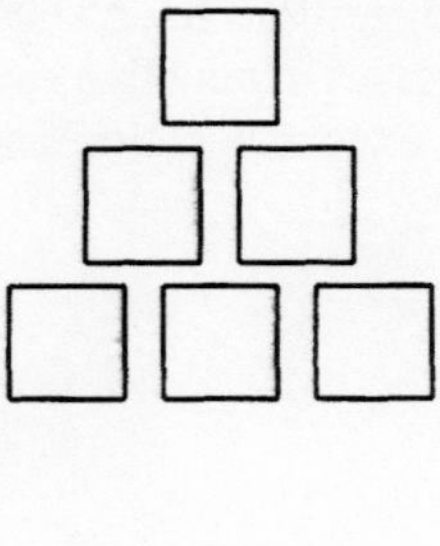

Reasons:

F. Try another patterning of your own here and give your reasons:

The postcards might, for instance, be arranged in terms of colour, subject matter, style, artistic intention, historical chronology. With the help of the teacher, students may came to see that, for instance, colour plays a different role in contemporary abstract art than in medieval art, where subject matter is more important. The patterning process should cause the students to look more closely and think more widely about possible ways of defining – and arguing for and against – art. Along the way they are likely to broaden their vocabularies and conceptual understandings.

Finally the students return to the question 'What is art?' and to what they wrote originally. Using the following kinds of question to guide them, they should then write a further response to the question:

Do any of the postcard groupings reflect what you wrote first? Do any of the groupings fall outside your definition of art? What definitions of art are possible besides your own? If some of these groupings aren't art, what are they? Could art be a way of challenging definitions of art?

The same kinds of patterning can be used with other sources: poems, short argumentative statements, pictures and writing relating to a particular (social or political) theme or to a contested concept, such as 'Propaganda', 'Literature', 'Happiness', etc.

Why is argument important?

The reasons why argument is important are found in all the things that argument does: argument breaks apart and brings together; it transforms the meaning of what we think and what are told to think about; it is a way of challenging positions, but also a way of establishing them; it brings together shared purposes and individual goals.

Argument is about passion and sense of purpose and about posturing and play. It is a social process: by engaging in it we gain a sense of how we act our social roles and purposes and conversely of how we are acted upon by the arguments around us. Each of these functions make developing students' skills in argument an important goal for teachers of language.

Learning a language, like learning any subject, should enable us to use language to interrogate what we are given, to make new meanings and to adapt these for our various purposes. My practical suggestions have aimed to facilitate this way of learning language and I hope – in an argumentative spirit – that they may be a stimulus for discussion, a basis for experimentation and themselves, open to change.

Chapter Fourteen

LEARNING TO BE CRITICAL AND CORRECT – FORMS AND FUNCTIONS OF ARGUMENT AT 'A' LEVEL[*]

Sally Mitchell

Whenever I happen to mention casually that I am involved in a project which addresses the nature of argument, I am greeted with raised eyebrows and not uncommonly the repost 'No you're not!'. (Remember that Monty Python sketch?) In more 'serious' contexts, students – of the Arts and Humanities in particular – seem to know what I am talking about and expect me to find examples of it when I come into their classrooms; teachers too see the relevance, sometimes adding quizzically 'Ah, but do they do it?'

In this chapter I discuss some of the kinds of argument engaged in by sixth-form sociology students. I detect some mismatches between its different functions and manifestations, principal of which is a disjunction between spoken and written forms. I argue that the rhetorical constraints of the essay form may inhibit the development of active critical thinking and suggest that written argument might be improved by practice outside these rhetorical constraints.

The chapter takes as its primary evidence work observed in a sixth form sociology classroom on health and related issues. It starts by looking at a small group discussion.

The students have been introduced to a theory put forward by Ivan Illich which contends that medicine and its institutions can have a detrimental effect upon health and well-being. This phenomenon he calls *iatrogenesis*. The topic of health and Illich's theory are particularly interesting, since they implicate the personal experiences and values of the students in the wider consideration of society and social issues. This relation of the personal to the sociological seems to be one of the subject's defining characteristics. Moreover it contains within it a strong potential for the generation of argument: a site of conflict where everyday 'common-sense' values are challenged by sociological theories. This conflict to a great extent drives the small group discussion.

The students are asked to do three things:

---

[*] First published as Mitchell, S. 1993. 'Learning to be critical and correct: forms and functions of argument at A level', *Curriculum* 14 (1).

1. To think of examples of iatrogenesis (illness caused by doctors – the concept framed by Illich).
2. To list supporting arguments for the concept in more general terms than offered by the examples.
3. To list counter-arguments to Illich's theory.

The task given to the group has an argumentative structure and sequence. It guides the students from the concrete to the abstract, building a case first for one side then the other. In the discussion this 'macro' structure is largely adhered to, though the talk itself has a dynamic which is charged by the students' individual agendas.

Each student in the group plays a distinctive role. Susan is passionately opposed to Illich's argument – her most frequent exclamation is 'What a load of rubbish!' Much to Susan's exasperation, Andrew is keen on the idea of iatrogenesis, and wants to get on with completing the task. His interest is more dispassionate; he seems to enjoy pulling out implications. He frequently comes into conflict with Susan whose feelings impede her interest in the idea. Liz is less vocal and is non-committal; when she does speak, though, it is often to clinch a point which her companions have been tussling over. Her role is, in a sense, enigmatic, difficult to assess: does her thought develop from listening to her companions or are her contributions already obvious to her?

The following extract from the discussion illustrates the dynamic which is typical of the whole. It occurs as the group are moving on to discuss counter-arguments to Illich. Andrew invites Susan to begin since this is clearly, he thinks, where her forté lies:

S: Alright, things like heart disease and stuff and – you need treatment. You can't just get over it, sat at home in bed. Like AIDS and stuff.

A: There again you get over it anyway – I mean if you've got ...

S: No you're not. You're not ...

A: If you've got a bad heart, you're not going to ...

S: What about leukaemia, chemotherapy and all that?

A: You still die though don't you? It don't usually ...

S: Yeah, but you want to live longer, you want to live as long as you can ...

A: ...cure you. Eh, you're living longer, but you're in like pain. It's costing more money as well isn't it?

S: Rubbish. No sorry Andrew I don't agree.

A: Why?

S: Because I wouldn't want to die and I don't think you would and if it comes to the choice where you'd have to [breath] got a chance o'living, would you treat me? You'd have it. You would have it! [very emphatic: crescendo]

A: Depends on – how you were living. Depends how you were living.

S: You would have it. [softer]

A: If you were living w' no hair and in total pain all the time, then what's the point?

L: When you're going to die anyway.

S: Yeah! [shouts]. But I'm on about heart disease and stuff. If you have a heart attack and you get taken to hospital, you want the ...

A: Yeah but, Yeah, yeah, alright. [Conciliatory]

S: ...treatment to get over it.

A: Yeah, but you see, you're going back to the symptoms aren't you? They're only looking at the symptoms aren't they? Doctors, they're not looking at the causes, so once you've got it yeah, fair enough, you need the doctors, but ... it's getting it in the first place.

S: Yeah – but you've ... that's the argument. [tapping paper]

A: You're eating fatty foods and that, just thinking, 'Oh, if I do get it ...'

S: [exasperated] Don't you want hospitals or sommat?

For Susan the real-life situation overrides the academic argument. She values life above everything, whilst Andrew is able dispassionately to draw a distinction between the quality of life and life at whatever cost (and indeed actual cost). Whilst Andrew talks in terms of 'it depends ...' Susan is arguing from absolute conviction. This is automatically a conviction about the priorities of people in general and her point takes the form of a personal attack on Andrew. Where Liz joins in with 'When you're going to die anyway', the emotion escalates. Susan lacks support from both companions and is unable to defend herself. It is worth speculating how she might have done this. If she had moved from the particular to the general and articulated a value or principle (life over death), which, if held, would justify any attempt at treatment and cure, the status of her point would have changed from subjective to objective, from common-sense to 'sociological'. The tone would have changed accordingly from 'unreason' to 'reason' and her point would have become useful rather than obstructive in compiling the list of counter-arguments.

In this feelingful turmoil how does reasoning progress? It is not by a clear or 'reasoned' path and yet insights do occur and are formulated. The following extract occurs shortly before the one above. In it Andrew formulates the idea he resorts to above that doctors treat symptoms rather than causes:

Teacher: Well, just to start you off then. I mean he would argue that if I said to you 'Do you look after your health?' you'd sort o'say 'Oh yes, well I'm reasonably careful. I don't smoke too much and I don't eat too many beefburgers and so forth, but o'course if I do get ill then, yes, I go to the doctor's. I look after my health like that.' The very existence, the fact that there's doctors and hospitals here, perhaps that's a sort of safety net that makes us take ...

A: It's an excuse for being ...

T: Right.

A: ... to put off smoking. If you're going to get ill, you're going to get help.

T: Now just pursue that idea just a little but more, because that's the sort of approach.

A: So it's a, it's an excuse ...

S: ... for taking risks.

A: Yeh, so you've got the back up of knowing you're going to get treated.

L: You go to the doctor [flippant]. You go to the doctor [joking about general practitioners for a bit]

A: Right, is that it? Is that all?

S: And he thinks they're a load of rubbish because ...

A: Yeh, but he was saying that ...

S: [over the top of him] Cos they do treatment, they do treatment that,

L: They don't look for the causes [sounds flippant]

S: No no no no. They do treatment. What they don't ... No [tapping with pen]

A: No that's a point that ... No it's a point, that. That 'cos most hospitals and doctors only do treat the symptoms don't they? They're not actually... treating the causes.

S: [loud] Don't place enough emphasis on the causes. [writing down]

L: Don't treat the causes.

A: Yeh they're just doing the symptoms. [pause]

L: [soft] Pretty obvious really.

A: So it's an excuse for, like, the government not intervening in causes of ill health, isn't it?

S: Oh it's not the government.

The teacher helps the students to tackle the second task – arguments supporting Illich – by creating a hypothetical concrete situation. His intervention bridges the gap between the abstract ideas of Illich and their particular manifestation. He begins to generalise from his role-play by referring to 'a sort of safety net'. Andrew picks this up and reformulates it – 'It's an excuse ...' – into a general reasoning statement 'If you're going to get ill, you're going to get help'.

Having focused the students in this way the teacher leaves them. The statement they arrived at is uncontested, but the conversation begins to degenerate, Andrew reacting defensively to Susan's dismissive tone. When Liz casually slips in the comment 'They don't look for the causes', Susan doesn't seem to hear her, pursuing instead her own thought. Andrew, however, seizes upon what she says as if it crystallises something for him. He expands the idea, building onto untreated causes the idea of treated symptoms. Susan concedes the point by writing it down, but doesn't share the enthusiasm; her writing is a way of closing the discussion. Liz can't see what all the fuss is about, but Andrew is quite excited. He takes the idea a great leap further, suddenly seeing a connection with the government: the idea of medicine as an 'excuse' is taken beyond an individual level and applied at a political one. If people are happy that medical services treat the symptoms only, government need not concern itself with causes. The two preceding points form this third one where both the 'excuse' and the 'cause' take on new significances and applications. Andrew has reached a level of abstraction from which individual instructions and practices can be seen as part of a larger over-reaching pattern of relationships. It is not clear whether his insight comes from co-operation with the group or whether it has an intuitive impulse behind it. Certainly it is not methodically reached.

Susan, predictably by now, does not receive Andrew's idea well; the idea of government investment in iatrogenesis simply makes that theory seem even less commonsensical. Andrew - perhaps in recognition of her view - does not pursue the idea. Later, though, when the whole class are asked to pool their ideas, he offers it as a contribution and it is accepted by the teacher as a good point.

How can this short interaction and its complex nature - the independent and dialogic learning which seems to be going on, the mixture of reason and unreason - be understood as part of a larger context of learning and disciplinary behaviour? One important thing it reveals about argument is that it cannot be defined as a simple or single thing; in the discussion both argument and arguments were generated. What were these and how do they function within the larger context?

Manifestations of argument can be broadly divided into the cognitive and the rhetorical, where the former is largely concerned with process and the latter with product. The functions of argument can be divided into at least four, frequently overlapping categories. These functions elucidate the forms in which argument is manifested.

Argument as process

The first is social. Taking part in argument (as class discussion) is a social skill; it means having the courage and conviction to make one's own voice heard; it suggests an active rather than a passive role. Classes which involve active participation tend also to have an air of conviviality about them, often relapsing into humour and digression. This kind of conviviality is sometimes a prerequisite for other forms of argument.

In presenting argument as polite, friendly and facilitative, however, there is a danger of oversanitising its meaning. As part of my research sixth formers recently completed a questionnaire, which relied on a largely academic model of argument. Several of their comments gave an alternative or rather a more immediate meaning - that argument is 'an angry replacement for discussion', 'a strong expression of disagreement, often purposely caused through boredom'; it 'enables you to get what you want', 'can be used to show many kinds of self-feeling - to demonstrate love, hate and so on' and is 'used when it's a last resort'. One student commented: 'Physical violence is the best way to settle arguments'. These comments serve as an important reminder that argument is a strong and sometimes destructive social force. Except in the safe guise of role play, argument which functions in this way is not generally encouraged in the classroom. Teachers tend to operate with a prevailing sense that becoming educated is also becoming reasonable, a quality which is not allied in our culture to passion. The impetus behind this view is both moral and academic. ('Academic' means 'abstract, theoretical, cold, merely logical'.)

One effect of the small group example given above, however, is to disrupt the ease with which 'reason' and 'unreason' may be opposed. It suggests that what, within the educational context, seems unreasonable, may from a common-sense social perspective appear to be entirely reasonable. In the same way the students who responded to the 'research' questionnaire with definitions and uses of argument taken from their everyday, unschooled lives, were asserting the common-sense necessity of their view and wresting the definition of argument back from the narrow parameters of my pedagogically motivated research project.

It remains the case, however, that Sarah's common-sense view was in many ways inappropriate to the academic framework within which she was operating, and that Andrew's disinterested approach made him a better sociologist. The sense that Sarah's common-sense view was a hindrance to other forms and functions of argument shows the extent to which argument is contextually defined and implemented. The various forms and functions of argument, that is, have validity only within certain parameters and in this sense all of its functions are social.

It should be noticed too, that the differentiation between 'reason' and 'unreason' ('right' and 'wrong') in the above extracts is as concerned with tone and style as with content. The importance of presentational form in terms of what it can achieve in distinguishing – or better, persuading – right from wrong is relevant everywhere in this discussion. But it needs, I go on to suggest, to be treated with some scepticism.

Argument – as discussion – has another social function too. When students are encouraged to question and to challenge, they are offered control over – and ownership of – the content with which they are presented; this in turn implies control over their own learning and a certain autonomous status within the institutional structure.

Argument also functions as a way of assisting the learning process, a way of enhancing students' understanding. This function is related to a sense that argument is a cognitive process of making sense, which involves abstracting from the given to more general and inclusive concepts, making connections between evidence and conclusions, making comparisons between disparate phenomena and, crucially, evaluating them.

In my experience this kind of argument is largely regarded as taking place through speech – as discussion either with the teacher or in groups. Lesson time in many subjects at A level is taken up with discussion characterised by questions and more or less developed lines of reasoning. Such discussions, like the extract above, do not consist purely of argument, but are a hybrid in which a variety of factors – the transmission of material, the authority of the teacher, the unspoken sense of what is proper – play a part. Why the notion of argument as cognitive process should be largely associated with speech is clarified below when I turn to the written form. Argument may also occur as a private and internal process of cognition, but when it takes on a public form it may come into conflict with another set of criteria associated with argument: argument as rhetorical product.

Speech situations from which the teacher is absent – in which, that is to say, the institutional structure to some extent effaces itself – can enhance students' participation in argument and are frequently used. It was this sense of increased participation that probably motivated the sociology teacher to organise his class into small discussion groups which gave students an opportunity to think critically about the stimulus material. The sense in these situations that there is no-one who is already in possession of the answer or outcome, facilitates guesswork and speculation and validates the contributions of all participants. In the example above a space was created in which the personal and sociological could, without inhibition, come into contact.

What are the outcomes of such learning situations? How do they go on to be used? The validity of any contribution may be enhanced when it is presented to the teacher or person in authority – as was the case with Andrew's insight. The teacher may also reformulate it at a higher level of abstraction: when, on another occasion, the teacher did this the class collectively breathed an 'Ah!' Articulating at this level – abstraction – seemed to secure their thought. The concrete example that a student in this case had suggested did not hold the same degree of satisfaction as the essential point which the teacher had been able to supply – and in supplying it the teacher validated the exploratory processes the student had independently been involved in.

The context change may, however, diminish as well as enhance the validity of contributions made in a small group. A view that is freely aired amongst peers (the personal) may never surface in front of the whole class and may also be absent from resulting written work. Not only views but also modes of operation – guesswork, speculation, critical and discursive approaches – may disappear. Notions of permission and propriety – whether real or merely perceived – always have some eventual bearing on what can be said or argued. And the context of reception always to some extent determines its status as process or product.

Argument as product

Implicit in much of what I have said has been the notion of assessment; how argument is to be judged. Assessment drives much of the learning which takes place in schools and it generally emphasises products and outcomes. Where evidence of argument is required by the examiner its form and scope is in a sense already decided; a conventionalised and standardised end-point for learning. Rather than operating as a vehicle for learning, argument is now displayed.

The point where presentation and display become important is also the point where the product enters a new arena of argument: the point where it is judged for its effectiveness, its power to persuade. Argument is now understood as public product, rather than personal or private or even collective process: rhetoric rather than cognition.

This shift of emphasis leads to a fourth function of argument: a way of belonging to a disciplinary community. Argument can be understood as concerned with the real status of practices within the discipline, the activities in which real practitioners engage. Argument takes place at the highest levels of disciplinary study and at the cutting edge of all disciplines where boundaries are reinforced or shifted. At this level argument can be conceived of as the production, distribution, exchange and reception of information, insight, opinion, theory. A discipline is a community of dialogic exchanges, communication; it can, in fact, be understood as argument. To what extent this description is acceptable will in part be dependent on the conceptions of practitioners within the subject: in competing theories of knowledge argument will be accommodated to a greater or lesser extent. Generally however the higher up the educational system students go the greater access they are given to the argumentative constitution of their discipline – until finally they are in a position to advance arguments themselves. At this stage argument becomes doing.

Thinking in these terms of the small group discussion, it seems clear that the arguments generated there did not function as doing. Partly this was due to Susan's 'unsociological' role, but it was also inherent in the small group context. Students' talk becomes doing through validation. This begins to occur when the teacher intervenes and when at the end of the lesson, he conducts a plenary. He acts as a gateway to the discourse community of sociology, accepting the students' comments as valid or invalid, not in terms of everyday judgement but of the academic field.

The ability to argue, to generate argument and to differentiate one's own position from others' through argument is an index of the degree to which one can be said to belong to an academic discourse community. Belonging is, however, contingent upon the context and manner in which one argues, the forms and organisational structures one employs. In the academic world the process of belonging largely culminates in the written form. Postgraduate research students win their colours through recognised genres such as the research paper (the challenge for postgraduates from overseas is not so much concerned with the content of their study, but with becoming conversant in the appropriate genres – see Swales, 1990). Lower down the educational ladder the essay is the major form through which an individual enters the public arena and is assessed.

If argument were a simple thing, one might expect that as the A-level sociology students moved from small group discussions to teacher-arbitrated situations to the writing of essays, they would come closer to 'doing' sociology. My observations suggest however that when the transition is made from speech to writing there is a fall off in argumentative content. Moving away from speech seems for many students to mean a movement away from argument and consequently a deferral of 'real' status within the discipline. At the same time though, they are grappling with the appropriate means of expressing themselves, attempting to be rhetorically correct. This results in a confusion – which is not always clearly recognised – between the form of the essay and the mode of argument, where the first, successfully executed, stands in for and becomes, to a degree, synonymous with the second.

Analysis of sociology essays written as a result of the lessons on health did not show students operating upon their material at levels beyond 'knowledge and understanding'. There was a failure to engage in critical analysis or evaluation and to develop alternative perspectives: a failure, that is to say, to argue. Instead, the essays I looked at were all organised on a largely narrative pattern.

The influence of form over content was evidenced by considering the relation of the essay titles to structure and content. One title asked only for an account: 'What explanations have sociologists offered for variations in health and illness between different sections of the population?', whilst the other invited evaluation: 'Examine the argument that health and illness are socially constructed and distributed'. What is significant is the fact that the different titles did not produce vastly different essays in terms of the way material was organised and handled. The explanation seems to be that there is something about the organisational structure of the essay that overrides the specific title that is set. These seem to be what Flower and Hayes (1981a) have described as learned 'writing goals' which the writer draws on automatically without reference to, or in addition to the goals of a particular writing task. They will be, for example,

> Those goals associated with writing in general, such as, 'interest the reader', or 'start with an introduction', or on goals associated with a given genre, such as making a jingle rhyme. (p. 381)

Put another way, the essay form imposes on the writer a requirement that a certain set of functions be fulfilled. In general structural terms these can be listed as: introduction, middle, conclusion. Though these are employed in the service of the particular title, they also have independent characteristics and expectations attached to them. For example, whether the title asks for evaluation or not, the conclusion is anticipated as a site for some kind of evaluative summing up. The introduction, too, is to offer an overview of what the reader may expect, often raising questions which it is the promise of the rest of the essay to answer. Rhetorical notions of what the essay involves are often crudely offered or interpreted, creating the misguided impression that there are categorically right and wrong ways in which to approach a task. To a degree it is true that there is right and wrong, yet the quality of ideas and of argument often finds no place in such definitions.

The common requirement on the student to write an essay as the outcome of a period of learning seems, in addition, to bring with it a deference to the subject's authorities and a strong tendency to report rather than critically – much less hotly – debate the views of those authorities. Writing an essay also conventionally requires an impersonal style. This rhetorical detachment seems – at this level of study – to bring with it a cognitive detachment. It is as if impersonality is most successfully achieved through the neutrality of reportage. Opinion, readily associated with passion and with speech, is effaced. The rhetorical constraints of the essay overcome the active engagement of the cognitive processes which was evident (in however inappropriate a form) in the group interaction. In part at least the rhetorical effect of narrative knowledge coherently presented within a standard three-part essay form seems to stand in for argument and argumentative engagement. In other words a statement or conclusion convincingly presented within an accepted rhetorical structure is to an extent automatically manifested.

What I mean by the distinction between rhetorical coherence and cognitive engagement can perhaps be clarified by the following example from one of the essays the students wrote. Rachel wrote this paragraph on the work of Marxist theorists Doyal and Pennell:

> They go on to argue that Capitalism doesn't only destroy its workforce's health, but also the health of the outer workforce, via pollution such as radiation damages to the community, and pollution from factories, like Sellafield, Chernobyl and Capper Pass, as these tend to be situated in working class areas.

The paragraph achieves a rhetorical coherence by supporting a general statement with a list of examples – this balance of proposition and illustration evidence is a major criterion for the rhetorically satisfying essay. Yet what gives the game away is the examples themselves. In class discussion Chernobyl had been used to question Doyal and Pennell's anti-capitalist theory since the disaster there occurred under a Communist system. It was the teacher's encapsulation of the power of the example as 'They are confusing Capitalism with Industrialisation' that produced the satisfied hum which was mentioned above. In the essay, however, the critical argument contained in the example is suppressed – as is the potential of the VDU screens example, which might successfully have been used to criticise rather than illustrate the Marxist position. The risk – to the ordering of material – that might be involved in abstracting from the concrete is avoided in favour of a safer option, which also appears at least to strike the right tone for an impersonal academic essay and therefore to be rhetorically satisfactory.

It may also be significant that it was the teacher who came up with the abstraction about Industrialism and Capitalism, whilst a student supplied the example. It is at the level of exemplification that students are frequently invited to begin their reasoning: this seems to offer a way into the subject by linking existing knowledge with new ideas. To demonstrate their understanding of a concept explained by the teacher, students are often asked to give examples which illustrate it. The examples are either suitable or not. Students are rarely asked to explain in their turn the reasons why such an illustration is appropriate;

what in particular it illustrates. Examples as a result often remain in the form of lists, tacked onto concepts without really illuminating them. These lists, as we have seen, can find their way into written work, fulfilling the rhetorical demand for supporting detail, but without indicating any cognitive ability to connect by abstracting.

Putting process into product

It may be that the option Rachel took to eschew critical argument really was safer. Research by Freedman and Pringle (1980a) has suggested that teachers look for evidence of rhetorical coherence when marking essays rather than for evidence of cognitive development and intellectual processes. Certainly when this essay was marked no comment was made about the unexplored and faulty argument. By implication – and at first sight, paradoxically – the emphasis placed by teachers on the well-structured essay may be a reason for the relatively weak performance of students in terms of the higher cognitive skills of analysis and evaluation – a weakness commented upon by A-level examiners (AEB 639 examiners' report, 1991). Whilst this emphasis remains, it seems probable that the processes by which students move towards legitimate doing of their subject will be hindered and delayed. As Freedman and Pringle comment:

> They need to know ... that writing involves more than the mastery of the norms and forms of expository prose as articulated in the traditional texts. They need to be introduced to the broader conception of the writing process...which recognises the epistemic and cognitive dimensions of the process; beyond this, they need to recognise the fact of development and that development is not linear, that intellectual growth, for example, may involve temporary setbacks in rhetorical control.

When writing essays – public products – it is perhaps little wonder, given the strong rhetorical bias which accompanies the written word, and particularly the essay form, that students put aside their own uncertain ways of arguing in favour of the certainty of narrative knowledge and simple structure. If presentation really is to the detriment of generation, might it not be worth employing intermediary stages of writing or considering a redescription of the essay, which emphasised the mode of argument and of critical thinking? Critical thinking is an important term to use here, since it is more exclusively concerned with active cognitive process than the term argument. The inclusiveness of 'argument' in referring both to process and product is perhaps to a degree responsible for the confusion; like the word 'essay' it is both a 'trying out' (*essai*) and a handing-in. And too often in institutional settings the latter sense holds away. If education is a process of becoming, then the forms and situations offered to those involved in the process need to give potential for change and development. Alongside an awareness of rhetorical structures must be an awareness that writing can and must involve critical thinking processes. This may mean deferring emphasis on essay structure, in order that writing – like the small group discussion – may be thought of as a place to challenge and develop, both tentatively and assertively. It is not enough to provide students with the opportunity to argue amongst themselves: this does not provide them with the assurance that their contributions can be risked in wider contexts. If access to these contexts comes through writing, then writing has to be experienced as a form through which it is possible to think creatively and afresh rather than to repeat what has already been thought, usually by others.

Chapter Fifteen

ENGLISH 'A' LEVEL AND BEYOND: A CASE STUDY[*]

Sally Mitchell

Question: At this early stage how do you feel about the transition from sixth-form life to life in higher education?

Answer: I'm rather unsure as I expected that the standards expected would be harder but they're not; e.g. in English instead of expecting a greater understanding of certain 'principles' we have already studied, the subject has taken a shift in a different direction...Instead of doing character studies and interpretation of texts, we are applying headings such as 'sonnet and ode', 'authority', 'varieties of non-fictional prose'. (Laura, in a written questionnaire completed in her first year at the university)

When we talk about the development of understanding, we commonly draw on metaphors of dimension and proximity to express the direction in which we expect to be going or to be led. We talk about greater depth, wider perspectives, closer analysis, distanced evaluation. For Laura, in her first term at university, these metaphors come into conflict: for depth she gets width, for closeness, greater distance. Her sense of what it is to study English is shifted out of its expected path of development. How did Laura's sense of English at A level manifest itself and how did it change?

This discussion uses Laura's work in English in the upper sixth form and as a first-year undergraduate on a Combined Arts degree course in an attempt to characterise the kinds of 'principles' and shift that she recognises in each phase and to speculate more widely about the nature of English.

A level

At A level, Laura was considered to have a particular 'literary sensibility'. By this was meant, not so much the possession of 'a good brain', but such qualities as quickness of apprehension, intuition, flashes of insight and a 'quivering' to language. Despite these, however, Laura was not guaranteed the highest grade

---

[*] First published as Mitchell, S. 1994. 'English A level and beyond: a case study', *English in Education* 28 (2): 36–47.

at A level. Her fallibility lay in sustaining her insights in writing or building them into a case. In a sense, her very 'literariness' – the close attention to the details and nuances of texts – seemed to contribute to the unpredictability of her writing and work against the construction of argument. The gamble, then, was whether her examiners would recognise her qualities and value these as highly or above a well organised but less engaged essay. In the event, they did. Laura got the A grade her teacher was convinced she deserved.

To explore Laura's qualities I want to look at a coursework essay she wrote on Graham Swift's novel, *Waterland*. The title provides clues both to the essay itself and to the literary practices at A level more generally:

> How far is Tom Crick responsible for the bleak situation which he faces at the chronological end of the novel?

Waterland is structured by the juxtaposition of events from different eras and perspectives of history, and the chronological reading thus involves the reordering of the text: a skill and action assumed by the title rather than focused upon. The title does not address any effect of the novel's non-chronological order on the way in which Tom's responsibility can be read. In effect, the title allows the novel to be read as a mirror to Tom's life as a chronological, coherent entity, rather than, as would be equally possible, a complex textual mechanism, through which the notion of chronology is challenged. What the novel argues (about history as a chronological progression) is subordinated to what it narrates (a series of lives). By effacing textuality, the title invites a 'straightforward' concentration on character and event. Here is one of the central principles identified by Laura: the character study.

The title asks the reader to evaluate the degree of the character's responsibility, but on what basis she should go about this is not made explicit. Should she bring a moral code to the book or should she examine the degree to which the book itself suggests Tom's responsibility? The ambiguity is, I think, significant; if the reader is to achieve as close an identification as possible with the characters as people then there is a necessary glossing of those moral codes within the text and those brought to it.

The assumed consensus on moral value detectable in the title can be traced to the A level syllabus:

> The JMB recognises that the aim of a sixth form English course is to present the subject as a discipline that is humane (concerned with values), historical (setting literary works within the context of their age) and communicative (concerned with the integrity of language as a means of enabling human beings to convey their feelings one to another). (JMB, English Literature, Syllabus C)

The wording refers only tangentially to *texts*: it is the *discipline* that is humane, historical, communicative. These descriptions characterise the work done to texts, though by implication texts also become humane, historical, communicative. The merger of text, individual reader, collective readership, operates on an assumption of transparency, in which value, positionality, textuality are not at issue.

Laura's essay complies to a great extent with what I take to be the hidden assumptions of the title and syllabus. In the following paragraph, where Laura's recounting of the story (in italics here) is interspersed with direct quotations from the text, it is possible to see how closely reader and text are identified:

Parr's death draws us dramatically into the summer of 1943,
For this something was a body and body belonged to ...
this summer was also the beginning of Tom's awareness, and also the beginning of his Bleakness ...
and your teacher was no longer a babe.
He is linked with Parr's death simply because Dick, the murderer, is his brother, but also because of his and Mary's 'generosity', and their desire to educate Dick.
Dick killed Freddie Parr because he thought it was him which means we're to blame too.
Perhaps Tom's curiosity was driven to explore Dick's mind, Mary's to explore the contents of his swimming trunks
Mary's eyes – we all notice this – goggle,
but however innocent and charitable their childish love games were, they had dire results. The death of Freddie Parr.

The integration of the novel's text into her own suggests familiarity, a kind of empathy. At the same time, the origin of the question of responsibility or the linking of cause and effect is directly attributable neither to text nor reader. These appear as identical points of view – suggesting and complementing the novel's unity – until the word 'perhaps' is used, and here a slight gap appears. There is a tentative weighing of motive against consequence, leading to an evaluation of the characters' actions within the parameters of the story. But the story is not the same as the narration, and the issue of how the book itself might seem to beg the question of responsibility is not addressed. Nonetheless, the interweaving of the reader's interpretation with evidence from the text means that these distinctions blur; proximity is everything.

Laura's approach is highly valued by her teacher. She reads Laura's essay for evidence of close attention and imaginative engagement, reflected partly in her allusive use of language. She writes:

The whole of this page and the next in its analysis of Mary – a complex character – and of the marriage – equally demanding for a young reader – is impressive. I was constantly having my breath taken by Laura's insights. The ones I enjoyed most are marked:
... in doing so she killed the only thing likely to retrieve her spirit ...
and in Tom she willingly subjected herself to a life of emptiness ...
She had no illusions about marriage. She was not duped.

He never tried to retrieve the old Mary, or put excitement or purpose
into her life.
Perhaps he was a scared child still pretending not to notice.
... he could have taken some responsibility for past sins, past events –
but he just followed dazed ...

The teacher couches her evaluation in terms of enjoyment, subjective experience
– as with a literary text, the writing reflects the written about. She seems to
feel, moreover, that through her engagement Laura demonstrates an insight into
life.

The separation of text and reader and the attribution of point of view and
judgement – crucially important to the presentation of argument in other
subjects – does not seem, at this stage at least, to be part of 'literary sensibility'.
The use of the word 'perhaps' is the crux of this difference: it indicates the
reader's interpretative activity working on ambiguities and complexities in the
text, and at the same time stands in for an explicitly articulated position in
relation to it. Thus it mediates a position between sameness and otherness.

Perhaps Mary's curiosity was not to blame. Her curiosity, a need
always for exploration, was produced from the flatness, the deadness
of the fens. The responsibility she had of her father and his house
might also produce a necessity for something more. She may also have
been rebelling against her virtuous upbringing at St Gunnhildas ...
... Tom could have kept this knowledge to himself, as Henry had.
Perhaps he was trying to explain the events to himself.
Better not to learn. Better never to know. But once you've ...
I'm the one who had to dig up the truth.
Perhaps it was his historical mind, probing into the past, witnessing its
effect. Either way he should have considered the consequences, the
hurt he would have caused –
But once you've ...
But like Mary he was just a child. Just maturing ...

'Perhaps' shows the reader engaged in what Scholes (1985) has called the
construction of 'text upon text' (p. 24). The text Laura produces is one of
tentative, provisional meaning prompted by the moral question of responsibility.
It is in sympathy with the literary text, working with it to explore and uncover
meaning rather than taking a position in relation to it.

If understanding literature is in some sense always a case of 'perhaps', the
setting forth of a clear argument is of secondary importance, and in fact seems
almost a contradictory approach, to engaged and imaginative interpretation.
Interpretation does take place as argument, however:

In the same way Tom should not be blamed for his kindness, but he
could have stopped the events with Dick and Mary (perhaps), instead
of encouraging the seduction, which suggests a lacking in his own

character. A lacking of strength which is again shown in his own marriage, but we must not forget that Tom was only 15 and it seems without the guidance of his father, a man who worked all night, and was still preoccupied with his dead wife.

The argument here is a moral one. The first sentence contains two points of view, one exonerating Tom from blame, the other attributing it to him. Tom becomes blameworthy not simply because of a failure to act on one occasion – the failure to prevent the seduction – but because of a more general flaw in his character – a lack of strength. To reach this conclusion Laura interprets the event to give it meaning in terms of character, a generalisation that allows her to make a connection with another part of the book, Tom's marriage. Against this strengthening of her argument in favour of his guilt, she mitigates the blame in the second half of the last sentence by returning to the circumstances of the particular event.

The return to the particular is managed by the phrase 'we must not forget'. Looked at one way as just a figure of speech this phrase is, nonetheless, remarkably powerful. It signifies the position from which the statement is made as collectively agreed upon and in this sense it is ideological. It calls upon generalised social and moral standards of fairness, the need to show a balanced case. Whilst the phrase takes the argument away from the text and shows it to be constructed at one remove in a moral system that may or may not be that of the book, it also makes the writer a transparent cipher for these values. They are originless but also everywhere. Laura talks for the text through her interpretations of it, but she also, in the same breath, talks for the world. The combination of close, engaged, imaginative reading with an unarticulated, originless moral system points to the powerful paradox of collective subjectivity underpinning the discipline at this level.

Only when Laura writes '(perhaps)', qualifying her assertion of what Tom 'could have done', does the text 'talk back'. In the immutable 'world of the book', Tom didn't stop the events with Dick and Mary; what he 'could have' done is extratextual speculation. The text offers up no alternative endings and its fixity acts as a rein to the interpretative activity of the reader and to the argument. It is not in fact possible to go 'deeper' into character without abandoning the text. For the argument to be taken further whilst retaining a grounding in the text, a shift is required in which reader, text and world are prised apart. Being separate, the text is no longer transparent, but is in itself substantial, opaque, textual. The change in the text signals also a change in the reader: the text is read differently.

First-year undergraduate

When Laura got to university a shift was immediately signalled in a handout entitled 'Texts, modes and methods: how is level one English literature ... different from A level?' The writer suggests that what students have hitherto learned in a 'piecemeal' way will now be learned more systematically in a development from concentration on texts towards modes and methods, such as genres and 'topics like irony, rhythm, historicity and imagery'. Though the course begins by raising questions about the nature of literature and the purpose of studying it, generally a continuity is assumed with study at A level:

> The work in literature you are beginning is going to involve, for many of you, a change in the habits of study you have built up over the last few years. But, of course, your attraction to particular texts and authors is still at the heart of the whole process. If you continue with English you will find yourself coming to the texts you have chosen to study at levels 2 and 3 with a much wider, richer and more creative sense of how you can talk about them and in so doing explain yourself.

The model of learning here is circular: patterns are disrupted in order to allow for new forms of engagement motivated by the same basic principle. The belief in the subject as personally fulfilling accords with the humane objectives of A level and the sense in which Laura's *Waterland* essay could be read as a mature insight into and sophisticated handling of lived dilemmas.

An essay Laura wrote in her first undergraduate term illustrates the shift away from text towards modes and methods. Its title immediately suggests a new kind of focus:

> Who tells the story, why they tell it, how they tell it may be more significant than the story itself. Discuss in relation 'The Haystack in the Floods' by William Morris and 'My Last Duchess' by Robert Browning.

The texts are approached through a generalised statement aimed at confronting the difference between story and narration. Two texts rather than one are to be used, though in fact Laura manages only to address the first of them. In the written questionnaire which asked her to comment on her writing she put this down to:

> my own limitations in manipulating order of argument ... I wrote in too much detail for the first poem, and had difficulty in deciding how much relevance I should give to each point. I thus could not 'reduce' the essay.

Her comment indicates the constraints that working with the concept of narrator imposed; a need to select and prioritise in order to illustrate an understanding, not primarily of the poem, but of the concept. Reading for the way in which the poem made use of devices was not at this stage easy for Laura. Her reflections on the essay are highly perceptive and directly record her sense of the transitions she is being asked to make and her difficulty in shedding one literary habit for another:

[I] argue that the narrator's techniques and strategies have an important role in the production and success of fictional writing. That a series of events is not enough to create a 'great literary piece'.

I had great difficulty in keeping to the above argument. I kept referring to the text and its characters too often, instead of the mechanism behind the narrative ...

I think I had difficulties because I'm used to just giving an interpretation, instead of focusing upon the narrative style and production of a text ...

During the writing I began to realise how involved, and manipulative, the narrative process is. I usually don't analyse how the author attracts the attention of the reader etc. ... (From the questionnaire)

No longer a close interpretative relation between herself and text, reading is now mediated by a distancing awareness of the conditions under which interpretation is possible. There are traces of confusion here about where to attribute origin, which seem to arise in part from imprecise terminology. The 'mechanism' is described as behind the narrative, and the 'production' of the text is referred to as if separate from the text. Both the narrative and the text seem to be thought of as story.

The essay itself shows evidence of the struggle Laura senses. There is some confusion throughout between the 'omniscient narrator', Morris (the poet), and the heroine Jehare. Where Laura talks about the function of the narrator it is often in generalised terms, as if she cannot quite reconcile her reading with the particular kind of analysis she is trying to apply (square brackets contain the teacher's comments):

How the narrator portrays [is used to portray] the characters is also of importance, because this is how one obtains [what establishes] the mood and emotional depth of the poem. Again Morris refuses to fulfil the reader's romantic appetite, or conform to convention. With Robert and Jehare the sexual roles are reversed ...

Notice how the teacher's comments pick up on Laura's attribution of origin and point of view: the narrator does not portray but *is used to portray* – behind the narrator is the poet – in order *to establish*. Where at A level there was a blurring of the origins of effects and judgements, which, whilst it heightened the empathy of the reading, inhibited the development of a critical position, here the text is broken down into a constellation of attributed techniques and effects. The teacher guides Laura towards locating these within a precise model of the communicative structure, in which the narrator is the agent of an unspecified authorial source. The separation begins to make possible a judgement of the text, based on criteria other than and in addition to character and event. In the case of 'The Haystack in the Floods' Laura is able to see how the effects of the poem are brought about by narrative choices and to make a link outwards to how the poem is situated within a tradition. She needs the idea of the tradition, of course, to do this:

> The narrator focuses more upon Godmar than Robert, thus we identify more with Godmar. His speech is more powerful, his emotions more intense and compelling.
>
> Thus by focusing on Godmar and Jehare, instead of the conventional Hero and Heroine, the narrator is able to mock the ineffectuality of love. Faced with the callous, unemotional and demanding Godmar, Robert is a submissive parody relationship between Godmar and Jehare, the narrator also creates a fascinating sexual tension which has to be resolved. We are compelled to read on, and Robert is merely incidental.

The analysis is not fully developed. The narrative reading creates Godmar as a kind of hero, whilst a character reading shows him to be 'callous, unemotional and demanding', but the contradiction is not examined. To go further Laura would need to draw significance from or 'read' the clash itself. This is where the metaphor of distance begins to turn back into a metaphor of depth: by operating at one further remove, she would, one could say, move closer to an understanding of how the text works. This movement is a kind of dialectic in which contradictory positions are brought together to form a new level of understanding. Such a synthesis is only possible where positions are first differentiated.

Given the approach developing in the first term of study, Laura's essay on realism, written towards the end of the first year for examination purposes is in one way surprising, in another, confirmatory. There is a fundamental difficulty in the way that Laura understands the essay title:

> Realism does not tell us how it is. It is through various artistic devices that the writer of realistic fiction gives to his characters and action that familiarity which makes them seem like actual people and events. Discuss with relation to two texts.

Though the title appears to prompt a move away from the treatment of characters and action as people and events, Laura does not seem fully equipped to achieve this. Her comments on the essay reveal an underlying confusion between the implicit discourse of A level (about believability, psychological wholeness, life) and the more technical approach of the undergraduate course:

> That to reproduce a realistic situation is not enough. You have to make the reader believe in the characters/situation. You have to evoke a response using structural devices etc.
>
> I feel I have shown how the author makes the text 'familiar', but the beginning of the essay title 'Realism does not tell how it is' produced

some concern. I wasn't quite sure just what they were trying to
establish. 'How is it?' (From the questionnaire)

Laura's explanation obscures the distinction between Realism, the realistic and
the real. By suggesting that the mediating actions (structural devices) of the
writer distinguish between mere reproduction and believable reproduction, she
avoids confronting the crucial fact that in each case reality is mediated. Her
confusion over the real and the represented, the believable and the stylised,
continues in later comments:

> I think a work achieves 'real' success if it mirrors and appreciates the
> haphazard reality of society. If it is believable it doesn't generally have
> to be wooden or predictable. I think an individual's idea of real life is
> obtained from experience. If one can empathize with the
> characters/situation in the novel, one can believe in it more. (Perhaps it
> also has to be heightened experience so that the reader is startled by the
> intimacy or force of the emotion, to create a more intimate relationship
> between reader and novel.) (From the questionnaire)

It is characteristic of Laura that she should describe the reading experience so
eloquently and engage with a sense of complexity, rather than formula. At the
same time she seems to sense, though not articulate, the paradox of appealing to
both the real life experience of the reader and the 'heightened experience'
offered by the literary encounter. Her account corresponds to the approach and
beliefs underlying the *Waterland* essay, and testifies to the ideology of collective
subjectivity identified there. For, if Realism's success is measured by its appeal
to an individual's experience, then it is likely to be different for every reader.
Only by an assumption that all readers' experiences are in some way similar,
can Realism be said to be about the real. What Laura describes in terms of an
individual psychological truth is in fact based upon a social consensus, a set of
conventions.

Laura makes this general introduction to her essay:

> We experience familiarity when reading a text because it provides a
> sense of comparable recognition of human nature as it is in our lives.
> For example we rarely believe heroics because few people are really
> heroic in real life, at least not in contemporary Britain. Having
> established that realism has to be believable, one also has to recognise
> that when told 'one-dimensionally' it may be felt as insipid, or too
> close to real existence. The individual aspires all one's life to escape its
> negative side, its unpleasantness, unless one is inspired or strangely
> invigorated by it. When one reads a work portraying reality, one is
> exposed, if the work succeeds to an intense paradox. One is comforted
> by the realism; the tragedy. One's isolation is reduced; one empathises
> with the characters within the text. One is familiar with their emotions.

Again this overview is imbued with Laura's strong emotional and imaginative sense of the reading experience, but also with unexamined contradictions. What is noticeable is the extent to which her idea of real life is drawn from literary representations of life – tragedy, the cathartic power of suffering – so that her understanding of realism is, in a sense, a constant reconfirmation of itself. The metaphor of depth is lurking somewhere here, for it is as if the 'work portraying reality' allows one to see life in greater profundity, in more than 'one-dimension'. Again, the text is transparent, a pool of meaning; yet, in fact, the text is only surface.

Laura's misreading of the Realism title seems to derive from the centrality which characterisation still plays in her reading. Her text is smattered with references to what it is 'really' like to be human:

> They are strange creatures – restrained, suppressed, preoccupied with trivialities – but we recognise the relationships, we understand why they are so suppressed (because of the colonel), and we recognise their system of values. They are also primarily human. They are weak – 'But it seems so weak', said Josephine, breaking down. 'But why not be weak for once Jug?' (page 228) – they put things off, they are cowards and have been all their lives. We can forgive them for this though, because we are all weak, we are all afraid, at some stage, of the bogeyman in the cupboard.

Again, the position taken by the reader is not articulated or made explicit (again the 'we' is ideological): which readers, whose values? The argument goes that the characters are realistic, because they are 'essentially likeable'; they have emotions that are 'human ones'. The moral frameworks of the reader and the characters coincide. Laura is complicit with their evaluation of themselves as weak and with the sense that weakness is a moral fault, however forgivable. She makes no move to consider what the characters might be being 'used to portray' or to consider the validity of the weak/strong criterion for judging moral worth (which was also used in the *Waterland* essay).

In the following extract the link with Realism and a particular set of social beliefs and behaviours is again unconsciously made:

> The language also helps to create the illusion of reality. The sense of the upper middle classes is continually affirmed by the use of 'dear boy' and 'your dear father', and the use of adjectives, for example 'You're perfectly right. Father's most frightfully keen on meringues'. It all serves to re-establish the sense of middle class niceties, and good manners. Even the names themselves conform to our expectations of the 20s – Cyril, Constantia and Josephine.

The equation of 'reality' with the life of the upper middle classes reads rather startlingly as false consciousness. The presumption that this is what life was like in the 1920s can be based only on representations, and these representations become the touchstone of reality; she is caught in an ideological double bind.

Ultimately Realism conforms to humanistic values and the essay becomes a celebration, rather than a critique of these. This is the conclusion:

> Thus Realism is primarily about reader response and the emotions that are evoked. If the author is successful, he will have intuitively presented us with a living body of work, not just a realistic situation. The characters will live on in the memory like friends, or even enemies. They will continually conform to reality. This does not mean that they will not surprise us, however, because that is real too.

Again textuality has disappeared and the characters have taken on an independent life of their own. They become the world 'as it is'. What the world is, though – to return to Laura's question 'How is it? – seems rather banal. That in reality people are capable of surprising, that they are 'primarily human' are less truths than truisms.

Much of Laura's essay displays sensitivity and insight entirely consistent with the approach recognised and valued at A level, but working obediently with the incompletely understood idea of Realism limits her development. My surprise at the essay stems not from Laura's lack of awareness of the double bind she is in, and the consequent slippage between Realism and the real (which oversimplifies them both), but the uncritical response of the essay marker, who praises the conclusion as excellent and who gives the essay an A grade. This teacher fails to give Laura the analytic tools with which she could identify the Realist encoding of a text and thereby examine its moral presuppositions. If, through such an examination, she were led to foreground and reflect on her own value systems, the function of English in helping the reader to 'explain herself' would be realised much more powerfully – through reflexivity rather than reflex.

Open questions

The teacher's assessment seems to me to question the degree to which the consensual values of study at A level (if my limited interpretation is correct) are undermined at undergraduate level. The follow-on question is whether the values and the 'literary sensibility' which Laura showed at A level through an empathetic, largely uncritical approach to character are *foundational* to English as a discipline. It is perhaps no coincidence that this question should be raised in relation to an essay on Realism, a convention that was flourishing at the time when the foundations of literary study were being laid down. If such values are foundational, then to what extent can we expect them to be challenged later on?

What difference would there be if students were to undertake earlier the kind of structural analysis Laura encountered in her first term at university? Would we worry that something (say, pleasure) would be lost? If so, are there other sorts of pleasure (than that derived primarily from stories and characters)? Are other sorts of foundations possible or desirable or would English, if it adopted these, cease to exist as a discipline?

I have two suggestions about foundations, both of which disrupt the idea of foundations itself. The first is developed from Scholes' hierarchy of progression in English: reading 'text within text', interpretation 'text upon text', criticism 'text against text' (Scholes, 1985, p. 24). These operations seem to me useful, but I would suggest that they need to be seen as a circle of recurrently refined and developing skills rather than as a hierarchy. A reader who has articulated a critical position returns to reading with an enriched repertoire of interpretative codes and these in turn challenge the critical perspective. With a circular model it is less determined where literary engagement should begin or end, each activity being valid in relation to the others and each – and this is most important – suggesting a possible further move.

My second suggestion is that the engagement with literature be thought of as dialogic. This is important in fact if the student is to operate with the model above, since she cannot make effective switches in activity, without a sense of distinction between the text and herself.

Dialogue is predicated upon separation, the difference between points of view (the text, the reader, the social convention), but is also a process by which contact is made and meaning generated and exchanged. The dialogic principle resists the subsumption of one position into another; it resists the monologic 'we' of ideology (and impersonal discourse) and insists on clarification and questioning. This is, I think, as important in the relationship between teacher (assessor) and student as between student and text. I can't help thinking that a sense of dialogic relation is the way in which Laura might reconcile both closeness to and distance from the texts she reads. This would not preclude the role of subjectivity, but would require awareness and expression of who and what the subject is.

Note

1. See also Mitchell (1992) for a discussion of the tendency towards consensus in discussion in English.

Chapter Sixteen

THE AESTHETIC AND THE ACADEMIC – ARE THEY AT ODDS IN ENGLISH LITERATURE AT 'A' LEVEL?[*]

Sally Mitchell

This discussion largely concerns a single essay written at English A level. The essay is only a fragment of evidence yet it provides a rich stimulus for thought and speculation about the nature of English at this level of study. The subject of the essay is poetry – more specifically, the poetry of Sylvia Plath. What might be expected of such an essay? What responses to poetry might be possible within it?

Possible responses to poetry

Rosenblatt (1978) makes what seems to be a basic distinction between different reading responses; one which is highly relevant to the institutional setting in which my fragment of evidence was produced:

> As the reader responds to the printed words or symbols, his attention is directed outward, so to speak, towards concepts to be retained, ideas to be tested, actions to be retained after the reading.

> To designate this type of reading, in which the primary concern of the reader is with what he will carry away from the reading, I have chosen the term 'efferent', derived from the Latin, 'efferre', to carry away ...

> In aesthetic reading, in contrast, the reader's primary concern is with what happens during the actual reading event. Though, like the efferent reader of a law text, say, the reader of Frost's 'Birches' must decipher the images or concepts or assertions that the words point to, he also pays attention to the associations, feelings, attitudes, and ideas that these words and their referents arouse within him. 'Listening to' himself, he synthesises these elements into a meaningful structure. In aesthetic reading, the reader's attention is centred directly on what he

---

[*] Previously published as Mitchell, S. 1993. 'The aesthetic and the academic: are they at odds in English literature at A level?', *English in Education* 27 (1): 19–28.

is living through during his relationship with that particular text. (pp. 24-5)

Rosenblatt's account suggests that the object of attention is constituted as meaningful by the response which is made to it. An efferent or non-aesthetic response is essentially recognitive; the object of attention made meaningful when it finds a place within an existing cognitive or affective structure. A non-aesthetic trip around an art gallery, for instance, would be satisfactorily completed once the viewer had determined what the paintings and sculptures depicted and to which schools and genres they belonged. Such considerations might form part of an aesthetic response, but they would not be the end of it. In aesthetic responding, the object of attention is the point of constant reference and return. Attention is paid to surface shapes and textures, to nuance and ambiguity. Aesthetic response is typically developing rather than developed; it is dissatisfied with simple recognition of, say, a theme, image or style – and resists closure, the categorical arrival at meaning. Aesthetic meaning is not a singular thing but is provisional, dependent upon context; a kind of perceptually-grounded questioning.

The efferent or non-aesthetic response is, then, one which derives from and arrives at consensual public meanings, whilst those developed through aesthetic engagement are more likely to be personal, idiosyncratic, speculative and untested. In the educational context it is important to consider which form of response is most frequently elicited from students and - importantly, too – to what ends it is elicited. This question is central to what we understand by the subject of English.

Efferent or aesthetic responses in the essay

It may be that it is students' initial responses to poetry that are best characterised as aesthetic, though most school readings carry with them from the outset an efferent imperative. If the response is to have a final form it is usually a written one: an essay. The essay is the outcome of a process which is likely to have had several stages of development, from private to collective readings, group and class discussions. In writing publically and in an assessable form about poetry, what then becomes of the personal and experimental? Is the process of discussing, sharing and eventually writing about poetry a process in which aesthetic reading eventually becomes efferent reading?

To characterise the process of reading and writing this way is in a sense an oversimplification. It detracts from the potentiality in the writing process itself for a new discovery and insight. The question remains, despite the status of the essay as final product, whether the responses it communicates are full formed (carried away) before writing begins or whether there is space in the act (task) of writing itself for the development of (aesthetic) response. The essay I look at here suggests that these two different forms of writing and response may indeed be part of a single writing task. As a result there is a conflict in the way the poems themselves are characterised.

Jack's essay

There is a space here to examine closely only part of the essay; nevertheless this provides an indication of the approach taken by the writer, Jack, in the text as a whole. The essay is entitled: 'Sylvia Plath: illness and death in her poetry'. In this formulation the emphasis is on the poet who is juxtaposed with two themes to be found (by implication) in her poetry. This title is a significant clue to the structure and content of the rest of the essay. Did the writer simply write his response to the poetry and afterwards find an appropriate title? Or did the title come first? The evidence of the essay itself suggests that the latter is the case, though the origin of the title – student or teacher? – is unknown. There is, of course, a standard decorum about such an activity: choose (or more likely, particularly in assessment situations, be given) a topic, make a plan, write the essay.

The title proposes three subjects: the poet and two themes; the absence of a verb means that no transaction takes place between them, neither is a connection brought about by a question. The effect is one of stasis, an implication that the task is one of categorical recognition; exposition rather than exploration. In a crude sense there may be a connection here between the positing of categorical – as opposed to transactional[1] – meaning and authority. It would certainly be characteristic of Jack to have transformed an essay *question* into a succinctly thematic title, thereby reconstructing the actual student/teacher context of his writing as one of author/general reader. The claim to authorial or authoritative status through the creation of categories or generalisations is a feature which suggests itself again in the body of the essay. And in a related sense the absence (or disappearance) of a question in the title here also has significant resonances further on. Answers rather than questions are the preferred means of resolution, even where this leaves inconsistency unaddressed.

The essay's title, then, can be seen as the first clash between academic writing and aesthetic response. The essay is carefully organised: it contains an introduction, conclusion and five paragraphs on each of the themes. The themes are treated separately; illness first, located in individual poems, followed by death, located in largely the same poems. In between these two 'halves' of the essay is a pivotal paragraph concluding one treatment and making way for the other. Jack has a fluent style which in part seems to derive from a strong sense of audience; language used to persuade. He seems highly conscious of the

---

[1] Rosenblatt uses 'transaction' to describe the relationship between text and reader, describing it as "an ongoing process in which the elements or factors are, one might say, aspects of a total situation, each conditioned by and conditioning the other". (1978, p17)

conventions to which he is working, at least as far as the essay form is concerned.

What of this form? At A level the essay assumes great importance in the work of students, particularly of the humanities and arts; it is the primary form of both expression and assessment. The situation remains throughout higher education: essay writing is the pursuit of the academically-oriented, degree-destined student. Described as a genre, the essay is a recurring type of text, defined and understood by the context of its production and reception: a text, which in a sense speaks to its context through the forms and strategies it employs (introduction, conclusion, coherently linking middle paragraphs, and so on) as much as through its particular content. How does this generic voice affect the student's responses to the poetry of Sylvia Plath? How does form structure content?

The introduction

The introduction is a major feature of the essay form, functioning structurally and generically to organise what is to be said and to establish the level and nature of the relationship between writer and reader. Jack's introduction has a framing effect on the scope and stance of writing which follows:

> (1) Many of Sylvia Plath's poems explore the theme of illness and death, yet this does not make all these particular poems the same. (2) Plath treats these two subjects in several different ways; she considers the aspect of illness and death being welcome, in the sense that it allows for relaxation and genuine recuperation. (3) In this way illness can be regarded as a chance to revitalise oneself. (4) Contrasting pieces of her work let her vulnerability show through, and her sense of insecurity with the prospect of facing death or a long illness. (5) It has been said that Plath was almost schizophrenic, and the varying ways she approaches writing about illness could well suggest this. (6) Some poems convey a very positive attitude, where it seems that Plath is at one with the world and herself. (7) Then there are poems in the collection which suggest that Plath was angry and frustrated. (8) Other strong feelings in Plath's work include insecurity as in the 'Bee Meeting', and 'Fever 103' shows how active her mind was even when ill, turning ideas over in her head. [Sentences numbered by me]

As well as a sense of the writer's reading of Plath's poetry, the introduction creates a general context – a system of rules and taken-for-granteds. This interpretive or recognitive framework is used by Jack to substantiate his particular reading of this particular poet. Immediately, in the first sentence, the notion of thematic sameness becomes the bedrock from which he will argue his reading. Generically (that is, regarding the form in which the student is writing) it seems important that the sentence should convey an impression of logic; there is authority in the argumentative or argued form of the syntax. Yet this thematising is an efferent response, which results, not ultimately, but as a prerequisite, in closure. The poems do not so much end up, but rather begin by being about two things: illness and death. These categories are unargued, unchallenged and inexplicit within the whole of the essay. How satisfactory is this? Should Jack be encouraged to articulate his general understandings and test them against his reading experience? Is there a place for such self-questioning in essays of this kind?

The second sentence develops the implications of the first in referring to the themes as *treated and considered* by the poet. Plath, the active poet, is the subject or agent of the sentence. The poems themselves are, by implication, transparent ciphers to the action and intention of the poet. She, however, is not straightforwardly the origin; Jack seems also to sense that other agents of meaning are at work, principally himself as reader. He is, though, unable to articulate these sources; in sentences 3 and 4 the agents are invisible or effaced. In sentence 4, for example, does Jack mean that when he contrasts the poems he gets a sense of the poet's vulnerability or that different poems all reveal her vulnerability?

Very rarely in the essay as a whole does an aspect of or quotation from the poem form the subject of a sentence; the words of the poems themselves are not shown to have a function or to elicit a response. In these sentences, for instance, the use of 'pebble' indicates Jack's knowledge of the poem, but overrides attention to what and how the word itself means *in* the poem:

Sylvia Plath's sense of vulnerability and inferiority amongst others is a source for her writing to be resentful and bitter. But in 'Tulips', being ill and her body being a 'pebble' for others to tend is something she seems to regard as enjoyable, even cleansing and therefore she becomes pure.

It may seem pedantic to pay such close attention to the construction of individual sentences but it is these which offer clues to the way the writer is organising his response. The sentences raise what is for me the crucial question of ownership; who is responsible for the interpretation of the poems and what is the role of the reader within the essay?

Since he does not locate himself within the essay, Jack is caused to name Plath as the agent of the themes and effects he (in fact) identifies within the poems. As a result the themes of illness and death appear to belong to Plath and not be a construction of the essay's title and the student's writing. This conflation of Plath-with-the-poems-with-the-themes becomes more explicit in sentence 5 of the introduction where a suggestion about the poet's biography is substantiated not through the poems but through a linguistic construction in which Plath 'approaches writing'; Plath's schizophrenia is in direct relation to her act of writing, which can in turn be imputed directly from the poems. The implications contained in this sentence are more explicit in the next, where what the poems convey is directly attributable to their author. In these sentences the poems themselves seem to disappear.

The introduction sets up a framework through which the poems are analysed or treated. Though apparently comprehensive, this framework is an oversimplification of the act of writing (Plath's authorship) and a constraint upon the act of reading (Jack's response). There is little sense of the poems as worked on by any agent other than the poet. The student himself is absent from the text he is writing. In order to acknowledge his position Jack need not necessarily write in the first person: to disguise himself as an anonymous general reader would do just as well, perhaps better, given the academic convention. But if a poem or any literary text is to be understood – as I would argue it should be – as a construction made meaningful only through 'transaction', then a position for the reader in a written response seems vital.

By way of comparison here is a section from the opening paragraph of another student's essay. She writes:

> Instead of exploring the options for women, Plath attacks the roles present, and this way, through a narrator, we can grasp many of Plath's emotions. In fact because the poems are so assertive, so extreme, it is difficult not to feel that these relate to her own life, that these poems are Plath's experiences.

This student also asserts that there is a relation between the poet and the poems, but she makes explicit two other factors: a narrator and a reader. She justifies a biographical interpretation of the poems by a reference to their effect: 'so assertive, so extreme' so that the reader is compelled to understand the poems by reference beyond them. This it seems to me is a comment about the poems before it is a comment about their author. Though the reasoning is not entirely consistent, the positions through which meaning is constructed are in place. These positions enable the writer to bridge the gap between subjective and public response, by creating (making explicit) positions of self and otherness which are rooted in the textual transaction. As a further development of this response the transaction itself might become the object of the writer's critical reflection or reflexivity. Aesthetic response is nurtured by such awareness and acceptance of personal voice.

Conflict between categorical and narrative readings

The second paragraph of Jack's essay begins the more detailed consideration of the poems. It enacts a representative conflict between the thematic unifying framework of the essay and the reading response of the student:

> (1) Plath considers, sometimes, illness to be a state worth welcoming, it takes away responsibility and can be a period when one can relax properly with no expectancy or dependency being laid upon you. (2)

This is a positive view of illness and an opinion incorporated within 'Tulips'. (3) However the overall outlook of this poem is not so optimistic, Plath does not relish any prospect of spending time in hospital. (4) Being made to feel helpless by the nurse invokes a sense of emptiness within her, and she begins to see herself as inadequate. (5) She has 'let things slip' and the nurses 'swab [her] clear of [her] loving associations'. (6) The poem could be written after an attempt at suicide. (7) She says 'I am nobody'. (8) This sense of desperation in the first half of the poem mellows as the piece progresses. (9) Plath is enjoying being free and peaceful. (10) The 'peacefulness' is 'so big it dazes you, and it asks nothing'. She is quite happy to be left alone. (11) 'To lie with my hands turned up and be utterly empty. How free it is, ... you have no idea'. (12) Perhaps Plath is exhausted, desperately in need of rest, and so the hospital peacefulness is what she needs as 'it asks nothing'. [Again, my numbers]

The paragraph opens with a reiteration of the first point made in the introduction about the welcomeness of illness – according to Plath – as if stated by her. The opinion is described as *incorporated within* the poem 'Tulips'. As I have suggested, there is no position in the essay, which would allow it to be *interpreted from*. Jack's evaluation is in a summarising form: 'This is a positive view of illness'. Though he does not say that the opinion constitutes the whole poem he does imply that it is a whole entity within the poem and that it is somehow extractable from it. This tendency towards a categorical reading is undercut however by a number of suggestions: the tentative 'sometimes' in the first sentence, the more obviously signposted qualification 'However' which begins sentence 3 and then the concession that the rest of the poem is in fact 'not so optimistic'. This revised assessment is supported by statements, which again are referenced to the poet rather than the poem or the reader.

What is apparent here is Jack's need to attribute the feelings of the poem. There are a number of options. The reader, the writer, the words themselves (which may constitute a narrative voice); though these, as we have seen, are not all available to this writer. According to my view of the text, only the reader and the words are actually present in the reading situation and yet it seems here that the sense of the words is most easily attributable to the absent factor. John writes, for example, that the 'sense of emptiness', is within 'her', the poet, rather than in the words (which, yes, the poet has chosen and arranged) and/or in the responding reader: a sense of emptiness created by the reading transaction.

How useful might the notion of *narrative voice* be to Jack? The complementary role to the narrator is that of the narratee. Having a sense of these two positions might allow him to deal with his awareness, and at the same time prevent him from operating at a remove from the words by recreating the poet herself. The sense he has of a speaker would then become a product of the reading experience in which he himself plays a vital constituent role.

Towards the end of the paragraph the poem is approached in a different way; whereas in sentence 3 it had an 'overall outlook', now it is treated as a progression (sentence 7). Increasingly quotations from the poem are integrated with Jack's ideas, suggesting a developing attention to the text itself. Jack notes a change in the poem; it does not, in fact, all say the same thing. The 'overall outlook' (3) which is 'not so optimistic' is actually a reading of the 'sense of desperation in the first half of the poem' (7) whilst the 'positive view of illness' (2) (an opinion incorporated within 'Tulips') develops 'as the piece progresses' (7). When Jack, then, having categorised the poem, goes on discursively to explore (to read) the finer details (a search, perhaps, for illustrative material), he reveals that the poem resists categorisation; it has a changing mood. Jack does not remark explicitly the contradiction between his thematic approach and his narrative reading (the poem from beginning to end), but the paragraph's final sentence (12) could perhaps be seen as an attempt to resolve it. He draws again on the possible biography of the poet and by suggesting that she may be exhausted he is able to reconcile the positive with the negative aspects of illness he detects in the poem. The figure of the poet thus has a similarly organising and unifying function as, say, the phrase 'overall outlook'. It brings the reading of the poem back into line with the thematic intent set out in the introduction.

But the resolution is uneasy, excluding as it does consideration of internal contradictions and developments within the poems and silencing the role played by the reader in the co-production of the poems' meanings. By a kind of paradox, the paragraph might have been better ended by the formulation of a question or the articulation (voicing) of the problem: 'Why can't I reconcile these moods?'

Generalising in order to belong

Jack's approach can be contextualised, however, by the observations of John Dixon (1989). In examining the ways in which established literary critics discussed Wallace Stevens' poem 'Not Ideas about the Thing, but the Thing Itself' he notes as interesting the critics' use of 'the generic choices':

> *It is a ___ poem*
> *It is a poem of ___*
>   *a poem of having ___ed* (p. 123)

He comments:

> The impulse, it seems to me, is to categorise, and to offer a single unifying category. What is more, the category is treated as if it is reported in the poem (as a previous event), not dramatically enacted (within the poem). (p. 123)

Where the critics did refer to shifts in the mood of the poem they did not pursue their observations, nor could they make much comment on the several different interpretations they came up with. Dixon wonders:

> ... How is that possible? Basically, I believe, because the generic choice is to generalise, not to narrate. Narrative could hardly fail to incorporate feelings and speech acts within its structures; in generalised discussion and argument they can too easily be excluded. (p. 124)

These observations make it possible to read Jack's essay as displaying characteristics derived from a literary, critical and academic practice which excludes 'feelings and speech acts'. Such generalising practice may also be part of the conventions of essay writing. How far does the essay form promote a tendency to work from generalities and apparent (because unchallenged) certainties? Did Jack open his paragraph in a categorical way because he sensed that a well-constructed paragraph argues a point, presenting it first in summary form – a mini-argument: 'This ... However, that ...' – before going on to substantiate it? There certainly seems to be this generic element to the writing. Jack's adept use of stylistic convention orients his writing towards a display of confidence in *judgement* (supported by the unchallenged underlying assumptions) and in *intention* – the essay has a clear structure and sense of direction; it knows what it wants to say. The form, that is to say, is used to structure thought.

In terms of academic writing, referencing to knowledge beyond the poems themselves is a way of establishing oneself within a public collectivity and of giving oneself authority. Consider, as a final extract, the paragraph I mentioned above as a pivot between the two thematic halves of the essay:

> These contrasting ways of approaching the theme of illness I think show a strength in Sylvia's writing. By writing about the same theme in several different ways shows that Plath was objective in her work. The amusement at cutting herself with the desperation at the pain and her suffering when she is ill and the contented peacefulness in hospital are three different aspects of being ill. A poet could easily have written all these poems in the same vein, but Plath didn't. That it was a conscious thing to make the poems different and deliberately approach the theme of illness in several ways is unlikely. From what I have learned about Plath, it is more likely that each poem was written separately and reflected how she was feeling at the time.

The paragraph fulfils a structural necessity. The thematic treatment demands consolidation; the theme becomes a theme by being generalisable. The paragraph appears to be given over to summary, evaluation and argument; a kind of detached standing back from the individual treatment of the poems. Yet what does it, in fact, argue? The writer's evaluation takes the form of praise for thematic variation; Plath has exceeded expectations of the role of poet (implicitly, to explore themes) by managing to do this in several different ways. Jack accounts for this achievement by a psychological idea suggesting that Plath's writing was a sporadic and unconscious activity, prompted by individual circumstances. Plath, so the argument suggests, is differentiated from other poets in this respect.

There is something obvious about all this and I am tempted to dismiss what is being said as 'pseudo-argument'; based, that is, on factors which are spurious or fallacious. Yet something else is perhaps going on here: we get an insight into how a poet can be individualised and valorised amongst the community of poets. In a very real sense it is the decision to treat the poems thematically and as a single 'authorised' unit which allows this process of acceptance to take place. The argument perhaps has little to do with an aesthetic engagement or evaluation of Plath's work; it may, though, be forging a valid place for Plath within a different set of criteria. Do these criteria constitute a collective and public domain: the academic study of literature, the literary critical establishment?

Can the academic and the aesthetic coexist?

Looking closely, though by no means exhaustively, at this single student text has raised a number of questions about the practices in which students of literature are engaged and, I hope, opened some of these to challenge. What do we expect from students: that they be both critical and perceptually engaged, that they be both rigorous and sensitive in their thought? The JMB A level syllabus C, for which this essay was written, says something like this when it asks for students to:

> ... express in writing responses to reading that are first-hand as well as appropriate to the matter; that is, neither self-indulgently idiosyncratic nor mere restatements of received opinion.

How can students achieve such a difficult balance? How can both the public academic and the personal aesthetic features of literary study be reconciled in a form of writing which is both critical and perceptually engaged? The problem, I believe, revolves at least in part around the written form in which students are required to respond.

It is often assumed that the standard essay form (introduction, middle, conclusion) is a sufficiently adequate structure within which to develop thought. The essay form, that is, is seen as providing a structure for argument. Yet the disciplinary activity itself is not constituted by the formal features of the essay. It is something different; it has its own peculiar internal structures and ways of making meaning. The essay form represents only an external structure. What has a conclusion to do with aesthetic response? How can an introduction interrogate the reading of a poem? These are not the structures, which will allow for a critical treatment of the ways meaning is made in literary study. Yet they are often the only structures to which students at this level of study are given access.

Thought, which is true to the fundamental and defining activity of the subject – in this case, reading – needs to be structured internally as a critical understanding of the activity itself. To provide well-thought-out responses students need access to organising tools besides those of point-making and paragraphing; they need access to the fundamentals of their study, to an understanding of the processes they are engaged in, the ways in which meanings are made and structured. Such awarenesses would legitimise open aesthetic response, making space for tentativeness, provisionality, and renewal. Theories of the text and of reading are accepted as the legitimate and, I believe, necessary concerns of teachers and researchers. Are they really too sophisticated for the students who are engaged most intimately in the practice of the discipline? I'm not suggesting that awareness of possible responses and types of engagement should become a separate focus of study – critical theory tacked on – but rather that this be integrated into a practice which is rigorously and fundamentally reflexive, questioning and ongoing. English approached in this way might have a transforming effect on the essay, make it subservient to developing thought rather than the straightjacket for it. There is, after all, no imperative reason why the essay form need favour answers rather than questions, reduction rather than complexity; these are no less successful at structuring thought.

If in general terms academic study is about learning to structure and control material, then this discussion has I think suggested that there are alternatives as to where this structure should originate: external structuring provided by the learned form of the essay or internal structuring derived from the defining activity of the subject itself; from reading. In providing students with a structure for critical self-awareness – the notion, for instance, of narrator and narratee – thought is organised less by the conventionalised constraints of the written form than by a reflexive awareness of what is involved in response itself. An awareness of process, which would include the generation and pursuit of questions, might be the very way in which living, aesthetic response to poetic form could be reconciled to the critical demands of academic study – and the efferent demands of the essay form be surpassed with a more vital but no less rigorous form of structure.

CHAPTER SEVENTEEN

LEARNING TO ARGUE IN ENGLISH [*]

Sally Mitchell

This chapter emerged from the 16 to first-degree level project (the third project mentioned in the Preface) on argument. It attempts to offer a flavour of the project's general approach to the teaching and learning of argument and the kinds of outcome it resulted in. Its central theme is a critique of the essay form.

The methodology of the project was broadly ethnographic. I was interested in *instances* of argument and, more than this, in the contexts in which it took place, the systems of power and access which shaped it, the ways in which it could be legitimately expressed, the conventions of communication, the other activities or areas of competence on which it was perceived to be grounded and which it, in turn, enabled to take place. So the 'argument' I was concerned with was far from being an abstract or ideal formulation or process; it was far more – to quote Clifford Geertz (1983, p153) – 'muscular' than that. Geertz in fact has the phrase which sums up my main approach: he talks about 'an ethnography of thought', constituted around:

> The belief that ideation, subtle or otherwise, is a cultural artefact. Like class and power, it [thought/argument] is something to be characterized by construing its expressions in terms of the activities that sustain them. (1983, 152)

If this approach was largely descriptive and analytic, seeking to characterize and interpret what was there in the field situation, the research had an additional orientation: it was pedagogical. It was looking, that is, for ways in which what was observed of the practice of argument might be done better (the better achievement of existing goals) or done differently (the re-evaluation and reworking of the goals themselves).

The relation between the ethnographic and pedagogic was central to the findings of the project and I want to explore them here through a particular instance – learning to argue in English Literary Theory.

[*] First published as Mitchell, S. 1995. 'Learning to argue in disciplinary discourses' in *Proceedings of the Third ISSA Conference on Argumentation Volume III: Reconstruction and Application*, University of Amsterdam: SICSAT, pp. 304–12.

Radical content/conservative form

When I observed the subject of English at A level the primary activity of students appeared to be interpretation – the uncovering of coherent meanings or narratives within a text – rather than argument or criticism which would be more suspicious activities, interested in change, incoherence, discontinuities, contradictions. The objects of literary study were on the whole validated, reinforced, shown to be unified by the types of reading and writing used at A level, and at the same time this approach was naturalised by being thought of as unmediated response.

This situation looked set to change when in the first year of undergraduate teaching in English which I observed, students took a course on Literary Theory. One impulse behind the course was to allow students to see themselves as historically and culturally situated, part of a tradition going back to Matthew Arnold: this can be seen as a motive to unsettle, destabilise. A second impulse was to introduce the students to a range of alternative ways of reading and making meaning from texts. The potential for argument now seemed to be far greater than before, with students bringing their own experiences of reading into line with the new possibilities. Crucially it seemed to me they might be able to articulate a position for themselves in relation to the explicitly stated theoretical perspective as well as to the literary texts.

Despite this it was noticeable that in the writing that eventually resulted from the term's seminars argument continued to play at best a small part. Many of the students were now operating in a way more reminiscent of students' work in the humanities which again often falls short of argument. They were offering, that is, *accounts* of the theoretical approaches without evaluating them or using them to evaluate each other and without asserting a position in relation to them. There are two ways of looking at this: one is that the students needed experience in forming accounts of the complex ideas they had newly been introduced to; in addition these accounts often included the extra dimension of applying the theory to a literary text. To expect a student to add to this an evaluation of what she had done would perhaps be asking too much. I would go along with this to a certain extent – it certainly looks commonsensical. Yet I also think it is possible to look at the situation in a different way. This way involves attending to the situation's 'vehicles of meaning' (Geertz); in this case the essay form in which the students were uniformly required to write and the conventions which this form carries with it in terms of what and how one can write.

When the students wrote their essays I asked if they would also complete a questionnaire I had prepared. What is particularly striking is how different the questionnaire responses are to the essays, though the topic overlap is potentially very similar. Cathy's essay, for instance, is a thorough descriptive account of how a psychoanalytic reading works. The essay synthesises the work of a number of critics, but does not deal directly with a literary text. She uses the essay, it seems, to give a coherent account of the theory and to demonstrate her comprehension of it. What Cathy feels about the theory – how she evaluates it –

does not surface in the essay. But in the questionnaire Cathy writes quite differently.

> Psychoanalytical readings of novels and horror genres offer a severe interpretation of the text. It leaves little to the ingenuity of the author and rather sees his work as a failure or 'shortcoming' in dealing with unconscious works of art. Sometimes it offers an extremely limited view and 'cripples' the potentiality of the text to develop. Not all texts are as easy to read in this way as horror fiction or the classic *Sons and Lovers*. (Cathy, questionnaire)

In response to another question she also explores the difference the introduction of literary theory has made to her enjoyment of the primary activity of reading.

> A text now presents itself as an enigma waiting to be discovered. Sometimes this removes the initial enjoyment of a text, but it enables you to feel you have got much more out of it. Re-reading a text is no longer a 'déjà-vu' experience but a delight at finding things you missed in the first reading ... The student is better equipped at deciphering language and studying a text from his/her *own* opinion. (Cathy, questionnaire)

Here too the questionnaire suggests a more advanced reflective response to the possibilities of literary theory than was evident in the essay. The difference between what was expressed in these two forms in the particular instance of the Literary Theory course adds weight for me to a more general impression that the essay is used by students as a closed form in which certainties are expressed. It is also, as several of the students testify, used as a way in which certainty is arrived at, but equally students may be reluctant to redraft their written work in case the rewriting starts to change or question their understanding. Understanding is tested through the writing of an essay, but at the same time the sense is that understanding is also limited or, to put it slightly differently, that the writing is limited in understanding. Questions, doubt, evaluation, tentativity tend correspondingly to be omitted from the essay form.

Part of the reason for this seems to be the omission of the personal pronoun from the writing students do – they have no direct way of voicing their own opinion (as, by contrast, they are *invited* to do in the questionnaire) and correspondingly no position of their own in relation to the authoritative figures and ideas with which they are dealing. Where students are not encouraged to name themselves, the potential for argument which was apparently so full in the introduction of Literary Theory is in fact diminished rather than enhanced. The theoretical texts offer students a chance to realise their own ideological positioning, but at the same time, treated through the written form as authoritative texts within an academic context, the theoretical texts reassert the dominant ideology. The use or avoidance of the personal pronoun is more than a matter of style. It is of course quite possible to write as a critical 'person' without using the pronoun, but it is equally true that at certain stages in learning the licence to write about 'what I think ... ' or 'what I perceive ... ' gives direct access to an area of thought and experience which might not otherwise be expressed or explored and not, therefore, valued.

What I am suggesting here is that the texts the students are asked to write are in as great a need of critique as the ways in which they have learned to read. If the English department's emphasis on the nature of *what* it teaches (content) leads to or includes the disregard of *how* it teaches, then it seems to me that however radical the content, the institutional basis remains essentially conservative.

The conclusion I reach here seems to me to have been facilitated by the ethnographic approach to the abstract idea of argument and it's easy now, I think, to see how the pedagogical impulse (which in addition to the description of practice was an objective of the research) was generated. I wanted to explore different ways of writing which might enable students to be less wedded to certainty and reproduction and more inclined to questioning and argument. The questionnaire itself had proved to be one such way. Behind this exploration of alternative forms is the sense that, as Vygotsky (1978, p. 126) put it, 'if one changes the tools available to a child, his mind will have a radically different structure'. To change a way of thinking, it may also be important to change the possibilities for expressing that thought.

Radical form/radical content?

I want now to suggest what an alternative form might be. The examples I give are based on a dialogic principle; the idea that there are two or more perspectives or speaking voices. Writing argument in academic disciplines nearly always involves multiple voices but as I've suggested these can often force the writer of the argument into obedience to each voice in turn. The result is then not an argument but a narrative account or series of accounts. In the examples here the linearity and exclusivity of such accounts begins to be broken down.

The first example (Table 1) is of a student's essay in philosophy assessed dialogically by a peer. It illustrates that the status of the essay (roughly, either as process or product) is dependent on the reading and writing practices that are brought to bear on it. The comments on the essay work against its status as closed product and position it in an open-ended conversational frame. For it to be most effective the writer of the essay needs to engage with the comments; many of which take the form of questions.

Figure 1

Essay / Comments

Essay

Even if you accept that there is actually is a God there are still many problems involved in tying morality to religion. A religious view of what is good and what is morally correct to do seems to be "what God wills". It is right to do what God wills you to do. Therefore, to act morally you would need to do what God willed you to do in every situation. This seems fairly straight - forward on the surface. You can learn of God's will through reading a bible and through other religious teachings which give basic idea of what it right and wrong to do. However, no teachings can allow for every situation that will occur in your life. How will you know what God wills at every given moment? This would seem implausible. You can know what you think God would want you to do, but you can't really know if it is what he really wants you to do. In respect of this, whatever you do will be what you think is right and what you think you should do, not what God thinks you should do.

Another problem with the idea that it is right to do what God wills is the question of how we know that what Gods wills really is what is right. If you believe in a God it would seem natural to assume that God is good and actually knows what is good. However you have no way of knowing for sure that God is good, you may believe that what he wills is what is good, but you can never be sure. The only way you can know that what God tells you to do is good is if you know what good is. The problem here is that is you knew what was good you wouldn't need a God to tell you what to do. You would need no spiritual guidance to help you lead a good life.

Comments

(VII)
Do you here suggest that if there is a God then what you read in the Bible is an "accurate" manifestation of God's will? That in the particular situation (portrayed in the Bible, or whatever religious book with the claim of speaking of the will of God) God's will can be taken as God's will, since the manifestation of his will is revealed in that particular situation?

(IX)
What do you mean by "really wants to do?" If it refers to what you said in VIII, then how can one be sure that this is really what he wanted the people, in that particular situation to do, since we do not even know anything about that situation apart from what we read in e.g. the Bible. So how do we "know" that that which they refer to as being the will of God *really* is the will of God? Is there even a question of "knowing" when it comes to the Bible?

(X)
Is the claim of the believer different from "merely" believing? And if that is not so then what significance does that have for claiming something being "true" in relation to belief? And if so, then in what sense?

(XI)
Once again do we *know* what "good" is ?

The 'conversation' initiated here by one student commenting on the work of another could run and run, though in practice it will be a limited exchange. Working against it is the institutional need to assign a grade (a final judgement) to the work (and 'work' here is usually understood as an individual endeavour).

Students are often as concerned, if not more so than their teachers, to have this closure imposed.

The form taken by the essay and comments above suggests other possibilities for students writing dialogically but on their own rather than in actual dialogue. The comments question divert and extend the 'main' text, making points and objections which are excluded from its argument. The juxtaposition also creates a further text: a dialogue across the dividing space. In the next example (Table 2) two films, *Gorillas in the Mist* and *Aliens* are 'compared and contrasted' (a formulation frequently used in essay titles). The student writes 'I see these two films as embodying two sides of the same debate: what *is* natural?' He then structures the text around four points of comparison, the first of which is 'The Technology of the Look'.

Figure 2

...Crucially, early in the film, at a moment when the frame is entirely occupied with the image from a VDU, that image flickers leaving the screen/frame momentarily blank. So, from an early moment in the film, the attention of the audience is drawn to the technologies of communication and how they do not always work.

No one mode communication is privileged over others within the film. There is no master code into which all information may be translated. There is no possibility of 'perfect' communication: communication is not impossible, yet the appearance of noise and interference in many technologies within the film indicates how systems are open rather than closed, actual rather than ideal.

A metaphor for this is found in the visual nature of the film. The point of view of the camera is frequently occluded. The colony is an industrial space of artificial lights, steam and smoke, galleries and service tunnels. The extreme chiaroscuro effect created by these light sources means that it is often difficult to see exactly what is going on. The unknown is the unseen, the threatening and horrific .

...Yet this serves to heighten rather than to diminish the sense of realism. The interference comes from the environment represented. It does not rise from the technology of communication.

The magic of this realist style of photography arises from the juxtaposition of perfect and imperfect technology: Where Fossey can only make notes, or take (black and white) photos, or where Campbell makes visual but not sound recordings, the cinematic eye/I show us everything(except itself) in a tour-de-force including widescreen, Dolby stereo, and naturalistic colour. It is a master code into which other codes may be translated, showing them to be by comparison, limited and partial.

Filmed largely in the open, the light is 'natural' and falls evenly over the scene. Yet to suggest that the lighting of the film *is* natural is another trick of Realism. It belies the way that the effect of 'natural' light was painstakingly achieved - a fact underlined by the inclusion of lighting technicians in the list of credits.

The total illumination of the naturalistic lighting serves as a metaphor for the all-seeing but disembodied point of view. Where the aliens occupy an area on the threshold of the light, the gorillas in the mist bask in the broad daylight which renders them unthreatening - in fact the gorillas are seldom seen in any kind of mist whatsoever.

In the final paragraph in the right-hand column, the two films are brought together in a classic comparative sentence which closes the section. The form is an excellent way of juxtaposing two textual analyses, which in a sequential text would be separated from one another and therefore limited in the extent to which the closely focused interpretative arguments of one could resonate with those of the other. This way, the narrative tendency of the textual interpretation (critique is as often embedded in the choice of descriptive words as in abstractions and generalisations) becomes argumentative by virtue of its constant contact on the page with an alternative narrative. The 'explicitness' of the argument is visual as much as verbal.

It is interesting to note the context in which the writer of this piece (an MA student of Cultural Studies) gives:

> It was unassessed; the tutors on the course got us to write a couple of short essays in between the 'important' assessed work. In them, we were invited to try out ideas, explore new areas, and so on. I think the idea was that these short essays would keep us in touch with the art of writing.

The writer goes on to say how much he enjoyed the piece, finding it playful, allowing him to experiment with languages and strategies used by established theorists without taking them too seriously. He notes however that the freedom of the piece derived in part from the fact that it was not assessed.

> It is perhaps significant that the only other adventurous piece of work I submitted was marked down. The rest was occasionally daring in content, but conservative in form.

Ideas for change, including a recognition here of the formative value of experimental writing are, it seems, in advance of institutional mechanisms for valuing them as product. This is the problem of diversification in essentially normative institutions; it does not mean, however, that change is impossible, rather that it is slow and must be negotiated, based, paradoxically, on consensus.

Another way in which a 'split text' may be used is not in juxtaposing critiques of different material, but in juxtaposing different responses to the same material. This is how the form might most obviously be tried in Literary Theory. Different 'lines' of thought governed by different kinds of criteria can be pursued in each column. These 'lines' may be different theoretical stances in relation to the same text or issue: a Marxist analysis or critique, next to a functionalist, next to a structuralist, next to a ... – the number of columns does not have to be limited to two. In the case of English one column might usefully be taken up with an initial 'untheorised' reading of the literary text.

I should point out that I don't see the voice of one side as being more 'authentic' than the other. Neither side has, in a sense, the greater claim to truth about the text. What the split text does is to offer students the space to explore a variety of different voices and perspectives. They don't discover their true selves so much as discover the different roles they may play and therefore the possibility of distance and critique. This possibility comes both from the opportunity to write differently but also, it seems to me, from the difference itself made visible in the dialogic form. The split text would, for example, be a good way to explore the different kinds of argument and writer/reader relationships which are created by statements on the one hand (literally) and questions, on the other.

In some ways the dialogic forms I've described highlight and clarify functions which are performed in academic essays, but which can be obscured or overlooked there particularly by inexperienced writers. It is possible, for instance to imagine a synthesis of the two columns in the '*Aliens* and *Gorillas in the Mist*' text. According to cognitive development models of writing which value the presentation of a unified thesis very highly (see, for instance, Freedman and Pringle, 1984) this would probably be seen as an advance. Looked at another way, however, it is possible to see the act of synthesising as a way in which the writer takes possession of meaning, closing the spaces in which a reader might interpolate herself and reducing the possibility of multiple interpretations. The text a writer chooses to write, that is to say, has implications beside cognitive ones. It also reflects and affects the status of the writer and the status of the content that is written about.

Looking at argument this way sees it as a process hedged about, constrained and enabled by its contextual embeddedness. In English its potential grows when alternative meanings are shown to be possible through the introduction of a range of perspectives. But this potential is also determined by power and licence; not only the permission to speak but also the structural, organisational opportunities that make it possible to listen, question and be heard. These factors are as potent in the conduct of spoken as written argument and in fact have emerged everywhere in my research in some form or other, both in describing what is and in envisioning what might be more widely possible.

CHAPTER EIGHTEEN

LEARNING TO OPERATE SUCCESSFULLY IN A LEVEL HISTORY[*]

Sally Mitchell and Richard Andrews

The ability of students to conduct arguments is now generally recognised as an area of interest and concern. Recent research and comment has focused on pre-school and school experiences,[1] much of it, at secondary level, within English and then again with a different emphasis on the genres employed by postgraduate students.[2] While there has been some research on the way undergraduates develop disciplinary specific skills[3] there has been little focus on argument in the final two years of secondary school. Yet it is at the 16–18 stage (at least in Britain) that the ability to argue – more often than not using the standard academic forms and within the constraints of specialised disciplinary discourses – becomes increasingly important.

This chapter investigates some of the tensions generated by the dual demand on students at this level to display both complex cognitive operations and confident rhetorical form.[4] We take, as an example, a history course in which particular emphasis is placed on the students' skills of historical argument and examine closely the evidence for these skills in the written assignments of two students. We note that at this level students of the arts and humanities adopt a standard form of extended academic writing – commonly referred to in Britain as the 'essay' – and that this form is often associated with the presentation of an argument. We argue, however, that successful adoption of the essay form – in terms of its features of style and overall organisation – does not necessarily result in or reflect successful argument.

To put this another way, argument is generated by ways of organising and operating upon material that are not intrinsic to writing in the standard form. As a result we argue that the development of students' argumentative skills should not be assumed to take place in the composition of the final written form, but should be fostered by increased access to ways of operating upon content and concepts in order to generate argument prior to essay writing. We further argue that attention to the interface between argument and the text-types in which it finds expression leads us in two pedagogic directions: to the writing of better

---

[*] First published under this title in Freedman, A. and Medway, P. 1994. *Teaching and Learning Genre*. Portsmouth, NH: Heinemann/Boynton-Cook.

conventional academic essays on the one hand, and to experimentation with more explicitly dialogic written forms on the other.

The disciplinary context

Our discussion in this chapter concerns a course of study in history, which in 1992 was being piloted by the University of Cambridge Local Examinations Syndicate and was subsequently officially approved by the Schools Examination and Assessment Council for England and Wales.[5] The Cambridge History Project (CHP) reflects a movement (currently reversing) in British education towards active forms of learning, which emphasise appropriate disciplinary skills. The CHP exercises greater control over the materials to be used and topics covered by individual schools than usual for examination boards. It supplies simulation exercises and historical sources as verbal and visual evidence, which relate to events in history chosen for their relevance to larger topics, such as 'People, Power, and Politics': such a topic is broken down into a development study – political change through time – and an in-depth study of one particular era. The exercises and materials are supplied as modules, based on procedures rather than content: for example, 'Approaches to the Problem' and 'Comparative Analysis'. The 1992 syllabus offers this rationale:

> CHP is designed to develop students' understanding of history as a form of knowledge. It starts with the premise that any serious attempt to teach history must involve students both in tackling important historical questions and in explicit reflection on the nature of the discipline. The point of historical enquiry is to give us knowledge of the past, but students cannot acquire genuine knowledge without understanding how it is grounded, and this understanding involves a grasp of concepts and procedures, which make history what it is. In turn, such an understanding cannot be acquired without a study of some part of the past, not as a mere vehicle for the concepts and procedures at issue, but as the activity, which gives them their point.[6]

When these statements are translated into syllabus objectives and assessment criteria it is apparent that reflection on the discipline, knowledge with understanding, and understanding as an activity are manifested largely through the skills of argument. The connection is made explicitly by the CHP's director who comments:

> Candidates who do not put forward an argument and merely provide a narrative account are awarded level 0 on all domains.

Extrapolating from the syllabus, argument in this context involves: the use of evidence; the identification of problems; the selection, evaluation, and application of sources and explanations; the consideration of relative status and reasons for difference; the generation of interpretations through synthesis and modification; the analysis of events: and the construction and reconstruction of accounts. These skills are demonstrated in particular ways according to domains of historical operation (for example, using sources as evidence) and conceptualisation (cause and motive, change and development). Within each domain there are three levels of attainment, each of which can be understood to correspond to a level of sophistication in argument. For example, in the domain of 'Offering Evidence', students are assessed according to the following levels:

1. Can propose and evaluate explanations by establishing connections obtaining within or between patterns of ideas, actions, and events.
2. Can propose and evaluate explanations of ideas, actions and events by comparing them with similar phenomena or sequences of events.
3. Can propose and evaluate explanations of ideas, actions, and events by considering 'the actual' in relation to 'the possible'.

The levels can be thought of in relation to the six cognitive skills listed by Benjamin Bloom (1956): knowledge, comprehension, application, analysis, synthesis, and evaluation. The conceptual underpinning used by the CHP is not unique at this level of study – it can be widely detected in the syllabus objectives of arts and humanities subjects in particular – but the project is distinguished by its explicit articulation of how argument is manifested in differentiated domains of disciplinary thought. Level 3 involves a more complex and comprehensive interrelation of skills and a control of material, which extends to the point of hypothesis construction. The larger the bulk of material the greater effort of synthesis and evaluation required to contain it within a meaningful configuration. At level 3, therefore, the arguer is fully engaged with the restructuring and organising of material in order to make of it something new – in this case making the possible from the actual. This need for active manipulation has implications for the production of written work, as we go on to suggest in a later section. We want now, however, to make a few more suggestions about argument.

It is useful to think of argument as a mode – what the dictionary calls simply a 'way of doing'. The way we choose to do something affects to a great extent the outcomes and opportunities we go on to produce. Mode is used therefore as a way of describing types of process, rather than types of product (though it is necessary for analysis to extrapolate a process from the product). It does not then refer solely to the organisation (logical, say, rather than chronological) of a piece of writing, but rather to *the possibilities that are actively raised by organisational decisions*. For example, and as we shall see in the following analyses, putting two ideas together, rather than keeping them separate, can create the conditions in which a third, perhaps more inclusive idea is generated.

Argument as a mode

Argument is a mode which Kress (1989) and others have identified as exploiting difference. It enables new ideas to be forged out of the inadequacies of the old, making space for the creation of novelty.[7] At its fullest, operation in the mode of argument carries with it an awareness that however carefully a position has been established as the outcome of an argumentative process 'it could still act as the thesis for an antithesis and future synthesis; in other words no argument can be final but serves as the basis for future arguments'.[8] In the sense that it is contingent upon new evidence, fresh perspectives and competing theories, argument is open-ended and, potentially at least, ongoing. It is in this sense too that argument is associated with dialogue and dialogic thinking, even where the immediate or practical intention is to establish a monologue position.

Argument is also what Ricoeur (1970) described as the negative mode of interpretation – characterised by a 'willingness to suspect' and a 'vow of rigour'. In contrast the positive mode is characterised by a 'willingness to listen' and 'a vow of obedience' (p. 27). This positive mode seems to us to correspond with narrative, which, unlike argument, tends to organise material so as to resolve difference and to create an illusion of things, ideas, and relations existing in a significant sequence. Narrative as a mode is obedient; argument is suspicious.

What has been said here about argument as a mode holds true irrespective of whether it is written or spoken and it is, therefore, clearly distinguished from its form of expression. The distinction is important for practical and pedagogic reasons as well as semantic ones. The CHP operates both written and oral forms of assessment, but this chapter is concerned only with the written outcomes of the course. To understand how these are shaped and transacted we need to look to a wider context than the CHP.

The 'essay'

In Britain at this advanced level of school study there is a standard form of extended writing common to most subjects in the arts and humanities. This form is generally referred to as the 'essay'. It has the basic Aristotelian structure, which characterises persuasive discourse (anything from the two-part structure of 'statement' and 'proof' to the six-part oratorical structure). Its formal divisions – referred to in school vernacular as introduction, middle, and conclusion – do not always, however, perform the persuasive functions originally assigned to them. Students who study the arts or humanities beyond the age of 16 in Britain are greatly preoccupied with this form, experiencing the emphasis placed upon it as a significant change from the kinds of writing expected in earlier years. At this level of study the essay is scarcely ever a piece of personal writing, but is associated with work within a discipline. In a sense, then, familiarity with the essay symbolises the transition between a general and an academic education.

Because of its association with academic and disciplinary conventions we see the school essay as a text-type operating within generic conditions. With its rhetorically motivated features of introduction, middle, conclusion (however crude these divisions are), the essay is a standardised vehicle for conducting a transaction between the student-writer and teacher-reader; a transaction, which says among other things that work has been undertaken and can now be assessed.[9] In this sense the writing can be seen as a means of social action – participation in the academic community – which carries with it a certain formal license. The essay is used across the disciplines of the arts and humanities, where the rhetorical features are shared and where importantly students and teachers perceive them to be shared. Within this extensive category there are subforms that are defined by the differences that exist between them: a geography essay is not a sociology essay, and a CHP essay is not an essay elicited from another examination course in history.

The conception of genre promoted in the present volume is useful in this area since it enables a distinction between relatively more formal notions of text-type and relatively more contextual influences on the shape of a particular text. Sheeran and Barnes have described these latter as ground rules (1991):

> writing in school requires the writer to take over both new
> conceptual structures and (at the same time) to manage
> sets of ground rules, some general to the school as a
> whole, some related to the curricular subject, and some
> specific to a particular occasion and teacher. (p. 14)

As we have done, Sheeran and Barnes separate 'conceptual structures' from the socially negotiated rules. Writing in school is certainly a complex business with the actual written artifact the outcome of a number of operative factors: contextual, transactional, formal, conceptual, and modal.

Writing in A level history

At 16 the transition to academic status brings with it an increased expectation of the student's ability to argue. The nature of the school subject may itself change so that students are dealing with more complex materials and ideas. To state the case crudely, for history there is a move from the teaching and learning of historical narrative and facts to a form of study that addresses the construction of historical accounts as a problem and foregrounds the diversity of interpretations of the past. History becomes in the final two years the subject of historical analysis and, because analyses differ, of historical debate. To put it another way history is less concerned with subject content than with actual and possible ways of acting upon that content.

Writing and argument come together almost exclusively in the essay form in advanced level history and in practice; therefore any distinction between mode and form is blurred. When in the following extracts two students talk about what they mean by developing an argument, they are talking also of the form in which they are required to write. Referring to the transition between pre- and post-16 courses, the first student describes writing tasks as changing from being a 'precise thing' to being something far more complex:

> They ask you a question but then you're supposed to
> develop your argument within that.

She seems to be saying that at the advanced level a question no longer has a simple answer. It is, of course, more of an invitation to argue than a request for a neat solution. Asked what 'developing your argument' meant, she replied:

> I suppose it's expressing all sides of the question, attitudes
> and things, and then you come up with your own answers
> at the end of it.

Her friend then completed the description by adding:

> And then you have to criticise your own answer as well,
> which is really hard if you believe what you're writing.

These students have recognised the importance of active engagement with subject content. And they have also recognised that what they claim to be a personal viewpoint must be arrived at, paradoxically, through an *impersonal* process of dispassionate assessment and differentiation, or rather that it must be presented as having been arrived at in these ways. Being impersonally arrived at, the 'personal' view must then itself be open to impersonal evaluation. The notion of arguing from passionate conviction has no place in this academic context, unless it can be substantiated through the critical analysis of alternative positions. As we have said, students commonly have some notion – as these young women do – of what it means to develop argument but when it comes to actual practice the task does not seem so easy.

Learning the differing views of others – or that others hold views that differ – and that the world can be interpreted in different ways does not in itself mean that the student is able to argue or to operate in the argumentative mode. It is perfectly possible to show evidence of arguments learned while at the same time revealing no evidence of the ability to argue. In the course of our research we have read a great many clear presentations of the authoritative views of notable critics, historians, and sociologists, which have, however, failed to engage with these views argumentatively. In other words they are expository rather than argumentative – not untypical in the writing of 16-year-olds, as Berrill (1990) has argued based on her work with Canadian students.

The written form is not synonymous with the mode of argument. In fact, the most common account of an essay's structure – introduction, linking middle paragraphs, conclusion – can as well accommodate a narrative mode of organisation as an argumentative one. Where the student relies on this distilled three-part structure to organise content, the result is often a linear sequencing of unprocessed material in the body of the essay with evaluative comment postponed to the concluding paragraph. More often than not the writer has run out of steam by this stage and the conclusion merely functions to close off the writing.[10]

The sequential organisation of material isolates rather than integrates the cognitive skills referred to earlier. The so-called higher of these skills – analysis, synthesis, and evaluation – cannot be developed in isolation from the lower skills. That is, analysis, synthesis, and evaluation must take place alongside the operation of knowledge and comprehension. Argument, we take it, thrives where the full range of cognitive skills are dynamically interrelated and is not facilitated by their structural separation.[11]

Cambridge History Project essays

The insistence of the CHP on modes of operating makes the written outcomes produced by students particularly interesting. While the CHP places strong emphasis on argumentation it does not specify the form in which this should be presented, beyond mention of 'written or oral assignments'. However, as we hope we have argued, an appropriate written form within the wider educational context usually goes without saying – the essay is the legitimate currency of student–teacher transactions at this level of study.

The following analysis is of two student essays that achieve different degrees of success with regard to argument. They draw on the same source material from the domain 'Change and Development' and are written in response to the same question:

> On the basis of the available evidence how far would you be prepared to accept that the First World War was a turning point in the development of the position and role of women in English society?

The question requires argument: the writer must process the available evidence and scrutinise it in relation to the analytical category turning point. The case is unlikely to be cut and dry as the phrase 'how far' suggests and whatever the degree of agreement or disagreement, it must be justified by a weighing of the evidence.

Figure 1 is the detailed assessment scheme for the essay. Students had copies of it when they set about the writing task. Notice that the scheme supplies certain specific vocabulary and conceptual characterisations such as 'false dawn', 'turning point', 'continuing trend'. These provide a repertoire of alternatives to those terms explicitly given in the title.

Figure 1

Assessment scheme for Cambridge History Project essay assignment

---

On the basis of the available evidence how far would you be prepared to accept that the First World War was a turning point in the development of the position and role of women in English society?

LEVEL 1 – Demonstrates understanding of the ways in which significance may be attributed to events as turning points, dead ends, and false dawns.

N.B. In order to achieve level 1 (and beyond) the student must demonstrate understanding that significance needs to be assessed by means other than simply describing the changes made in this period. Characterisation of the changes as a turning point or, alternatively, a trend ... within the development of this position and role of women in English society is necessary. Such an assessment will require the student to analyse and interpret the events and relate their findings to an appropriate characterisation.

1A. Demonstrates understanding that the characterisation of events as a turning point signifies a break with the past and is also forward referencing. Applies this understanding to the events of World War One. From this answers may conclude that the First World War did or did not constitute a turning point in the development of the role and position of women in English society.

1B. Chooses a different characterisation of events to that of turning point ... demonstrates understanding of what this characterisation signifies and, by applying their understanding to the events of the First World War, concludes that the period should be interpreted not as a turning point but instead as a false dawn/dead end.

N.B. At this level the student may show understanding of more than one characterisation in order to justify their argument that an alternative is more appropriate but the events will only be analysed and interpreted to support one characterisation. The student does not progress to show how the same events may be interpreted as being different and of competing significance.

1C. Chooses either the characterisation of turning point or an alternative and illustrates why it may be difficult to conclude either in the affirmative or negative because of the different perspectives ... temporal, spatial, and historical against which the events of the First World War may be interpreted. The candidate at this level shows understanding of some of the problems which may be involved in characterising the significance of a period of time but does not progress to show how it is possible to interpret the same events as being of differing and competing significance.

LEVEL 2 - Demonstrates understanding that lines of development are theories as well as representations of the past and that differing and competing lines of development may be advanced to describe and make sense of any part of it.

N.B. Answers at this level develop the understanding of historical characterisation of change and development to show *how* it is possible for differing and competing characterisations of the same events to be developed. The student will identify, evaluate, and compare the criteria upon which competing characterisations of the First World War are based. At level 2, they will continue to treat them as parallel, separate accounts.

2D. Answers and appreciates and illustrates how it is possible to put forward differing and competing characterisations of change and development from differing interpretations of the same evidence.

2E. Answers show how different historians give different *emphasis* to the available evidence ... conclusions will vary according to which aspects of the First World War are emphasised.

2F. Answers demonstrate the effect that variations in the temporal or spatial context in which the events of the First World War are interpreted may alter the significance attached to the events.

LEVEL 3 - Demonstrates understanding of the reasons why and the ways in which different and competing lines of development may co-exist and be integrated into a single historical account.

N.B. Answers at this level demonstrate understanding of the many aspects of change and development at any one period in time. The significance of the changes and developments of the First World War will be shown to be varied ... some aspects may be turning points, others accelerations of existing trends ... yet others possibly false dawns/dead ends. No one characterisation will allow a balanced analysis and the student understands that the incorporation of competing analyses into a single account may increase the ability to answer the question. The full complexity of change is explored.

3G. Answers demonstrate that it is possible to analyse the significance of the First World War by reference to more than one characterisation ... different aspects of change and continuity within the same period and different interpretations of the same events are shown to be capable of integration into one line of development.

3H. Answers demonstrate that it is possible to interpret the significance of the First World War within a more varied temporal and spatial context to show some of the complexities of characterising periods of change.

The scheme provides an instance of the different levels at which, as was described earlier, students may conduct their analysis. At level 1 the student will deal with single interpretations, demonstrating comprehension but not attempting to complicate or integrate the view with any other. At level 2 there is greater recognition of multiple viewpoints and the relativity of each. And at level 3, levels 1 and 2 are extended by an awareness of what extra might need to be done in order to resolve inconsistencies and develop a new hypothesis – in the form of a personal opinion or new narrative. Level 3 is in some ways a shift from a reactive to a more active role for the writer and thinker.

From the opening paragraph of each essay it is not easily possible to predict which will be the most successful in terms of argumentative development:

> *Mike*
> The question of how far would you be prepared to accept that the First World War marked a turning point in the development of the position and role of women in English society can be answered providing that it is kept in mind that there are many different aspects which could judge whether it is a turning point or not. Such as the kind of evidence an historian concentrates on, the different perspectives used, spatial or temporal, or the different strands of women's role in society, for example their economic or political roles. If all these elements are taken into account then it can be shown that the First World War is both a turning point, trend and false dawn for women.

> *Robert*
> In order to answer this question it is necessary to recognise that within the development of the position and role of women in English society there are many different strands – for example VOTING RIGHTS, JOB OPPORTUNITY RIGHTS and EQUAL PAY claims. Each of these strands are affected at different rates over the passage of time and any analysis of a turning point must take account of this. We must in other words explore the full complexity of change.

Both students (aged 17) show an awareness of the task, acknowledging that the claim for the First World War as a turning point for women is open to debate; similarly with the conclusions, both of which are credited by the teacher as displaying level 3 reasoning:

Mike
So it has been shown that using the right evidence, strands and perspectives the First World War with regard to women's role in British society can be seen as a turning point, continuing trend, or false dawn.

Taking all these aspects into account the evidence tends to lean towards the idea that the war had very little effect on women politically or socially and that it was part of a continuing trend, especially when it is taken into account that progress was first made for women in these areas decades before the war, and that throughout the twentieth century women's role in society has moved ahead only very gradually, rather than the massive step forward that has been suggested took place.

Robert
What we must draw of importance here is that the development of women in relation to men is a very ongoing thing. It is by no means resolved and it by no means started only in 1914. The First World War doubtless has had a lot of influence on the rights and position of women in society. What we have to recognise is that change is not always constant and in all directions. It can affect different strands at different times and to different extents. I have attempted to integrate the strands and demonstrate that change is an ongoing thing. It is fair to comment that some of the modern day changes had their roots in the First World War, but by no means all. I regard the First World War as an accelerator not a turning point.

Our problem with these introductions and conclusions as evidence of argument is that they seem at least to a certain extent to be rehearsals of the language of the highly explicit mark-scheme and what it suggests would constitute a level 3 response. When, for instance, Robert states his intention to explore 'the full complexity of change' he is echoing the mark-scheme's description of a level 3 answer in which, it says '[the] full complexity of change will be explored'. In a sense then these parts of the essay can be learned, so that the correct analytical phrasing disguises the presence – or absence – of reasoning itself. Nevertheless, the explicit criteria and analytical framework provided by the mark scheme and the syllabus generally do seem to help students become aware of the complexities of the historical evidence and help them deal with it in critical ways. It is very clear in this syllabus that repetition alone is not sufficient.[12]

If we put aside the introductions and conclusions, which we have shown to be triggered by the surface cues provided by the syllabus rubric itself, how are we able to say that one of these essays displays a higher level of argument than the other? The answer lies in the organisation and treatment of substantive material in the middle sections of the essay. It is not possible to look at the texts of these in any depth here. However, it is not so much the minutiae of the writing that are revealing, as the way in which the material is structured and arranged.

In the introduction to his essay Mike made mention of the various ways in which the impact of the First World War on women could be characterised: not only as a turning point, but also as a continuing trend or false dawn. These characteristics become the means by which he structures his essay. Paragraphs 1–4 contain evidence that suggests that the war is a turning point; paragraphs 5–10 consider there was a continuing trend; and paragraphs 11–14 use the idea of a false dawn. Each possible interpretation is conscientiously covered and in each section taken separately the evidence could be considered plausible, since conflicting evidence is structurally and therefore temporally separated (see Figure 2).

Figure 2

Mike's Essay

Points of Interaction
between Conflicting
Interpretations

World War   Turning   Continuing   False
One as . . .   Point   Trend   Dawn

As a result of Mike's decision to treat the interpretations in a compartmentalised way, he rarely achieves more than a level 1: he is dealing with one narrative account of the war at a time. Simply by making the transition from one narrative to the next, however, he achieves level 2. As he makes the transition, the two alternative interpretations are juxtaposed and a spark of argument is generated. Moments such as this are rare though: the material is organised *in such a way as to minimise contrast and comparison.*

If we think again about Ricoeur's two modes of interpretation – the positive and the negative – then Mike could be said to be operating in the positive mode, under 'a vow of obedience' to each interpretation as he deals with it.

It is to the negative mode – characterised by a 'willingness to suspect' and a 'vow of rigour' – that Robert's essay tends. He seems to recognise that the argumentative potential of the material lies not so much in the substantive issues themselves, which in the terminology of the course are referred to as 'strands' and which he instances as voting rights, job opportunity rights and equal pay claims, as in the different interpretations that can be offered of these. He therefore organises his essay around his three chosen strands. Presented as complex yet complete bodies of evidence these become the still points around which argument rages.

The 1918 Voting Reform Act, for example, which took place just at the end of the war, is presented by Robert as the cause of contention between historians, who disagree as to whether the war was the decisive factor in bringing about the vote for women. Robert weighs these issues in his own words:

> It is certainly fair to comment that women had been striving for the vote well before the war; therefore we should judge the impact of the war in relation to this. Having said that, the immediacy of granting the vote seems to suggest that the war was of some considerable impact.

Robert also places this debate within a longer term context, by considering subsequent improvements in women's rights and insisting that the issue of voting rights cannot be entirely divorced from the issue of equal pay – this point effects a transition, of course, from discussion of one strand to discussion of another.

The essay's structure is depicted very simplistically in Figure 3.

Figure 3

Robert's Essay

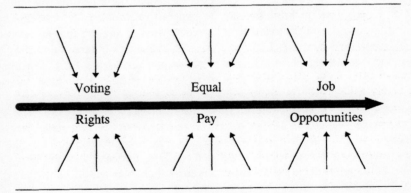

Each arrow represents a different possible interpretation of the substantive material. (Incidentally, looked at from the language point of view this kind of structural arrangement creates a great deal of opportunity for the use of argumentative diction of the 'however', 'nevertheless', 'on the other hand' variety.) In fact, in Robert's essay there are not as many alternatives as the diagrammatic representation suggests. Robert has a tendency to reject the idea of a turning point without fully considering the arguments in its favour.

In another way the diagram is not an accurate representation of Robert's essay since it suggests too neat a division into sections. In fact the organisation is more complex than this: there are other organising factors at work. The essay begins, for instance, with a consideration of the debate about women *before* the war and tends towards the end to deal with present-day evidence in the form of statistics: so there is a kind of underlying temporal structure. In addition there are occasions when Robert steps back from the material to justify or clarify his approach – as when, for instance, he comments that women's position can only be seen as relative to men's and that he has no 'control' group against which to measure his conclusions. He is explicit too in monitoring the progress of the argument, pointing out where gaps in the configuration of evidence still lie. Here, for instance:

> So we see that the role of women within society was already under debate. We must now examine what happened during the war and also afterwards to women in order to determine what impact World War One had on the role of women in society. On this impact there are two distinct camps ...

Even though both writers achieve a similar degree of argumentative strength at the conclusions of their essays, Robert displays a greater degree of rhetorical skill, employing a style that allows retrospective and prospective control and suggests an awareness of overall patterning,

Ostensibly the theme of these two essays is the same: the effect on women of the First World War. In Mike's essay (to generalise) three versions of this theme are offered and brought together at the conclusion to suggest that no one version is satisfactory in itself. In Robert's essay, however, it seems that the theme becomes something more than the effect on women of the First World War. Robert in a sense takes argument itself – that is, the exploration of difference – as his theme. He anchors his activity in three major strands and uses these as sites for the attribution of different significances. *Bringing different views of the same phenomena into contact with one another like this generates argument.*

This seems like a simple formula and if it really is the case then the next question is: how can students be helped to organise their material in ways that maximise opportunity for such critical engagement?

Conclusion: suggestions for generating argument

One suggestion we would make – to return to our distinction at the beginning of this chapter – is the separation of the *form* of writing from the *mode* in which the material is to be handled. Planning an essay is not the same as engaging in an argument; essay plans tend to have a linear form that records only the substantive material that is to be included. Brainstorming exercises are often used as a way of breaking down the linear model of the essay plan; but while they may play a useful role, they tend to lack the element of rigour, which characterises the negative mode of interpretation and academic argument. Nor do they allow the student any systematic insight into the ways in which argument can be generated.

As our research progresses we have become increasingly interested in ways of empowering students to break away from narrative and expository accounts and to occupy positions from which they can marshal material according to second-order categories, which they themselves have arrived at. We want to insist that structure and organisation are not simply characteristics of form – the introduction, middle, and conclusion of the essay – but are essential to the active processes of argumentation. There are several useful ways in which these processes may be fostered: time spent on summary and differential classification rather than being exercises by rote can build towards confident critical evaluation. We can assume that summary is an important part of learning from the extent to which it is used in student essays. Explicitly asking students to summarise the arguments of others leads to a further step – to look for common themes and to differentiate between them. Handling sameness and difference implicates the students in processes of argument from which they can develop their own views.[13]

Another important strategy and principle in the generation of argument can be located in the CHP's emphasis on the 'understanding of history as a form of knowledge' and on 'explicit reflection on the nature of the discipline'. This emphasis exposes and names the conceptual underpinnings on which the practice of history rests. Thus the historical significance of events is determined by 'the context of prior and subsequent developments' and the nature of that significance depends on 'the amount of change that takes place and the nature of that change'. There are, as we have seen, a variety of terms by which types of change may be manifested: turning point, trend, and false dawn. We noted above how when one of these – turning point – was used in the essay title it brought others into play, hinting at the wider conceptual model underpinning its specific wording.

The argumentative strategy we want to suggest is one that exploits this conceptual underpinning. It involves a move beyond the words of the essay question itself and away from formal organisation, which requires linearity, towards a notion of hierarchy (where a large overall pattern subsumes smaller less inclusive ones, which can be combined and connected in a variety of different ways). The starting point is to decide what the most general and inclusive idea behind the essay question could be. Locating such an idea is not equivalent to formulating a thesis, but can be an important stage prior to it. The chosen idea or concept is a stable common factor around which the material can be moved – organised, integrated, and differentiated – while the thesis represents an eventual configuration of material expressed in prepositional form.

We would argue that students' ability to engage in argument is enhanced where they can identify wider conceptions and categories and use these in the service of the particular task. In the case of the Cambridge History Project these conceptions and categories are explicit: the course offers descriptions and diagrams of the concepts upon which it rests. An example, which bears closely on the essays we have been discussing here, is given in Figure 4.

Figure 4

The significance of events

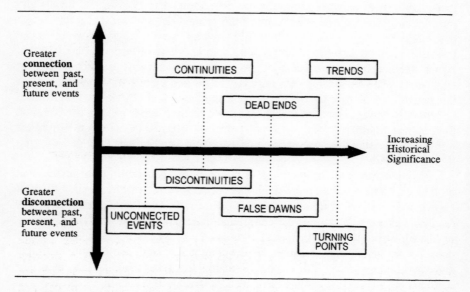

This diagram is based upon concepts of relative continuity and discontinuity and of historical significance. Students could beneficially be encouraged to use and adapt such a diagram for the generation of argument since it provides a structure against which actual accounts or interpretations can be matched and evaluated.

More usefully though they could create diagrams of their own that address their specific purposes and tasks and that have space for the substitution of actual events. Figure 5 is a suggested diagram relating (though not exclusively) to the essay discussed here.

The stable factor was chosen as 'change'. We then arranged some possible ways in which change manifests itself around the central idea. These possibilities can be combined to produce further ways of characterising change – the arrows drawn are not exhaustive. The labels can be thought of as representing condensed questions by which the event or account of the event can be evaluated or considered as historically significant. The diagram does not address the specific material, but could be applied to any strand that had been identified. The strand of 'voting rights' for instance could be examined with regard to the various aspects in the diagram, which would be a means of interrogating the evidence: where does so and so stand on this issue? How does her view differ from his? Have all the possible interpretations been considered?

Figure 5

A working diagram for generating argument

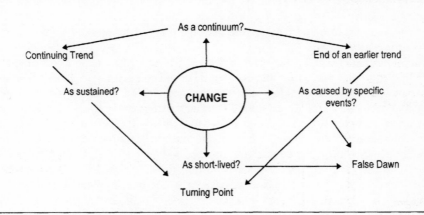

The diagram in Figure 5 differs significantly from the official CHP one. It is less coherent, authoritative, abstract and there are inconsistencies in the historical thinking it displays. Its function, too, is different: it is a working diagram to be drawn on and adapted; in it, meaning and understanding are emergent, not developed. The difference between using a given model and generating one of one's own is important. While we would encourage students to adopt the strategy of looking for an inclusive idea, we would resist any suggestion that they find the inclusive idea. The aim is to alert students to the organising and generative potential of wider concepts and hierarchical patterning. The use of diagrams such as Figure 5 does not generate an order or sequence for material to be put down in the essay form – that remains the function of the essay plan – but rather it represents an important preliminary step in which raw material is caused to be dealt with in an argumentative mode.

In emphasising the forms and structures that constitute history as a discipline, the Cambridge History Project has enormous potential for the generation of argument. Its highly explicit descriptions of historical thought represent one way of aiding students to go beyond the narrative repetition of given material and to operate at a level of conceptual complexity. However, there is danger, as we have seen, in assessment criteria, which in their explicitness and the way they are used by teachers and students, transform the how of students' thinking into what they should have thought.[14] The benefits of a meta-understanding of history as a form of knowledge, rather than a collection of facts, are lost if that understanding becomes a substitute right answer to be learned by the student. Our suggested strategy demands an active interrogation of the relations between concrete material and the conceptual interpretations that can be made of it and in doing so it increases the chance that the student's own voice will be heard. It is worth considering whether the CHP's syllabus might not be supplemented by practical suggestions as to how teachers and students could work together and independently to develop appropriate argumentative responses. Each individual task or question with which a student is faced poses its own problems of interpretation and method and we certainly do not wish to be prescriptive as to generative strategies. There are, however, insights to be gained and passed on to students and help them make the most of argumentative opportunities.

Researchers such as ourselves and many teachers often seem to be caught in a dilemma: we want, on the one hand to encourage and explore new and alternative forms of thinking and writing, and on the other we want to help students achieve as highly as possible within existing conventions. Too often the result is an overemphasis on conventional form as if repeated practice in that area will lead to the evidence of thought and engagement we are hoping for. Going against the strong educational impulse to cover all the possible content of a course and to mark that coverage with quantities of standard written products we want to argue for a changed emphasis in which development of the mode of thinking is given priority and students are freed – initially at least – from the conventionalised constraints of essay writing. In the long term, we can see the emergence of alternative forms of writing to the essay both within the CHP approach and in other syllabuses for this age range. Already, postgraduate students and those in middle and early high school are using more explicitly dialogic forms like the dialogue, Socratic dialogue, letters exchanged with teachers and lecturers, symposium and narrative-with-dialogue. Quotations – a staple ingredient of the conventional academic essay – have the potential for greater status within a student's writing, once we acknowledge that they enter as authoritative or questionable voices within the emerging thesis of the student writer. Rather than embed them within a conventional form, we can see the possibilities of their being used to generate thought and argument. The advantage of such alternative written forms in the educational context is that they might be closer to the spoken discourses that go on in classrooms and seminar rooms, and might give more ready access to argumentation than the conventional written outcomes.

The aim in the short term, however, remains to satisfy course requirements – 'the good essay' is certainly something we are anxious to help students to write. But to do this the criteria by which the good essay is defined and the ways in which it is commonly understood and used can usefully be re-examined and opened to change. If we want essays to be argumentative, we must pay attention to what operation in that mode really means and to ways in which we can help students achieve it.

Notes

1. Examples of reports into pre-school argumentation include Wilkinson (1990), Wilkinson et al. (1990), and Fox (1989, 1990). Research into school experiences includes the work of Pringle and Freedman (1979, 1980,1985), Freedman and Pringle (1984, 1989) in Canada; Reid (1991), Andrews and Costello (1992), Andrews, Costello and Clarke (1993), and Dixon and Stratta (1982, 1986a).
2. Swales (1990) provides a comprehensive discussion of work in this field. See also Bazerman (1988) and Berkenkotter, Huckin, and Ackerman (1988).
3. See Freedman (1987), Kaufer and Geisler (1989), and Geisler (1992).
4. This work was part of a research project funded by The Leverhulme Trust entitled 'An Examination of the Teaching and Learning of Argument in Sixth Forms and Universities'. It was based at the University of Hull and ran from May 1991 to May 1994. See Mitchell (1992a and 1994e).
5. In Britain, there are a number of regional examination boards, often associated with universities, which draw up course syllabuses and assessment criteria for examination at 16 (GCSE) and 18 (A level). Schools are therefore able to choose which syllabuses to follow. The Schools Assessment and Examination Council (up to 1993) was an umbrella organisation that controlled standards while allowing diversity. It has been replaced by the School Curriculum and Assessment Authority (SCAA).
6. The CHP syllabus is available from the University of Cambridge Local Examinations Syndicate. The domains and levels described here have been revised for subsequent years.
7. See Kaufer and Geisler (1989).
8. Andrews and Costello (1992, p. 58).
9. See Newkirk (1989).
10. We are not suggesting here that argumentative structures are necessarily opposed to narrative structures. There is plenty of recent argument (and evidence) to suggest that essay structure can take the form of what is conventionally assumed to be narrative structures. See especially the work of Hesse (1986, 1989a,b and 1992) and Myerson (1992). We also know from classical sources (Aristotle, 1926; Cicero, 1954) that suggestions for the arrangement of speeches were not prescriptive, but that it was 'often necessary to employ such changes and transpositions when the cause itself obliges us to modify the arrangement prescribed by the rules of the Art' (Cicero, 1954, p. 187).
11. We should say here too that we do not believe narrative to be any less concerned than argument with the full range of cognitive skills. We consider there to be at least two ways of defining narrative; one requires only a low level of cognitive skill and is the rehearsal or repetition, whether it be of story or argument, of material which is already given. Many of the student essays we have read are narrative in this sense. The other kind of narrative results from the full range of cognitive skills. Narrative may, for instance, be the outcome of a process of argumentation; a way of reconciling or ordering within a single unified structure elements that previously had seemed disparate or at odds. At this level narrative is the creation of a new ordering: when the process of argumentation is over, that is to say, a new narrative may be in place. This is recognised also by the CHP: while narrative – as the mere repetition of knowledge – scores 0, a new narrative which is the outcome of complex cognitive operations, can score highly. The level 3 student 'demonstrates understanding of the reasons why and the ways in which different and competing lines of development may co-exist and be integrated within a single historical account' or 'can select, organise and interpret material so as to construct coherent narratives that make reference to concurrent sequences of events and different lines of development'.
12. The CHP seems also to acknowledge a difficulty with its rigorous assessment criteria, in so far as teachers may be unused to 'levels of response marking'. The syllabus advises teachers to 'be aware of "the learned response" and be satisfied that rewardable statements are the candidate's own'. In an ideal situation the conclusions on their own would not be sufficient to merit level 3, unless they were the outcome of earlier level 3 argument.
13. Strategies such as these are put forward by Geisler and Kaufer (1989). We have adapted them ourselves in preparing students to write essays on general and social issues around which so much public debate rages that developing a coherent personal argument often seems impossible.
14. The mark scheme (see Figure 1) is intended merely as a series of indicators as to how students might answer the question. Where a student meets the requirements of the level in a different way, *post hoc* indicators are written and added to the mark scheme.

CHAPTER NINETEEN

ARGUING ABOUT RESEARCH: THE LANGUAGE OF ESSAYS ABOUT RESEARCH METHODS IN EDUCATION AT UNDERGRADUATE LEVEL[*]

Richard Andrews

Research at undergraduate level in the UK is a growing phenomenon, manifesting itself in various ways. For some time, undergraduates have been expected to undertake short dissertations (or long essays) of up to about 12,000 words. These long essays have conventionally been review-like in nature, and so have not been seen as research as such. But now that, in Education Studies courses (and also in Engineering, English, Dance and other disciplines), long essays or short dissertations are sometimes underpinned by original small-scale research (partly because of the shift from teaching to learning in thinking about education at university level) the recognition of the role of research in the undergraduate degree is heightened.

The interest in the increasing part that research has to play in undergraduate study in Education is shared by Sweden. Lena-Pia Hagman (1996), for example, notes that there is little research on undergraduate dissertations. At the Hogskolan in Kristianstad, where she works, teacher education students have to plan, execute and evaluate a small-scale educational experiment and work by themselves – with supervision – through the conventional steps of designing and writing a study in Education: problem formulation, literature reviews, collecting and analysing data, etc. She has begun to research attitudes towards supervision on these undergraduate dissertations.

The present paper describes one such course, currently running at Middlesex University, London, and analyses actual research as well as writing *about* research by students on the course. In doing so, it draws on a current research project at Middlesex University, 'Improving the Quality of Argument in Higher Education' (Mitchell, 1996) which takes as one of its principal hypotheses that students will perform better at their undergraduate work if they can argue better. In this particular chapter, I look at whether that hypothesis holds true for writing up and writing about research.

---

[*] Previously unpublished paper, delivered at European Conference for Education Research, University of Seville, Seville, September 1996.

The course itself

The course, 'Approaches to Educational Research' is a relatively new course at Middlesex University. It tends to be taken by second- or third-year undergraduate students studying for a degree in Education or a combined degree on the multi-disciplinary programme. The course lasts 12 weeks, and consists of two hours a week of a taught component as well as the reading and writing that accompanies every such module. Because the course is compulsory for students majoring in Education, each autumn semester about 70 students take this course. It is a prerequisite for anyone wishing to undertake a 'proposition module', i.e. a mini-dissertation (6,000 or 12,000 words) towards the end of their degree programme.

The course is taught in a variety of ways – lecture, workshop, seminar, individual tutorial – and assessed with two coursework assignments. The criteria for assessing these assignments are made explicit to the students and form the basis of grading and of written responses to the assignments. The criteria are:

- critical grasp of the subject

- emphasis on the methodology: throughout the course the emphasis is on how to conduct educational research; it follows that one of the main emphases of the assignment should be on methods of research

- reference to at least two authoritative sources

- structure, accuracy and presentation of the assignment.

It is the first and last criteria that I wish to focus on now as I turn to a consideration of how students argue about research in their writing.

Analysing two essays

Two students undertook the following assignment:

> Choose one of the approaches to educational research that we have covered during the course. Give a full account of its procedures, the situations in which you might use it, and its strengths and weaknesses.

At first sight, the assignment does not seem to give room for argument. It asks for an *account*, i.e. a story, a tally. To a weaker student, the invitation to write such a narrative or classificatory/descriptive account is swallowed whole. The better students, however, see that in the wording of the assignment title is an invitation to go further: a *critical* account is much different. It asks for a weighing up of that particular kind of research against other kinds.

Here is the first paragraph of a very good response by one student, whom I shall call Dahlia:

> The approach to educational research chosen for close examination and analysis is action research; a notably controversial approach. Definitions vary, indicative of implicit tension between ideologies that lie behind the two words 'action' and 'research'. Its essence is succinctly expressed in '... action research is a small scale intervention in the functioning of the real world, and a close examination of the effects of such intervention' (Halsey in Cohen and Manion, 1994, p. 186). Positioned within the qualitative boundaries of research, it specifically relies on the reflective action of the practitioner. The intention is not confined to illuminating problems but is extended to addressing the need to resolve issues as the research develops. Further, action research is concerned with discovering hypotheses as well as attempting to test them. Where conventional research seeks to minimise subjectivity, action research seeks to utilise it and give it a degree of credibility. Consequently, to what extent does this approach raise issues concerned with both subjective and objective concepts of knowledge and truth? Although the answer to this question is not within the remit of this essay it is useful to discuss action research within this framework. The approach would appear to cause unease within certain quarters of the academic fraternity whilst it is met with acclaim and enthusiasm within sections of the teaching profession. Why is this? In order to give a full account of action research and set it in some context, it would seem necessary to first briefly discuss the history and political implications of this method of discovery and action.

Like many good answers to assignment questions or invitations (note that the title is not a question) to write, this one starts by addressing itself directly to the wording of the title: the approach is chosen. But immediately the student begins to open up the possibilities offered by the title with the appended noun phrase 'a notably controversial approach'. As an assessor of such writing, you can instantly tell you are reading something that is probably going to score highly. By establishing in the first sentence that action research is controversial, the student has set up for herself the opportunity to explore that controversy. From the very start, at least, there is promise of a discussion of arguments surrounding educational research.

The second sentence begins to explore the controversy about definitions of action research: 'Definitions vary, indicative of implicit tension between ideologies that lie behind the two words 'action' and 'research' and there follows a sentence quoting Halsey on action research, establishing quickly the student's credentials in referencing. The interesting aspect as far as argument however, is that the student has used the conventional practice of ing the terms that make up 'action research' to explore the *ideologies* behind the two words'. In other words, the student has created a discoursal space for herself by revealing a layer of underpinning to action research that indicates its political and historical derivation. She can now explore the relationship between the two levels – the surface and the foundational elements – and thus develop a *critical* account of action research. Not only are there ideologies to chart, but also the 'implicit tension' (as there always is in dialectical shaping of ideas) between ideologies, or systems of ideas.

The fourth sentence uses another argumentative strategy as it develops its course, and in doing so it employs a term that is central to argumentative debate: '*positioned* within the qualitative boundaries of research ...'. Good argument is not only aware of the grounds, warrants and backing underpinning its claims (terms from Toulmin et al.), but is also aware of the *position* of propositions within a particular territory or forum for argument. To put it another way, students who write such essays have to be aware of where the various ideas stand in relation to other ideas; otherwise they cannot begin to relate them or – better still – compare them. In this case, Dahlia is placing action research within the broader frame of qualitative research. Although she may be making a category mistake in doing so, in that action research is an approach to research while 'qualitative' describes the nature of the research data – the contextualising of the topic under examination within a broader frame allows for further discussion. Argument, then, thrives when the frames that are brought into play – as they have to be – can be compared with each other as well as helping to inform the phenomenon under consideration.

The paragraph continues with further exploration of the nature of action research, and then, mid-way, uses another helpful technique in argument. As with previous rhetorical moves, the use of 'Where conventional research seeks to minimise subjectivity, action research ...' creates a space for the student in which to operate. The surface syntax ('Where conventional research ... action research ...') is a manifestation of a deeper, ideational structuring that is going on. Because argument thrives on the creation of difference, which it fosters in order to clarify, develop and resolve, students have to carve out a space for the development of their own ideas. These ideas may not in themselves be original, but the carving out of space lends them a degree of rhetorical originality that will more than suffice at undergraduate level. In this case, Dahlia uses the creation of a working space to raise other (very broad) issues about 'subjective and objective concepts of knowledge and truth', thus creating yet another frame of analysis. As with judicious research, she acknowledges that answering such broader questions 'is not within the remit of this essay' but at least indicates that – should there be space, time and opportunity – she could explore them and that they do impact upon the narrower questions she has set herself.

It is important to recognise that she has indeed set herself questions to answer in her writing, even though the title of the assignment did not explicitly pose these questions. Her questions are concerned with where action research stands in relation to other kinds of research, what its various elements are, how it breaks away from convention, and – crucially – how its underpinning ideologies inform it. By asking these questions, she will be able to 'give a *full* account of its procedures, the situations in which [she] might use it, and its strengths and weaknesses'.

Thus, by setting action research in a number of contexts, she is able to launch into the rest of the essay with a clear sense of where she is going and with plenty of scope for the exploration of arguments and tensions within the field. The essay then develops, in large structural terms, along the following lines:

para 1	introduction
para 2	history of action research
para 3	debates about action research
para 4	core procedures
para 5	situations in which it might be used
para 6	extending the discussion: from primary and secondary school to higher education; further questions raised
para 7	conclusion – and a look beyond

The structure is a clear one, and there is evidence that it reflects the structuring of the thought that provides the argument of the essay. In argument, as opposed to narrative, the large-scale structuring of a piece is usually reflected in the surface paragraphing. In this particular essay, Dahlia's paragraphs neatly set action research in context and then address the elements required in the title in systematic fashion before coming to a conclusion – and suggesting more beyond the frames of the discussion that has taken place.

In Natalie's case – in answer to the same title but an answer receiving a lower grade – the structuring (to start with that aspect of the essay) is less appropriate. The sequence of paragraphs is as follows:

para 1	introduction
para 2	classification: where does case study sit in relation to other kinds of research?
para 3	when is it best to use case study?
para 4	ways in which case study can be carried out
para 5	another major step in carrying out case study
para 6	what are the uses of case study?
para 7	problems with summarising strengths and weaknesses
para 8	strengths
para 9	weaknesses
para 10	summary

I am confident that the paragraph structure of the essays analysed in this paper reflects their overall argument structure. Research I undertook between 1987 and 1992 (Andrews, 1992a) established that such a relationship between argument and paragraphing was much closer than in the case of narrative writing.

It might be evident from a glance at the overall structure of the piece that, in comparison with Dahlia's essay, Natalie's is more programmatic, more slavishly following prescription – as she sees it – of the offered title. An analysis of the first two paragraphs will reveal the differences more sharply. First, however, it should be noted that Natalie does not write out the assignment title at the top of her work. Though this may seem a schoolteacher's gripe, it indicates to me (as an inveterate schoolteacher) that already the actual assignment – despite Natalie's programmatic approach to it – is already left behind as she embarks on something rather different from what is really required. The title provided by Natalie is simply 'The Case Study', her chosen approach:

> Every year, newspaper headlines greet results from the latest educational research project (e.g. the *Times Educational Supplement*). Results are important, according to those in authority, and are even absolute – however parents and teachers do not seem to think so. Doubts soon follow by *'experts in the field'* about methods, statistics and interpretations. The original researcher, sometimes, also announces that they were wrong all along. However, research is necessary in all fields of learning in order to bring new facts and information to light. Without medical research we would not be able to find the causes and cures of diseases; without educational research we could not diagnose and help backwardness. However, it must not be assumed that research is done only in order to seek causes and cures – it is also essential in devising new techniques and improving old ones. In this present study one shall be discussing the procedures of case studies, the situations in which this method can be used to its advantage and its strengths and weaknesses.

> Research involving collecting data for the purpose of describing existing conditions is known as *descriptive research*. This is in contrast to studies which attempt to manipulate or control the environment, in order to investigate causal relationship, known as *experimental research*. The case study is a construct of the former mentioned research. It involves the detailed investigation of a single individual or a group of people – it describes events, situations or behaviour. In research, the definition of the case study includes a detailed description and analysis of a single person, event, institution or community. In clinical work, the benefits of case studies accrue primarily to the patient in that the individual is the subject. This is known as the *idiographic approach* in that behaviour and attitudes are attempted to be understood without generalising the results to other people or to groups. In contrast, most studies attempt to develop principles and theories having a wider applicability, whereby findings can be applied to large numbers of people, institutions or events (e.g. child case

studies by Piaget, from R.D. Gross, *Psychology – The Study of Mind and Behaviour*). This is known as the *nomothetic approach* ...

What distinguishes Natalie's opening from Dahlia's, and in particular what argumentative moves are being made here that are qualitatively different from those made by Dahlia? The opening paragraph seems characterised by confusion – both in the field, according to Natalie, and also in her own understanding and expression of that field. The second and third sentences ('Results are important ... they were wrong all along') paint a picture of muddled incompetence and of 'absolute' results. In fact the opening is of such unsupported generality as to inspire little confidence in the reader that this essay will develop into anything sharp enough to answer the (albeit tacit) question set in the title. An analogy is made with medical research to make the point that research is useful. At the end of that first paragraph, almost like a tag-sentence, comes a repeat of the assignment title.

The orienting function of the first paragraph – so clear in Dahlia's essay, is attempted here but with little impact. It is as if the real question in Natalie's mind as she wrote this was not that of the assignment (and its implications) but 'How do I start this essay and relate "research" to my own experience of reading articles in educational papers?' and 'How can I justify looking at research at all?' – questions that might be important in the development of a student's thought, but not relevant to the assignment in hand.

The second paragraph gives us an indication of how Natalie will develop her essay. In this paragraph she places case study – her chosen approach – in the 'descriptive' as opposed to 'experimental' camp of research, and then further classifies by subdividing case study into 'idiographic' and 'nomothetic' approaches. The creation of a space in which to write is not achieved, because the classificatory impulse of this second paragraph is descriptive and information-driven rather than potentially argumentative. That is to say, she does not give herself space in which to develop a critique of any of the positions mentioned. They are arrayed, as in a textbook, and although they fulfil the request for an *account* of case study as a research tool, they do not read into the real intention of the assignment title which is supported by the more explicit criteria for assessment. Furthermore, references – so useful in positioning yourself initially in relation to existing writing in the field – are used only to illustrate, and not used according to the conventions set out by the course. The distinctions made between descriptive and experimental research, and between idiographic and nomothetic approaches, are not pursued or used to open up a space between them in order to weigh one against the other. As Natalie says at the end of her second paragraph, each of the two approaches 'can complement the other'. The drive of her essay is thus to lay out rather than to distinguish; to follow a 'vow of obedience' rather than the 'vow of suspicion' so necessary to first-class performance in argumentation and academic writing.

Initial approaches to research

So far in this paper my analysis has concentrated more on the argumentative side of the students' work than on the conduct of research *per se*. I have wanted to do so in order to suggest that in writing about research, students have to be good arguers; they have to have sufficient grasp of the field to bring critical frames to bear upon instances in that field.

I now want to turn attention to early encounters with research proper, i.e. the mini-research projects which students undertake as part of the Approaches to Educational Research course before they embark on proposition modules. The mini-research projects require a small-scale study that can be written up in about 2,000 words – the length of the essays we have just been examining. Students choose their own topics to research, with the emphasis in the assessment being on the methods used rather than on the results of the research itself.

Although the emphasis of the course as a whole is on research methods, one of the principal aims of the course is to put methodology firmly in its place as a means rather than an end. As a result, in exploring and choosing methods with which to undertake research, students are encouraged to think of topics for research and main research questions (rather than hypotheses in such a short time-scale) *before* they plan their methodology. Two examples of these mini-research projects which I will use to illustrate what happens in the early attempts at research are by Nefti and Sara. Nefti's – a study of how 14-year-old students responded to an arts project co-ordinated by the Tate Gallery in association with the Royal National Theatre and the orchestra of St John's Smith Square – was part of a larger research project in which six of the undergraduate students took part, though each devised their own approach to a part of the evaluation of the project. Sara undertook to interview front-of-house staff at the Palace Theatre, London, to discover their attitudes to work in theatre.

The overall structure of Nefti's piece is as follows:

> Introduction
> Aims and objective
> Method
> Results
> Discussion
> Critique of methods
> Conclusion

In it she set out a clear research question – 'How do year 10 pupils at a school in the London Borough of Lambeth view art galleries?' and uses a questionnaire as her principal research tool. A pilot was conducted, and the final sample consisted of 70 pupils from a single-sex school in Lambeth. The questionnaire itself, following a session on questionnaire design at the university as part of the course, contained four types of question: yes/no, multiple choice, attitude scale and open. Teachers' help was enlisted to administer the questionnaire and a 61 per cent response rate was achieved. The results are set out in tables, and there are copious appendices to show the data collected, the pilot and other relevant material.

To give a flavour of the writing, here is a excerpt from the critique of methods section:

> The teachers may well have influenced the replies [from pupils to the questionnaire] by giving examples of illustration. The language of the questionnaire was very important to ensure that students were motivated to give their own thoughts and feelings on the subject. To overcome this suspected undue influence the questionnaire should have been administered by a professional researcher who knows how to probe without prompting.
>
> The questionnaire could have been submitted to the school for approval prior to administering it to pupils: the special needs co-ordinator could have been consulted to ensure language appropriate to the pupils' current state of education was used.

While not attaining a first-class grade, this report on a small-scale research project did receive a borderline first/upper second grade. Sara's work, on the other hand, was in the pass category. She attempted to interview four members of the Palace Theatre backstage staff during a performance – largely opportunistically, as she also works there – and chose a structured interview approach in order to ensure reliability of results. Reliability was achieved, but at the expense of validity as the answers to questions were hurried and brief, providing little substantial data. The report is brief and unstructured, with no sub-headings, and consists largely of an account of the problems encountered in first-person narrative. There are some gains made, as illustrated in this excerpt from the report:

> The results of the interviews were encouraging; I was able to discover answers to the questions I posed … If I did this assignment again I think that I would spend longer on the interviews and would pose more further-reaching questions. I would also make sure that the people that I interviewed were really wanting to answer the questions. I think that I would still use a structured approach as this is the one that works best when it comes to interviews.

What part does argument play in the reporting of research? It is perhaps a truism (though I recently heard this described as a deeply held principle) that research should be written up as a coherent argument, from beginning to end; that if there is anything extraneous to the argument, it should be relegated to an appendix. It seems clear from a brief analysis of the early research work of two students that the sense of shape, direction and coherence is important not only to the writing up of the research, but also to its initial design. Nefti, therefore, in hanging her research on a clear single research question, is able to come up with results in a way that Sara is not; but more importantly as far as the course in question is concerned and the success of her written report, she is able to judge critically the effectiveness of her methodology because she is clear what it is trying to do. Whereas Sara is confirmed in her use of structured interviews even though they are probably inappropriate for the kind of research she was undertaking, Nefti is able to see how her approach might be refined and adapted on future occasions.

Conclusion

What are the implications for practice and for further inquiry in the area of undergraduate research? As far as practice is concerned, I think the element of consideration of research as well as the undertaking of small-scale research projects on undergraduate courses can only be of benefit. In this way, not only do students have the chance to explore empirically something they really want to answer; they are also acquiring skills that will be of help to them as they embark on longer dissertations within the undergraduate programme or masters and doctoral level research subsequently. Furthermore, in building up a research culture at undergraduate level, a foundation is being laid for further work and also for integrating undergraduate with postgraduate students who are engaged in research. And as a method of learning rather than being taught, research enables the student to discover for herself and through experience how knowledge is created and developed.

A further implication for practice concerns the argumentative dimension. Instruction in rhetorically tested formulae for good argumentative writing seems unlikely to be productive. Rather, examination of good models of argumentative writing with students; discussion of how argumentative and critical space is created in undergraduate essays and other forms; experimentation with different structures in the presentation and generation of small- and large-scale pieces of writing; exploration of criteria for the assessment of essays and discussion of the tacit assumptions made by lectures and embedded in assignment titles might all be of help to students as they aim to improve their work and their grades.

But the areas of undergraduate research and its relation to argumentative skill are in need of further research. Questions pose themselves such as: What learning methods does research encourage? How can these best be fostered by teachers and lecturers? What is the exact relationship between research and argument? And finally – perhaps the sticking point – How can we encourage lecturing staff to become more interested in the discourses – both disciplinary and textual – which they often take for granted and which some students struggle to understand?

CHAPTER TWENTY

THE UNDERGRADUATE DISSERTATION: IMPROVING THE QUALITY OF ARGUMENT[*]

Sally Mitchell and Mike Riddle

The study which forms the basis of this paper set out to investigate the quality of argument in undergraduate dissertations. In this paper we take an oblique approach to what we found out about the dissertations by exploring the processes we have been through *as researchers*. We extrapolate from the data we have collected to draw parallels between our experience and that of the students undertaking the dissertation exercise. Our emphasis is on the *process* of generating claims in relation to data and theory; on the process, that is, of discovering what it is we want to argue. Our further concern is to distinguish between the process of doing research and the options which then present themselves for writing. At the end of the paper we suggest that the student 'dissertation' might have two written outcomes: one which allows the vicissitudes of undertaking the research to be expressed; the other which constitutes an argument on the basis of what has been discovered.

Context

It may be useful to understand the context from which this study emerged. In September 1995 a three-year project was begun at Middlesex University in London entitled 'Improving the Quality of Argument in Higher Education'. The aims of the project are to diagnose the problems students have in conducting argument and to develop strategies and materials by which their abilities can be improved. Since an important thrust of the project is to make change, collaboration between researchers and teaching staff is seen as essential to its success. Thus, members of staff from a number of disciplines across the university have joined in formulating aims and outcomes, which address their particular perceptions of how the quality of argument can be improved. In some cases, these same members of staff have become co-researchers in the diagnosis of problems; in all cases the impetus is on them to carry forward the implications of the diagnosis into practice.

---

[*] Paper presented at the EARLI conference, Barcelona, October 1996.

The study of argument in undergraduate dissertations emerged from discussions with staff in one School of the Faculty of Social Science. Whilst they considered the final-year dissertation to be the defining exercise of undergraduate study, they were often dissatisfied with what the students produced. Much of their unease centred around argument and associated skills of reasoning and analysis. Involvement in the Argument Project might be a useful way of clarifying the role and nature of the dissertation and might provide pointers to improved student performance.

This paper is being written close to the end of the diagnostic phase of the study, which has been undertaken by us, neither of whom are specialists in the particular Social Science field. We see ourselves as in some way commissioned by the Social Scientists to investigate an area identified as problematic in terms of argument. They are therefore the most immediate audience for our findings and recommendations. We have to be good at making our case persuasive, because we rely upon them to test our ideas.

The dissertations

The data for our research was a sample of 16 texts, half of which were 10,000 words long (the dissertation proper) and half, 5,000 words (known as the 'Proposition Module'). From our first reading, we picked out a number of general characteristics. Organisation of the texts was generally according to the following sequence of headings: Abstract, Introduction and aims, Literature review, Methodology, Results, Discussion, Conclusion. The discourse was often fragmented and there was redundancy and repetition of material, which suggested that writers had approached each of the sections independently. The Literature review appeared to function as a report of what had been read, sometimes yielding models for analysis, but seldom advancing the theoretical position for the writer. Recording the processes of undertaking the empirical research (Methodology and Results) generally outweighed the goal of inferring 'new' conceptualisations from the investigation. Although writers sometimes wished to infer conclusions from their research, the moves they made were not motivated by an argumentative goal. The dissertation texts, we quickly concluded, did not represent arguments.

What they did represent was not, however, very clear. Our overall impression was of a continuum. At one end were writers who advocated a position very strongly and then elaborated it with descriptive detail and supportive documentation. At the other end were those who endeavoured to use models to examine their case, satisfying themselves that they had found out something through their investigation. Many texts were a mixture of approaches.

When we interviewed staff we found a corresponding lack of consistency about what a dissertation should be. Some appeared to advocate the investigation of a particular case, making descriptive statements as a basis for arriving at evaluative conclusions, with recommendations. Others insisted that theory should link in with the data analysis. Yet others would go further, and want these theories themselves be held up to scrutiny, and so on. In general though staff were agreed that students should show that they were writing 'in an academic context'.

Our overall sense was that students were responding to a mixture of messages from tutors, handbooks and their general notions of research and academic conventions – and that the single text of the dissertation was being required to fulfil too many functions. In part this overloading seemed to arise from a conflation of the writing up process with the process of undertaking the research itself – the word 'dissertation' standing in for both. We began to treat 'the dissertation' not just as the name of a text but as a concept to which a variety of academic beliefs and practices adhered.

Reflecting on the process of research

As we have developed our thinking about the data we have collected, we have also reflected on our own experience of doing research of this kind. We have increasingly focused on what a 'research process' needs to be, in order to place the researcher in a position to argue a case. We have therefore tried to make explicit, to ourselves, in our research meetings, the investigatory moves we have made and to speculate upon correspondences with the students' task: 'What has been important to us in the work and what can this tell us about the students' experience? Where are the similarities and differences?'

One thing we noticed was how challenging for us it had been to work collaboratively. In contrast, we realised, the students' experience must be very isolated. They have occasional tutorial time but no real collaborator. On the other hand when staff commented that in the modular system students could not be assumed to have a single discipline behind them, we saw parallels with ourselves. Whilst we both considered ourselves to be students of argument in the educational process, we had differing disciplinary and research origins. These differences forced us to clarify for each other why each of us used certain theories and methods and to inquire whether we are going in roughly the same direction. Working in isolation and often foregoing tutorial opportunities, students were less likely to examine their own assumptions even though the dissertation might invoke input from a number of disciplines. Moreover, advice often given when starting a project is to 'find something you want to study, a topic, etc.', and little emphasis is given to establishing 'where you are at'.

Where are we coming from?

For us, this early period of questioning presuppositions and establishing a frame of reference was important. We came to broadly characterise our approach as phenomenological; that is we would aim to explain what was going on in what we were studying. We found ourselves negotiating a number of overlapping paradigms, for example were we looking at the structuring of relevant courses (an institutional perspective), or at the potential of students to meet the demands of some highly valued academic convention? We noted that one of the geography staff was asking for students to do just the same: to keep their approach open to the different perspectives contributed by different paradigms.

At this early stage we were also aware that our orientation was decidedly towards argument: that is, we had a preference. For students too, holding a belief is a motivation to undertake a difficult investigation, and makes it worth doing. Whilst staff valued the empirical research that students did as 'competence forming', we would add that having the courage and permission to develop a belief is also competence forming. Many of the students showed evidence of such commitment but their opportunities to express and substantiate it seemed hampered.

What kind of approach?

Having worked out a shared frame of reference we were able to think about our methodology and to elaborate our theoretical apparatus. Following some standard sources we seemed to have the option of a descriptive approach (DA) or a hypothetical deductive approach (HDA). In so far as their difference can be characterised: an HDA results in a demonstration; a DA results in an explanation. The HDA is about verification and begins with a well-formed hypothesis; whilst the DA is about the generation of theory. As we talked it became clear that we were developing a descriptive approach. It would be no good to be driven by a hypothesis such as 'If a dissertation is good then it will be so on account of the degree of argumentation in it. And so, there will be a high correlation between the existence of argument in dissertations and marks given in assessment'. We needed to be more open and exploratory than that.

It is important to note at this point that our choice of the DA constituted no commitment to a descriptive/narrative account of our research in any eventual write-up. Writing up as we want to argue is a separate part of the work, in which the ultimate goal in terms of audience plays an important role in the choice of structure. There are, in fact, a number of options to choose from. For the students in our sample, however, the predominant way of writing up was to replicate the research chronology with a narrative approach.

Developing an overall hypothesis

Guiding our descriptive approach was what we termed an 'overall hypothesis' – a set of assumptions about what we thought dissertations were supposed to be, deriving from theoretical notions of structure, genre, discourse, the influence of staff practice on student performance, and so on. Taking our theoretical standpoint and relating it to the case in this way created a particular image of the object of our study. This overall hypothesis could then be modified, challenged and further explored as the empirical work proceeded. We anticipated in fact that aspects of the dissertations would re-adjust our conceptualisation.

Some students in our sample did describe some kind of overall hypothesis in the early parts of their dissertations, but they were on the whole reluctant to return to it and assess how far it had survived the findings. The general strategy, we found, was to veer off the original standpoints without acknowledging this – in the case of one student simply inserting a substitute set of objectives later in the text.

Turning thinking into action ...

The overall hypothesis was the basis from which we developed our strategies for gathering data. If, for example, we wanted to know how handout advice transferred to the texts, we would need to analyse the texts; and probe students' understanding of the terminology used and the advice offered. If we considered the beliefs and practices of staff to be important to our understanding of the dissertations then we would need a way of assessing their conceptualisations. When we devised our rather weighty staff interview schedule, the theories embedded in our overall hypothesis were important in determining our questions and in making sense of the answers we got. At the same time some of our questions were less clearly theoretical, deriving from hunches and drawing on the kind of academic folklore that we had both acquired by our interest in writing, argument, learning and assessment.

In the students' dissertations the framing of research questions is often a considerable weakness. They seldom seem to be located in theoretical positions, but rather aim to elicit basic factual material about the case being studied. Aims articulated as the intention 'to investigate', 'to identify', 'to analyse' suggest what *techniques* are being used but give no indication of the position which is shaping then. There is of course a fine balance between a genuine openness and the need to have some informed stance when starting an investigation of the sort both students and ourselves were engaged in. The difficulty seemed to be compounded in the students' writing by an interpretation of the academic writing task as a place for the neutral distanced reporting of an investigation, in which 'bias' is unwelcome.

... and back again

As we gathered and examined data we began to feel confident about making descriptive statements about the written form of the dissertations, and the way they are conceived by staff. We were also settling on a concept of the 'dissertation' and forming our theory about what the 'dissertation' might become. We 'instantiated our overall hypothesis' by moving between the phenomena and theorising. Different elements of emerging generalisations were pulled into view by the data we were gathering; at the same time the data revised and modified those generalisations.

Many students in our sample, as we've suggested, have not set themselves up to tackle the inter-connectedness of theory and data in this way. Instantiation for them is making statements about states of affairs as revealed by the methodology. The dynamic strategy of reinforcing or modifying emergent generalisations is very difficult for them. The conclusion in their write-up seems to be a closure on the case investigated, and seldom a set of generalisations that can function in the academic discourse as starting points for further study options. In our case, we are able to follow our conclusions with a set of *particular* hypotheses that can go on to be refuted or confirmed. We could, for example, assert that the dissertation is not functioning properly in the education of our sample of undergraduates and that, 'for the dissertation to function properly we recommend certain changes be made!'

Making particular hypotheses

What would these changes be? First, we suggest that if students' performance in the dissertation is to be improved, then revisions are required in the way students conceive of and go about research. The emphasis on technical skills needs to be balanced by understanding of the relations between theory, method and the interpretation of results. Students should understand, for example, what the function of reviewing the literature is in the overall process of research.

Second, we suggest that the role of writing as a way of assessing the 'dissertation' should be reconsidered. We have been experimenting with turning the students' existing texts around into various other kinds of text including the 'journal article' and 'essay'. This reveals that many of the students generally 'know' enough to be able to argue, but cannot seem to effect the switch out of the descriptive approach and the strait-jacket imposed by the 'section headings' they are given. We believe that when they have completed their empirical research, students should be prepared to ask new sets of questions. These will concern: a) the claim of hypotheses it is now possible to make – 'On the basis of my research where do I stand?' 'What kind of claim can I make? and b) the purposes and goals of writing – 'Who am I writing for?' 'How can I convince them?'. The writing, we suggest should be an argument, rather than a narrative account, and it should be nothing like as long as the 10,000 words presently demanded.

Alongside the argument, however, we also consider that the process of research should continue to be valued and that students should write this up too – but as they experience it, that is, all its complexity and disorderliness. So in our recommendations, this entity called the 'dissertation' results in two assessable products: a written log of the process undergone and a short argumentative essay or other text relating to the concepts, theories and phenomena that were researched.

Here, then, is a *particular hypothesis* to emerge from our process of research to date, and it is this that we will take to our colleagues in the Social Sciences trusting that they will consider it plausible enough to test with a future cohort of students.

BIBLIOGRAPHY

Andrews, R. ed. 1989. *Narrative and Argument*. Milton Keynes: Open University Press.

Andrews, R. 1992a. 'An exploration of narrative and argumentative structures in writing, with particular reference to the work of year 8 students'. Unpublished, University of Hull, Hull.

Andrews, R. 1992b. *Rebirth of Rhetoric - essays in language, culture and education*. London: Routledge.

Andrews, R. 1993a. 'Argument in schools: the value of a generic approach', *Cambridge Journal of Education* 23 (2): 277-85.

Andrews, R. 1993b. 'The future of English: reclaiming the territory', *English in Australia* 106, December 1993, pp. 41-54.

Andrews, R. 1994. 'Democracy and the teaching of argument', *English Journal* 83 (6): 62-9.

Andrews, R. 1995. *Teaching and Learning Argument*. London: Cassell.

Andrews, R. 1997. 'Reconceiving argument', *Educational Review* 49 (3): 259-69.

Andrews, R. and S. Clarke. 1996. 'A pile of iron filings: information, information technology and the English curriculum', *The English and Media Magazine* 35: 35-9.

Andrews, R. and P. Costello. 1992. *Improving the Quality of Argument 7-16: Interim Report*. Hull: University of Hull, Centre for Studies in Rhetoric.

Andrews, R., P. Costello. and S. Clarke. 1993. *Improving the Quality of Argument, 5-16: Final Report*. Hull: University of Hull, Centre for Studies in Rhetoric, School of Education.

Andrews, R. and A. Fisher. 1991. *Narratives*. Cambridge: Cambridge University Press.

Andrews, R. and S. Mitchell. 1994. 'The development of argument in English and politics in 16-18 year old students', *Literacy Learning: Secondary Thoughts* 1 (2).

Antaki, C. 1994. *Explaining and Arguing: the social organisation of texts* London: Sage.

Aristotle. 1926. *The 'Art' of Rhetoric*. Translated by John Henry Freese. London: Heinemann.

Armitage, S. 1991. *Kid*. London: Faber and Faber.

Bakhtin, M. 1981. *The Dialogic Imagination*. Austin, TX: University of Texas Press.

Barnes, D., J. Britton and M. Torbe, eds. 1989. *Language, the Learner and the School*. 4th ed. Portsmouth, NH: Heinemann/Boynton Cook.

Barthes, R. 1966. *Introduction to the Structural Analysis of Narratives*. Birmingham: University of Birmingham, Centre for Contemporary Cultural Studies.

Barton, D. 1994. *Literacy: an introduction to the ecology of written language*. Oxford: Blackwell.

Bazerman, C. 1988. *Shaping Written Knowledge: the genre and activity of the experimental article in science*. Madison, WI: University of Wisconsin Press.

Bazerman, C. 1994. *Constructing Experience*. Carbondale and Edwardsville: Southern Illinois University Press.

Beard, R. 1986. 'Reading resources and children's writing'. In *Resources for Reading: does quality count*, edited by B. Ropopt. London: UK Reading Association.

Berkenkotter, C., T. Huckin and J. Ackerman. 1988. 'Conventions, conversations and the writer: case study of a student in a rhetoric PhD program', *Research in the Teaching of English* 22 (1): 9-44.

Berrill, D. 1990a. 'Adolescents arguing'. In *Spoken English Illuminated*, edited by A. Wilkinson, A. Davis and D. Berrill. Milton Keynes: Open University Press.

Berrill, D. 1990b. 'What exposition has to do with argument: argumentative writing of sixteen year olds', *English in Education* 24 (9): 77–92.

Billig, M. 1987. *Arguing and Thinking: A Rhetorical Approach to Social Psychology*. Cambridge: Cambridge University Press.

Billig, M. 1991. *Ideology and Opinions*. London: Sage Publications.

Bloom, B., ed. 1956. *Taxonomy of Educational Objectives: Book 1 Cognitive Domain*. New York: David McKay Company Inc.

Board, The Associated Examining. 1991. Reports of Examiners, June Examination 1991. Guildford: Assoicated Examination Board.

Booth, W. 1961. *The Rhetoric of Fiction*. Chicago: University of Chicago Press.

Bremond, C. 1973. *Logique du recit*. Paris: Editions du Seuil.

Britton, J. et al. 1975 *The Development of Writing Abilities 11-16* London: Heinemann

Britton, J. 1987. 'Vygoytsky's contribution to pedagogical theory', *English in Education* 21 (3): 23 ff.

Brown, J. et al. 1990. *Developing English for TVEI (The Technical and Vocational Education Initiative)*. Leeds: University of Leeds/The Training Agency.

Burningham, J. 1983. *The Shopping Basket*. London: Picture Lions.

Christie, F. 1984. *Children's Writing: study guide*. Geelong: Deakin University Press.

Cicero. 1954. *Ad Herennium*. Translated by Henry Caplan. London: Heinemann.

Clarke, S. 1984. 'An area of neglect', *English in Education* 18 (2): 67–73.

Clarke, S. and J. Sinker. 1992. *Arguments*. Cambridge: Cambridge University Press.

Cohen, L. and Manion, L. 1994. *Research Methods in Education*. London: Routledge

Coirier, P. 1996. 'Composing argumentative texts: cognitive and/or textual complexity'. In *Theories, Models and Methodology in Writing Research*, edited by G. Tijlaarsdam, A. van den Berg and M. Coulzijin. Amsterdam: Amsterdam University Press.

Davis, C. and R. Scheifer. 1991. *Criticism and Culture: the role of critique in modern literary theory*. Harlow: Longman.

Dearing, R. 1994. The National Curriculum and its Assessment: Final Report (The Dearing Report). London: The School Curriculum and Assessment Authority.

Democrats, Liberal. 1993. *Facing up to the Future: Enduring Values in a Changing World*. London: Liberal Democrat Publications Ltd.

DES. 1989. *English in the National Curriculum* (The Cox Report). London: Department of Education and Science

DES. 1990. *English in the National Curriculum*. London: Her Majesty's Stationery Office.

Devitt, A. 1993. 'Generalizing about genre: new conceptions of an old concept', *College Composition and Communication* 44 (4).

Dixon, J. 1989. 'If it's narrative, why do nothing by Generlise?' In *Narrative and Argument*, edited by R. Andrews. Milton Keynes: Open University Press.

Dixon, J. and L. Stratta. 1982. 'Argument: what does it mean to teachers of English?', *English in Education* 16 (1): 41–54.

Dixon, J. and L. Stratta. 1986a. *Writing Narrative – and Beyond*. Ottawa: CCTE Publications.

Dixon, J. and L. Stratta. 1986b. 'Argument and the teaching of English: a critical analysis'. In *The Writing of Writing*, edited by A. Wilkinson. Milton Keynes: Open University Press.

Fitzgerald, B. 1992. 'A child-centred approach to genre', *English in Education* 26 (2).

Flower, L. and J. Hayes. 1981a. 'A cognitive process theory of writing', *College Composition and Communication* 32: 365–87.

Flower, L. and J. Hayes. 1981b. 'Plans that guide the composing process'. In *Writing: the Nature, Development and Teaching of Written Communication. Writing: Process, Development and Communication*, edited by C.H. Frederiksen and J.F. Dominic. Hillsdale, NJ: Lawrence Erbaum Associates.

Foucault, M. 1972. *The Archaeology of Knowledge*. London: Tavistock.

Fox, C. 1989. 'Divine dialogues'. In *Narrayive and Argument*, edited by R.J. Andrews. Milton Keynes: Open University Press.

Fox, C. 1990. 'The genesis of argument in narrative discourse', *English in Education* 24 (1).

Freadman, A. 1988. 'Anyone for tennis'. In *The Place of Genre in Learning: current debates*. Deakin: Typereader Publications no 1, Centre for Studies in Literary Education, Deakin University.

Freedman, A. 1987. 'Learning to write again: discipline-specific writing at university'. *Carleton Papers in Applied Language Studies* 4: 95–115.

Freedman, A and I. Pringle. 1980a. *Reinventing the Rhetorical Tradition*. Conway, AR: L & S Books for The Canadian Council of Teachers of English.

Freedman, A. and I. Pringle. 1980b. 'Writing in the college years', *College Composition and Communiction*, October 1980, pp. 311–24.

Freedman, A. and I. Pringle. 1984. 'Why students can't write arguments', *English in Education* 18 (2): 73–84.

Freedman, A. and I. Pringle. 1989. 'Contexts for developing argument'. In *Narrative and Argument*, edited by R. Andrews. Milton Keynes: Open University Press.

Freedman, A. and P. Medway. 1994. *Teaching and Learning Genre*. Portsmouth, NH: Heinemann/Boynton-Cook.

Gee, J. 1991. *Social Linguisitics and Literacies: Ideology in Discourses*. London: Falmer Press.

Gee, J.P. 1989. 'Literacy discourse and linguistics: introduction', *Journal of Education* 171 (1): 5–17.

Geertz, C. 1973. *The Interpretation of Cultures*. New York: Basic Books.

Geertz, C. 1983. *Local Knowledge*. New York: Basic Books.

Geertz, C. 1988. *Works and Lives: the anthropologist as author*. Stanford: Stanford University Press.

Geisler, C. 1992. 'Exploring academic literacy: an experiment in composing', *College Composition and Communication* 43 (1): 39–45.

Geisler, C. 1994. *Academic Literacy and the Nature of Expertise*. New Jersey: Lawrence Erlbaum Associates.

Geisler, C. and D. Kaufer. 1989. 'Making meaning in literate conversations: a teachable sequence for reflective writing', *Rhetoric Society Quarterly* 19: 229–43.

Gibson, H. and R. Andrews. 1993. 'A critique of the chronological/non-chronological distinction in the National Curriculum for English', *Educational Review* 45 (3): 239ff.

Giddens, A. 1986. *The Constitution of Society*. Berkeley and Los Angeles, CA: University of California Press.

Giltrow, J. and M. Valiquette. 1994. 'Genres and knowledge: students writing in the disciplines'. In *Learning and Teaching Genre*, edited by A. Freedman and P. Medway. Portsmouth, NH: Heinemann/Boynton-Cook

Glaser, N. and A.L. Strauss. 1967. *The Discovery of Grounded Theory*. London: Weidenfeld and Nicholson.

Goggin, M.D. 1995. 'Situating the teaching and learning of argumentation within historical contexts'. In *Competing and Consensual Voices*, edited by P. and S.M. Costello. Clevedon: Multilingual Matters.

Goodrich, P. 1996. *Reading the Law*. Oxford: Basil Blackwell.

Gorman, M.D. et al., eds. 1988. *Language Performances in Schools: Review of APU Language Monitoring 1979–1983*. London: HMSO.

Gross, J. 1991. *The Oxford Book of Essays*. Oxford: Oxford University Press.

Hagman, L.P. 1996. 'Supervision of undergraduate dissertations from a student perspective', 7–10 March 1996, at Lillehammer.

Halliday, M. and R. Hasan. 1976. *Cohesion in English*. London: Longman.

Harland, J., Kinder, K. and Hartley, K. 1995. *Arts in Their View: a study of youth participation in the arts*. York: National Foundation for Educational Research

Harré, R. 1983. *Personal Being*. Oxford: Basil Blackwell.

Harris, J. 1986a. 'Children as writers'. In *Literacy: teaching and learning language skills*, edited by A. Cashdan. Oxford: Blackwell.

Harris, J. 1986b. 'Organization in children's writing'. In *Children's Writing: a linguistic view*, edited by J. and J.W. Harris. London: Allen & Unwin.

Harris, J. and S. Kay. 1981. *Writing Development: suggestions for a policy 8–13*. Rotherham: Rotherham Education Committee.

Heilker, P. 1996. *The Essay: Theory and Pedagogy for an Active Form*. Urbana: National Council of Teachers of English.

Hesse, D. 1986. 'The story in the essay', University of Iowa, Iowa City.

Hesse, D. 1989a. 'Persuading as storing: essays, narrative rhetoric and the college writing course'. In *Narrative and Argument*, edited by R. Andrews. Milton Keynes: Open University Press.

Hesse, D. 1989b. 'Stories in essays, essays as stories'. In *Literary Non-fiction*, edited by C. Anderson. Carbondale, IL: Southern Illinois University Press.

Hesse, D. 1992. 'Aristotle's poetics and rhetoric: narrative as rhetoric's fourth mode'. In *Rebirth of Rhetoric: Essays in Language, Culture and Education*, edited by R. Andrews. London: Routledge.

Higgins, L. 1994. *Negotiating Competing Schemas for Discourse: Framework and Study of Argument Construction*. Pittsburgh: Carnegie Mellon University.

Honderich, T. 1995. *The Oxford Companion to Philosophy*. Oxford: Oxford University Press.

Hutchins, P. 1976. *Don't Forget the Bacon*. London: Bodley Head.

Ivanic, R. and D. Roach. 1990. *Academic Writing, Power and Disguise, Working Paper Series*. Lancaster: University of Lancaster, Centre for Languae in Social Life.

Johnson, N. and J. Mandler. 1980. 'A tale of two structures', *Poetics* 9: 51–86.

Kaufer, D. and C. Geisler. 1989. 'Novelty in academic writing', *Written Communication* 8: 286–311.

Kress, G. 1989a. *Linguistic Processes in Sociocultural Practice*. 2nd ed. Oxford: Oxford University Press.

Kress, G. 1989b. 'Texture and meaning'. In *Narrative and Argument*, edited by R. Andrews. Milton Keynes: Open University Press.

Kuhn, D. 1991. *The Skills of Argument*. Cambridge: Cambridge University Press

Labov, W. and J. Waletsky. 1967. 'Narrative analysis: oral versions of personal experience'. In *Essays of the Verbal and Visual Arts*, edited by J. Helm. Seattle: University of Washington Press.

Lamb, C. 1991. 'Beyond argument in feminist composition', *College Composition and Communication* 42.

Lanham, R. 1993. *The Electronic Word: Democracy, Technology and the Arts*. Chicago: University of Chicago Press.

Liberal Democrats. 1993. *Facing up to the Future*. London. Liberal Democractic Party

LINC. 1992. *Languages in the National Curriculum: material for professional development*. Nottingham: Nottingham University.

Lobel, A. 1973. *Frog and Toad Together*. London: Puffin.

Longacre, R. and S Levinson. 1978. 'Field analysis of discourse'. In *Current Trends in Text Linguistic*, edited by W.U. Dressle. Berlin: Walter de Gruyter.

Mandler, J. and N. Johnson. 1977. 'Remembrance of things parsed: story structure and recall', *Cognitive Psychology* 9: 111–51.

Mathison, M. 1994. 'Discourse about Discourse: constructing arguments in sociology'. Unpublished paper.

Matsen, P. et al., eds. 1990. *Readings from Classical Rhetoric*. Carbondale, IL: Southern Illinois University.

Medway, P. 1986. 'What gets written about'. In *The Writing of Writing*, edited by A. Wilkinson. Milton Keynes: Open University Press.

Meyer, S.L. 1993. 'Refusing to play the confidence game: the illusion of mastery in the reading/writing of texts', *College English* 55 (1).

Miller, C. 1984. 'Genre as social action', *Quarterly Journal of Speech* 70: 151–67.

Mitchell, S. 1992a. *The Teaching and Learning of Argument in Sixth Forms and Higher Education: interim report*. Hull: University of Hull, Centre for Studies in Rhetoric.

Mitchell, S. 1992b. *Questions and Schooling: Classroom Discourse across the Curriculum*. Hull: University of Hull, Centre for Studies in Rhetoric.

Mitchell, S. 1993a. 'The aesthetic and the academic: are they at odds in English Literature at A level', *English in Education* 27 (1): 19–28.

Mitchell, S. 1993b. 'Learning to be critical and correct: forms and functions of argument at A level' *Curriculum* 14 (1).

Mitchell, S. 1993c. 'Not so much a "trying out" as a handing-in-challenge to the academic essay', *CUE News: The Newsletter of the Council for University English* (5): 2.

Mitchell, S. 1994a. 'Argument in English literature at A level and beyond', *English and Media Magazine* 30.

Mitchell, S. 1994b. 'Learning to operate successfully in advanced level history'. In *Teaching and Learning Genre*, edited by A. and P.M. Freedman. London: Heinemann Boynton/Cook.

Mitchell, S. 1994c. 'A level and beyond: a case study', *English in Education* 28 (2): 36–47.

Mitchell, S. 1994d. 'Room for argument in English Literature at A level and beyond', *ETUDE Newsletter* 2.

Mitchell, S. 1994e. *The Teaching and Learning of Argument in Sixth Forms and Higher Education*. Hull: University of Hull, Centre for Studies in Rhetoric.

Mitchell, S. 1995a. 'Argument, rhetoric and reason: some practical suggestions for teaching' in *SELF Seminariernes Engelskloererforening* 95: 1.

Mitchell, S. 1995b. 'Learning to argue in disciplinary discourses' in *Proceedings of the Third ISSA Conference on Argumentation Volume III: Reconstruction and Application*, University of Amsterdam: SICSAT, pp. 304–12.

Mitchell, S. 1995c. 'Conflict and conformity: the place of argument in learning a discourse'. In *Competing and Consensual Voices: The Theory and Practice of Argument*, edited by P. Costello, and S. Mitchell. Clevedon: Multilingual Matters.

Mitchell, S. 1996. *Improving the Quality of Argument in Higher Education: interim report*. London: Middlesex University, School of Education.

Mitchell, S. 1996a. 'Institutions, individuals and talk: the construction of identity in Fine Art' *Journal of Art and Design Education* 15 (2).

Mitchell, S. and Riddle, M. 2000. *Improving the Quality of Argument in Higher Education: final report*. London: Middlesex University, School of Lifelong Learning and Education

Moffett, J. 1968. *Teaching the Universe of Discourse*. Boston, MA: Houghton Mifflin.

Moffett, J. 1981. *Active Voice*. Vol. 1. Upper Montclair, NJ: Boynton/Cook.

Moffett, J. 1986. *Active Voice*. Vol. 4. Upper Montclair, NJ: Boynton/Cook.

Myerson, G. 1992. *The Argumentative Imagination*. Manchester: Manchester University Press.

NCC. 1989b. National Curriculum Council Consultation Report: English. York: National Curriculum Council.

Newkirk, T. 1989. *Critical Thinking and Writing: Reclaiming the Essay*. Urbana, IL: National Council of Teachers in English.

Olson, D. 1977. 'From utterance to text: the bias of language in speech and writing', *Harvard Educational Review* 47 (3): 257–81.

Pavel, T. 1985. *Fictional Worlds*. Cambridge, MA: Harvard University Press.

Paz, O. 1974. *Alternating Current*. London: Wildwood House.

Pearson, R.A. and T. Phelps. *Academic Vocabulary and Argument: an introductory guide*. Sheffield: Sheffield Hallam University, Pavic Publications.

Perera, K. 1984. *Children's Writing and Reading*. Oxford: Blackwell.

Pringle, I. and A. Freedman. 1979. *The Carleton Writing Project. Part One*. Ottawa: Carleton University.

Pringle, I. and A. Freedman. 1980. *The Carleton Writing Project. Part 2*. Ottawa: Carleton University.

Pringle, I. and A. Freedman. 1985. *A Comparative Study of Writing Abilities in Two Modes at the Grades 5, 8 and 12 Levels*. Toronto: Ministry of Education.

Propp, V. 1968. *Morphology of the Folktale, American Folklore Society Bibliographical and Special Services No. 9*. Austin, TX: University of Texas Press.

Reid, G. 1991. 'Agree with me: the argumentative function in children's writing', MEd dissertation, University of Hull, Hull.

Ricoeur, P. 1970. *Freud and Philosophy*. New Haven: Yale University Press.

Ricouer, P. 1981. 'Narrative time'. In *On Narrative*, edited by W.J.T. Mitchell. Chicago, IL: University of Chicago Press.

Riddle, M, ed. 1997. *The Quality of Argument: A Colloquium on Issues of Teaching and Learning in Higher Education*. London: Middlesex University, School of Lifelong Learning and Education.

Riddle, M. 2000. 'Improving argument by parts' in Mitchell, S. and Andrews, R. (eds) *Learning to Argue in Higher Education*. Portsmouth, NH: Heinemann/Boynton-Cook

Rogoff, B. 1990. *Apprenticeship in Thinking*. New York: Oxford University Press.

Rosen, M. 1983. 'Today I ate'. In *Quick, Let's Get Out of Here*. London: Andre Deutsch.

Rosenblatt, L. 1978. *The Reader, The Text, The Poem*. Southern Illinois University Press.

Rumelhart, D. 1975. 'Notes on a schema for stories'. In *Language, Thought and Culture: advances in the study of cognition*, edited by D.G. and. A.C. Bowrow. New York: Academic Press.

Scholes, R. 1985. *Textual Power: Literary Theory and the Teaching of English*. New Haven: Yale University Press.

Schuster, C. 1985. 'Mikhail Bakhtin as rhetorical theorist', *College English* 47 (6).

Sheeran, Y. and D. Barnes. 1991. *School Writing*. Buckingham: Open University Press.

Snyder, I. 1992. 'Writing with wordprocessors: a way to develop students' argumentative writing skills', *English in Education* 28 (2): 35ff.

Stein, M. and C.G. Glenn. 1979a. 'The role of structural varieties in children's recall of simple stories', Paper read at Society for Research in Child Development, New Orleans.

Stein, N. and C. Glenn. 1979b. 'An analysis of story comprehension in elementary school children'. In *New Directions in Discourse Processing*, edited by R.O. Freedle. Norwood, NJ: Ablex.

Stein, N.L. and C.A. Miller. 1991. 'I win – you lose: the development of argumentative thinking'. In *Informal Reasoning and Education*, edited by J.F. Voss, D.N. Perkins and J.W. Segal. Hillsdale, NJ: Lawrence Erlbaum Associates.

Steiner, G. 1989. *Real Presences*. London: Faber.

Stratta, L. and J. Dixon. 1992. 'The National Curriculum in English: does genre theory have anything to offer?' *English in Education* 26 (2).

Street, B. 1984. *Literacy in Theory and Practice*. Cambridge: Cambridge University Press.

Swales, J.M. 1990. *Genre Analysis: English in Academic Research Settings*. Cambridge: Cambridge University Press.

Toulmin, S. 1958. *The Uses of Argument*. Cambridge: Cambridge University Press.

Toulmin, S., R. Rieke and A. Janik. 1984. *An Introduction to Reasoning*. 2nd ed. London: Collier Macmillan.

Van Dijk, T.A. 1981. 'Episodes as units of discourse analysis'. In *Analysing Discourse: text and talk*, edited by D. Tannen. Washington DC: Georgetown University Press.

Van Leeuwen, T. *The Grammar of Legitimation*.

Vonnegut, K. 1983. 'A bombing raid backwards'. In *Exploring Texts Through Reading Aloud and Dramatization*, edited by A. and A.S. Newbould. London: Ward Lock.

Vygotsky, L. 1962. *Thought and Language*. Translated by Hanfmann, E. and G. Vakar. Edited by E. Hanfmann and G. Vakar. Cambridge, MA: The MIT Press.

Vygotsky, L.S. 1978. *Mind in Society: The Development of Higher Psychological Processes*. Cambridge, MA: Harvard University Press.

Wertsch, J.V. and A. Smolka. 1993. 'Continuing the dialogue: Vygotsky, Bakhtin and Lotman'. In *Charting the Agenda: educational activity after Vygotsky*, edited by H. Daniels. London and New York: Routledge.

Wilkinson, A. 1989. 'Our first great conversationalists', *English in Education* 23 (2).

Wilkinson, A. 1990. 'Argument as a primary act of mind', *English in Eduction* 24 (1).

Wilkinson, A. et al., eds. 1990. *Spoken English Illuminated*. Milton Keynes: Open University Press.

Willard, C. 1989. *A Theory of Argumentation*. Birmingham, AL: The University of Alabama Press